Ph
21/7/06

SOCIAL NETWORKS AND SOCIAL EXCLUSION

Social Networks and Social Exclusion
Sociological and Policy Perspectives

Edited by

CHRIS PHILLIPSON
GRAHAM ALLAN
DAVID MORGAN
Keele University

ASHGATE

Published by
Ashgate Publishing Limited
Gower House
Croft Road
Aldershot
Hants GU11 3HR
England

Ashgate Publishing Company
Suite 420
101 Cherry Street
Burlington, VT 05401-4405
USA

Ashgate website: http://www.ashgate.com

British Library Cataloguing in Publication Data
Social networks and social exclusion : sociological and
    policy perspectives
    1. Social networks - Congresses 2. Alienation (Social
    psychology) - Congresses 3. Marginality, Social - Congresses
    I. Phillipson, Chris, 1949- II. Allan, Graham III. Morgan, D.
    H. J. (David Hopcraft John), 1937-
    302.4

Library of Congress Cataloging-in-Publication Data
Social networks and social exclusion : sociological and policy perspectives / edited by
    Chris Phillipson, Graham Allan, and David Morgan.
        p. cm.
    "This book originated from a seminar series entitled 'Social networks and social
    exclusion: conceptual and public policy issues'"--Acknowledgments.
    Includes bibliographical references and index.
    ISBN 0-7546-3429-9
    1. Social networks--Great Britain--Congresses. 2. Marginality, Social--Great
Britain--Congresses. 3. Children--Social networks--Great Britain--Congresses. 4.
Aged--Social networks--Great Britain--Congresses. 5. Social planning--Great
Britain--Congresses. I. Phillipson, Chris. II. Allan, Graham, 1948- III. Morgan, D. H. J.

HM741.S635 2003
302.4'0941--dc22
                                                                    2003054488

ISBN 0 7546 3429 9

Reprinted 2005

Printed and bound in Great Britain by MPG Books Ltd. Bodmin. Cornwall

Contents

List of Figures

List of Tables

Contributors

Graham Allan is Professor of Social Relations at Keele University. His research mainly focuses on aspects of informal social relationships. He is particularly interested in the sociology of friendship, family and domestic life, kinship, and community and has written widely on these subjects. His current research includes projects on stepfamily kinship and on marital affairs.

Vicky Cattell has researched and published on deprived and regenerating neighbourhoods, social networks, social capital and health inequalities, and taught sociology, social policy and politics. She is currently working at Queen Mary, University of London. Previously she has worked at the House of Commons, Goldsmiths College, University of London, Middlesex University, and University College London.

Graham Crow is Reader in Sociology at the University of Southampton, where he has worked since 1983. He is the author or co-author of four books and editor or co-editor of four more, on various subjects relating to families, households, communities and social theory. He has also co-edited the electronic journal *Sociological Research Online*. He is currently writing a book on modes of sociological argument, and working on a project exploring the issue of 'informed consent' in the research process.

Pearl Dykstra is a Research Professor at the Netherlands Interdisciplinary Demographic Institute at the University of Utrecht in Holland. Her research is principally concerned with social gerontology, especially in the areas of ageing, intergenerational bonds, childlessness and the life course. She has published widely on these topics.

Melanie Gironda is Lecturer of Social Welfare at the University of California, Los Angeles (UCLA) where she teaches courses on social gerontology and research on ageing. She received both her PhD and MSW from UCLA. She serves as Deputy Program Director of the Hartford Doctoral Fellows Program in Geriatric Social Work. Dr Gironda's research examines loneliness in various populations of the elderly, with a special focus on the nature of social support networks of older adults without children.

James Lubben is Professor of Social Welfare and Urban Planning at the University of California, Los Angeles (UCLA). Both his DSW and MPH are from the University of California, Berkeley. Dr Lubben serves as National Director of the Hartford Doctoral Fellows Program in Geriatric Social Work and as a regular consultant to the World Health Organization-Kobe Centre on health and welfare systems development for aging societies. Dr Lubben's research examines social behavioral determinants of vitality in old age, with a particular focus on the roles of social support networks.

David Morgan is Emeritus Professor at the University of Manchester and is a Visiting Professor of Sociology at Keele University. He has a part-time 'Professor 2' appointment at NTNU, Trondheim. He has written widely on aspects of family sociology, close relationships and masculinities.

Virginia Morrow is Research Lecturer, Department of Health and Social Care, Brunel University. Children and young people have been the primary focus of her research activities since 1988. Her most recent research explored the relationship between social capital and health in relation to children and young people, published as *Networks and Neighbourhoods: Children's and young people's perspectives*, Health Development Agency, London, 2001.

Victoria Nash is Policy and Research Officer at the Oxford Internet Institute and is also a Lecturer in Politics for Trinity College, Oxford. She was previously a Research Fellow at ippr, leading a programme of research for the Communities Initiative. Her recent publications include *Reclaiming Community* (ippr, 2002) and Making Sense of Community (ippr, 2003).

Ray Pahl is a Research Professor at the Institute of Social and Economic Research at the University of Essex and Professor Emeritus, University of Kent at Canterbury. He is the author (with J.M. Pahl) of *Managers and their Wives* (1970) in which he explored patterns of friendship in the middle class. His more recent publications include *Divisions of Labour* (1984), *After Success* (1995) and *On Friendship* (2000). He is currently completing a book with Liz Spencer on their research programme on Friendship and Personal Communities.

Chris Phillipson is Professor of Applied Social Studies and Social Gerontology at Keele University where he is also Dean of Postgraduate Affairs. His most recent books are *Reconstructing Old Age* (Sage Books, 1998), *The Family* *and Community Life of Older People* (co-authored, Routledge, 2001) and *Transitions from Work to Retirement* (Policy Press, 2002). Present research includes work on an ESRC-funded project on social exclusion in old age.

Thomas Scharf is Reader in Social Gerontology in the School of Social Relations, Keele University. His current research focuses on the situation of older people living in urban communities. He also has an interest in rural ageing and in the study of older people in different cultural settings.

Allison Smith is a researcher in the Centre for Social Gerontology at Keele University. Her research interests focus on the quality of life and social exclusion of older people living in disadvantaged urban areas of England and Canada.

Dale Southerton is a Research Fellow at the ESRC Centre for Research on Innovation and Competition (CRIC), University of Manchester. His work focuses extensively within the sociology of consumption and he is currently working on three related research projects: the changing temporalities of consumption, sustainable domestic technologies, and the diffusion of cultures of consumption. In addition to these subject areas, he has written about consumption and identity, cultural capital, social networks, parent-child relationships, community, a theory of social practice and innovation.

Liz Spencer is a partner in New Perspectives research consultancy and has been doing qualitative research for over 25 years. She has held research posts at the London School of Economics and Political Science, the London Graduate School of Business Studies, Brunel University, the University of Kent, the National Centre for Social Research, and the Institute of Social and Economic Research at the University of Essex. As well as carrying out research in a wide range of fields, Liz Spencer teaches qualitative research at the University of Essex and runs methods training courses for public sector organizations.

Marilyn Taylor is Professor of Urban Governance and Regeneration at the University of the West of England. She has been involved in research on community development, the voluntary and community sector, partnerships and neighbourhood renewal for many years, and has recently published *Public Policy in the Community* (Palgrave, 2003). She is currently Chair of the Urban Forum, an umbrella body for voluntary and community organizations in regeneration in the UK, a member of the Advisory Group for the Active

Community Unit at the Home Office and is on the Executive Board of the International Society for Third Sector Research.

Perri 6 is a Senior Research Fellow in the Health Services Management Centre at the University of Birmingham; in the 1990s, he was Director of Policy and Research at Demos. His most recent book is *Towards Holistic Governance*. He is currently writing books on public policy and personal social networks, on managing across interorganizational networks and on styles of political judgment, and conducting research on privacy and data sharing in 'joined up' government programmes.

Acknowledgements

This book originated from a seminar series entitled *Social Networks and Social Exclusion: Conceptual and Public Policy Issues*, funded by the Economic and Social Research Council (ESRC). The rationale behind the seminars was to review the academic and policy debate around the role of social networks in promoting different kinds of support to individuals and communities. The series of six seminars brought together a mix of both established researchers and students undertaking doctoral research around the topic of social networks. The series itself was a collaborative venture involving a number of academics and universities. The organizing group comprised Graham Allan (Keele University), Graham Crow (University of Southampton), David Morgan (University of Manchester), Ray Pahl (University of Essex), Chris Phillipson (Keele University), Clare Wenger (University of Wales, Bangor) and Perri 6 (King's College, London). Seminars were held at each of the above universities, with a final event at the Institute of Materials in London. The organizers would like record their gratitude to the ESRC for providing financial support, to the speakers at the various events, and all those involved in assisting with the administration of each seminar.

The seminar series brought together around 30 speakers and this volume provides a selection of some of the themes and issues discussed over the course of the programme. We are extremely grateful to the contributors for meeting the various deadlines and requests for information. The editors would also like to thank Katherine Hodkinson and subsequently Carolyn Court at Ashgate Publishing for their support for the venture. Sue Humphries provided valuable assistance in preparing the manuscript for publication.

Chris Phillipson
Graham Allan
David Morgan

Chapter 1

Introduction

Chris Phillipson, Graham Allan and David Morgan

A substantial literature has emerged exploring the nature and role of social networks in daily life. Social network analysis has itself been the subject of a number of reviews, not least those by Wellman and Berkowitz (1988), Scott (2000), and Wasserman and Faust (1994). Summaries of this tradition are provided in Allan (1996) and Crow and Allan (1994). From a sociological perspective, network analysis has been used to explore: first, the impact of informal ties both emotionally for the individual and for patterns of social organization more generally; second, the impact of particular configurations of social networks; third, the role of networks in the provision of support; fourth, the implications for public policy of adopting a social network perspective.

A more recent development (at least in the UK) has been the linkage between social networks and ideas about social inclusion and exclusion. Personal social networks may be viewed as 'structures of opportunity' (6, 1998) which may facilitate or frustrate access to different kinds of resources. This may be especially the case where deprivation is geographically concentrated, an important theme in recent academic research (Glennerster et al., 1999) as well as government social policy (Social Exclusion Unit, 2001). In addition, following Granovetter (1973), a number of studies have explored the impact 'strong' and 'weak' ties may have upon transitions through the life course. Ideas about 'social capital' have also contributed to this debate, these referring to the benefits which arise from membership of social networks or other kinds of social structures (Portes, 1998).

The above themes are also expressed in public policy concerns about the way in which particular network configurations may prevent people from moving out of poverty or unemployment. Membership of the 'right kind' of network is viewed by policy-makers as important in promoting access to employment, or preventing crime, or achieving support in old age. However more information is needed about the role played by networks, and bridges need to be built between research findings and the development of social policy. Social networks may also have 'antisocial' aspects that need better documentation and understanding. Strong social networks may operate to exclude outsiders from resources or opportunities; solidarity for one group may result in denial of access to opportunities for another. In addition, cohesive groups may exert pressure to conform. As a consequence, strong networks may place restrictions on people's ability to change of adopt new lifestyles.

The concept of 'social network' is both seductive and intuitively simple. Unlike some other social science concepts, the idea of the social network seems to link readily with the way in which individuals routinely live and understand their lives. There are few true isolates in the world. Each individual can be linked, in a variety of ways and with varying degrees of weight or significance, to a set of other people and these, in their turn, may sometimes be linked to each other or to others outside this original, ego-centred, network. The seductive character of this idea derives in part from this apparent everyday simplicity and in part from the fact that it seems to occupy a place and act as bridge between clearly bounded collectivities such as social groups, communities and so forth, and atomized individuals.

One of the origins of this approach was in British social anthropology and its attempt in the 1960s to develop an understanding of social connectedness in contexts not obviously shaped by clearly defined or bounded collectivities (Frankenberg, 1966). These contexts were as varied as residential areas in London or rapidly developing urban environments in Southern Africa. But the aim was perhaps less to remove or displace collectivities such as families or communities but rather to develop a more nuanced understanding of the ways in which they worked. Thus families are better understood as relatively fluid sets of connections across generations and between households rather than as firmly bounded entities. The idea of social network also seemed to be especially effective in capturing those relationships or social connections, such as friends, neighbours, workmates or acquaintances which could rarely be understood in bounded terms.

Social networks, then, are about linkages and connectedness and this idea of linkage may also serve as a metaphor for the many usages of social networks across a wide range of social sciences. First there is the link between theory and research with the social network perspective being viewed as an example of what Merton (1957) termed 'middle-range' theorizing. It is an abstraction from reality and a focus on particular aspects of social relationships to the exclusion of others. Yet it does not exist at the higher, more abstract realms of grand theory. The concept itself readily suggests ways of researching social life in terms of, for example, density of social network or the different weightings that might be attached to particular ties.

Another example of the links between theory and research is provided by the concept of 'social capital', a term which is now widely used across the social sciences, a development reflected in this volume. There does appear to be some kind of natural affinity between network analysis and the idea of social capital. Social capital can be roughly understood in terms of the social resources and connections that an individual has at his or her disposal and network analysis provides an elegant and visual way of understanding these resources and connections.

Another metaphorical linkage provided by social network analysis is between qualitative and quantitative research. The key elements of network analysis seem readily, perhaps too readily, open to measurement. But the best examples of network analysis recognize that the researcher is always encouraged to think further about the meanings of the social connections which may be mapped out, meaning in terms of the individuals concerned and in terms of wider theoretical or policy issues. An important objective of this volume has been to provide a range of examples from network-based studies drawn from quantitative as well as qualitative research.

The final metaphorical linkage provided by network analysis is that between research and policy, a question addressed in different ways by many of the papers in this book. Policy-makers and practitioners have become aware over the years that the unit of their concern is neither the isolated individual nor a theoretically bounded group such as a household or a community. Themes of interdependence and interconnectedness have come to the fore in recent exchanges between researchers and policy-makers, especially in the investigation of social exclusion. The three terms 'social network', 'social capital' and 'social exclusion' (and 'inclusion') are linked in a variety of complex and interesting ways and all of the work reported here focuses, with different degrees of emphasis, on these interchanges.

Structure of the Book

The chapters included bring together:

- an overview of the social network literature, summarizing the main sociological arguments and traditions;
- a review of the range of social phenomena which social networks seek to explain;

- examples of quantitative and qualitative studies using a broad network approach;
- a discussion of the implications for social and public policy of a network perspective.

In Chapter 2 Graham Crow provides an overview of the debate about the relationship between social networks and questions relating to social exclusion and inclusion. He notes the extent to which networks are increasingly important in shaping life chances and opportunities, suggesting as well that this may create new forms of exclusion as well assisting participation within civil society. The social network literature has been dominated by contributions from the USA and Canada over the past 20 years, and in Chapter 3 James Lubben and Melanie Gironda provide a summary of this work. They give particular emphasis to the links between social networks and health, and provide a detailed illustration of a particular approach to measuring social networks. Chris Phillipson extends this discussion in Chapter 4, examining how researchers have assessed the role of networks in the provision of support in old age. He reviews methodologies for assessing different types of networks and provides an agenda for future research in the field.

The next group of chapters explores, through empirical studies, the role of networks at different points of the life course. In Chapter 5 Virginia Morrow describes children's accounts of friendship-based networks. Her work reflects the new sociology of childhood that takes children as active participants during the period of socialization. Her research demonstrates younger people constructing informal communities with friendship a key element in the formation of identity. The following three chapters take different facets of the role of networks in the lives of adults. In Chapter 6 Ray Pahl and Liz Spencer explore the nature of friendship within what has been termed 'personal communities' (the set of intimate ties forged with friends, workmates, neighbours and kin). Their findings challenge pessimistic views about the decline of civic society, demonstrating that in their personal lives at least most people (with important exceptions) have access to robust networks of some kind or another – many of which are indeed communities rather than largely atomized and individualized social ties. Dale Southerton in Chapter 7 extends this theme by examining social networks and social capital within the setting of a New Town community, He focuses on the role both play in shaping the spare time practices of working class and middle class couples. Southerton demonstrates that access to different types of capital will influence styles of interaction and participation within social networks. The chapters by

Morrow, Pahl and Spencer, and Southerton, are all based upon different kinds of qualitative research. Pearl Dykstra, in Chapter 8, provides a quantitative study from the Netherlands looking at the consequences for network formation of diversity in marital histories. She examines the extent to which people are engaging in partnerships other than marriage, and the implications of this for involvement in social ties and the experience of feelings such as loneliness and access to close relationships.

To complete the empirical studies, two chapters consider social networks from the perspective of people living in areas of high social and economic deprivation. In Chapter 9 Vicky Cattell explores the dynamics between poverty and exclusion on the one side, and neighbourhood, and health and well-being on the other. Her research considers neighbourhood influences on networks and social capital. She notes how different network structures – dense and weak, homogenous and heterogeneous – appear to be involved in the creation of social capital – both carrying implications for individual well-being. Tom Scharf and Allison Smith in Chapter 10 examine issues about networks and social exclusion in relation to the lives of older people. They provide evidence of the multiple risks of exclusion faced by elderly people living in areas characterized by intense social deprivation. Their work also focuses on the extent of isolation affecting individuals in some settings and at particular points of the life course.

The final three chapters review different dimensions of the policy debate about social networks. Perri 6 in Chapter 11 examines the relationship between public policy and social networks. He assesses the various tools available to government for shaping individual and community-based networks and reviews the effects of such interventions. He concludes that social science has much to contribute in this area although empirical studies evaluating the impact of attempts to influence networks remain in their infancy. Much of the debate about social networks has focused upon issues concerning the changing nature of community life. Marilyn Taylor in Chapter 12 takes up this theme, exploring the different ways in which terms such as social capital, social exclusion and social network have been applied to policy-thinking in the field of community development. Taylor suggests how networks may be used to promote inclusion and secure participation within localities. In the final chapter, Vicki Nash explores ways of achieving better integration between research on social networks and the development of public policy. She notes that despite government interest in neighbourhood and community issues, research findings are often neglected or ignored. Nash concludes with a number of suggestions for developing a more integrated approach between academic research and the policy field.

The various chapters in this book bring together two sides of an important debate: the one dealing with research on the impact of social networks, the other with the policy issues surrounding inclusion/exclusion from participation in networks. By joining the two elements we hope to have provided a comprehensive overview of what has become a major area of academic and public policy interest. Our hope is that the book will stimulate further research as well as clarifying some of the possibilities for interventions aimed at improving the quality of people's lives.

Chapter 2

Social Networks and Social Exclusion: An Overview of the Debate

Graham Crow

Introduction

The analysis of social exclusion has frequently led researchers to think about their subject in terms of the operation of social networks, and in particular the capacity of such networks to exclude non-members. Following Simmel's analysis of secret societies (Wolff, 1964), it has become an axiom of sociological thought that the intensity of a social group's solidarity is related to the group's exclusivity. The strongest social bonds are found where there is a clear demarcation between 'insiders' and 'outsiders', and where this demarcation line can be policed effectively to restrict admittance to the group. 'Insiders' are bonded together in no small part by their shared identity based on the clear understanding of what sets them apart from 'outsiders'. The challenge for policy-makers that this situation presents is to find ways to enhance disadvantaged people's access to social networks that will empower them without undermining the supportive character either of those networks that they seek to join or of the networks of which they are already members. The promotion of social inclusion through the opening up of opportunities to participate in empowering social networks is a complex project with a range of associated dilemmas and paradoxes.

This chapter is devoted to the exploration of these issues. It will do so through the discussion of five linked propositions. These are that social networks present a methodological challenge; that diverse influences have a bearing on the character of social networks; that social networks may be antisocial; that social networks are not necessarily antisocial; and that the promotion of social networks is an intellectual puzzle and a political challenge. This discussion will draw on various pieces of published research on social networks in order to illustrate the sorts of concrete issues to which these sometimes rather abstract debates apply. It will also draw on studies of community relationships and of 'social capital', given that the literatures on these subjects are of direct relevance to the analysis of social networks and social exclusion.

Social Networks Present a Methodological Challenge

The remarkable impact of Granovetter's (1973) argument about the strength of weak ties can be attributed to its simple statement of a paradox of social networks: that dense and exclusive networks do not necessarily serve their members as well as looser and more open ones. People in patterns of social relationships that are heavily interconnected and overlapping may be less well-placed for activities such as job search than people whose social networks are more disparate in character. 'Weak' ties may act as a 'bridge' in the sense that 'they facilitate communication between different ... groups and across different strata' (Werbner, 1988, p. 178). Similar language has been used more recently by Putnam (2000) to describe different types of social capital, making the point that 'bridging' the gap between social groups can be just as important as the 'bonding' of members of well-established groups.

Harris's (1987) study *Redundancy and Recession in South Wales* took Granovetter's thesis as one of its starting points, but found it necessary to differentiate more finely between types of social network than the simple dichotomy implied in the bold distinction between strong and weak ties. Harris's conclusion from his project's attempt to operationalize the concept of social network was that it is fruitful to distinguish between 'size, density, dispersion, contact and setting ... in conjunction with identity and location measures' (1987, pp. 223–4) in the construction of empirical network types. In other words, the ties that make up social networks can be stronger or weaker in several different ways, in terms of the number of people in the network, the extent to which the people in the network have overlapping interconnections, the degree of geographical concentration or dispersion of the network population, the extent to which the relations between network members are characterised by equality and reciprocity, and the impact of the broader social setting within which the network is located. The links between members of networks thus have several aspects to them, and the distinction between strong and weak ties is insufficiently subtle to capture these nuances.

The more general points that this illustrates are that social networks are configurations of people rather than collectivities with definite boundaries, and that as such they present a fundamental methodological challenge. Social networks are distinct from communities, at least as they are conventionally conceived, in that networks are not necessarily restricted to one geographical location, and the focus in social network analysis is on the linkages between individuals rather than on the collective form of the group. The redirection of researchers' attention onto social networks has helped to reveal the shortcomings of assuming that people need to live in the same vicinity as those with whom they have meaningful social relationships, and of the related assumption that living in the same vicinity necessarily generates meaningful social relationships. Wellman has been a pioneer of this line of argument. He has shown in his work that technological developments in the field of communications (such as cars, telephones and more recently the internet) have liberated individuals from their reliance on neighbourhood-based social networks. In their place what emerges, Wellman (1999) argues, is the phenomenon of 'personal communities' in which the focus of attention is on the individual and his or her network of links to other people.

The use of the metaphor of a network for the analysis of people's patterns of social connections is an understandable response to contemporary social change. The transformation of community that Rosser and Harris (1965, p. 299) suggest has taken place involves the transition from the settled and interconnected relationships of 'the cohesive society' to the 'the mobile society' in which people are less likely than their grandparents were to live out their lives amongst people and surroundings familiar to them from their childhood. This 'deterritorialization' of community, as Albrow (1996) has called it, means that people's social networks are potentially far more extensive than the boundaries of the particular neighbourhoods in which they currently happen to reside. In principle they are global in scale, and the 'cosmopolites' identified in Albrow et al.'s (1994) empirical research show that some sections of the population do actually have global social networks in practice. Such networks pose a significant challenge methodologically, since network analysis does not exempt researchers from the need to identify the boundaries of the population being studied. Thus, as Knoke and Kuklinski (1991, p. 176) note: 'Before collecting data, a network researcher must decide the most relevant type of social organization and the units within that social form that comprise the network nodes.' Unlike place-based communities, social networks do not have any obvious points at which it would be appropriate for researchers to draw the line in terms of people to be included in their study. As a result, where the boundaries of people's networks are drawn may be somewhat arbitrary.

The fact that networks extend indefinitely is only one of the methodological challenges that network analysis raises. Further difficulties arise from the fact that the relations between the members of a network are not fixed, but vary in character in significant ways. Network links may, for example, be characterized by reciprocity, or they may be relations in which there are distinct donors and recipients. The things that pass between network members may be more or less tangible, ranging from hard cash, through information, to more abstract phenomena such as status and respect. Network links may be activated on a daily basis or much less frequently. And some networks will be more enduring than others that are recognized by their participants to be more short-term in nature. Longer-term networks can be likened to support convoys, with a core of people travelling together, periodically modified as new people join and others exit. Such 'convoys' often have members of the same demographic cohort at their centre, and have connections within them that have been built up over a lifetime, as for example Phillipson et al.'s (2001) study of older people's networks has shown. By contrast, short-term networks may endure no longer than the duration of one social gathering, and Bauman (2000, p. 199) has designated such phenomena as 'cloakroom communities' in order to capture their time-limited quality.

For all of these reasons, the diagrammatic representation of a social relationship in terms of a line between two nodes in a network is necessarily only the beginning of the social scientific inquiry into the significance of this connection. Researchers have to find out precisely what passes along these lines before pronouncements about the nature of the network can be made. This information may be shrouded in secrecy, as it is for example in the networks that make up the informal economy. Many other networks besides those associated with illegal activity may be 'hidden' simply because there is no reason for their members to draw the attention of outsiders to themselves and their activities (Crow, 1999). Network analysis involves much more than a simple mapping exercise, since it requires the collection and analysis of quite complex data (Degenne and Forsé, 1999).

Diverse Influences have a Bearing on the Character of Social Networks

Social networks vary considerably in the form that they take and the content of the relationships between the members who make them up, but it is nevertheless possible to identify what Barnes calls 'networky characteristics' (1995, p. 138). Networks cannot function unless their members operate with a shared culture and language, and in addition agree to abide by the (often unwritten) rules of the group, even where it is not in their immediate self-interest to do so. These conditions are necessary for trust to be present, as numerous commentators on the phenomenon of social solidarity from Durkheim onwards have noted (Crow, 2002). It is no accident that trust has been a key concern in the analysis of social networks, because networks cannot function without trust. Fukuyama's observation that 'Communities depend on mutual trust and will not arise spontaneously without it' (1995, p. 25) applies particularly to networks that do not have recourse to hierarchical organizations that can impose sanctions against people who break the rules.

It is unsurprising that family relationships figure prominently in social networks (Cheal, 2002). This is especially likely to be the case in circumstances where trust is low, because families are enduring and are thereby able to exercise a considerable degree of control over their members. Research has shown family and kinship networks to be central to many forms of community where people's options are relatively limited, such as in 'traditional' working class communities and in migrant communities (Crow and Allan, 1994). In circumstances where trust with others has not been established, families offer 'thick trust', that is: 'Trust embedded in personal relations that are strong, frequent, and nested in wider networks' (Putnam, 2000, p. 136). In such circumstances family networks can be important in securing employment, as Allatt and Yeandle's (1992) study of youth unemployment and Grieco's (1987) account of families assisting mobile workers show. Passing on information about opportunities in the housing market is another example of how family networks may act as conduits of very practical information, something that has long been the case (Tebbutt, 1995).

Family networks operate along gendered lines, with women being pivotal in their operation but not necessarily emerging as their chief beneficiaries. Dicks and her colleagues' (1998, p. 303) study of social support in ex-mining communities concludes that the networks that exist among women 'constitute a resource which prevents "an awful lot more trouble" occurring'. This is apparent, for example, in the field of care, where 'Most often, care-giving devolves on to those closest to the dependent person – and those deemed to be closest are generally wives, mothers and daughters' (Dalley, 1988, p. 7). Dalley notes that women of a particular age are most likely to be at the centre of caring networks, since in middle age women may find themselves called upon simultaneously by partners, children and parents. Such caring responsibilities will be influenced by geography, since they are more frequently activated among members of local kin networks, who may as a result come to 'feel too close for comfort' (Mason, 1999, p. 156). They will in addition vary according to household type, as is apparent when comparing the more restricted social networks of lone mothers compared to those of mothers who live with partners. Researchers have also highlighted the more limited and family-based networks of working class families compared to those of middle class families (Cochran et al., 1990).

These points about the way in which family networks vary according to gender, age, geographical location, household type and social class apply to social networks more generally. Nor is this list of factors that influence the character of social networks exhaustive. The importance that sexual orientation has for people's social networks has been highlighted in Weeks, Heaphy and Donovan's (2001) research on gay and lesbian lifestyles. Race and ethnicity is a further variable that has a bearing on how social networks operate (Ballard, 1994), and disability is coming to be more widely recognised as another (Pescosolido, 2001). In the case of the latter, Pescosolido (2001, p. 484) makes a distinction between 'naturally occurring and deliberately constructed social networks'. Socially excluded groups such as people with disabilities frequently find that they have to fall back on their own resources, and create their own social networks that are more receptive to their needs and supportive in more appropriate ways than the 'natural' networks of family and neighbourhood may turn out to be. Although they are not easy to sustain as on-going concerns, support groups comprised of people with disabilities such as that studied by Monks (1999) have the potential to be empowering 'artificial communities'. This is important in a broader social environment that is experienced as exclusive (Charlton, 1998). Similar points have been made about the 'encapsulation' of ethnic minority communities being a response to structured exclusion from mainstream social life (Crow and Allan, 1994).

Social Networks may be Antisocial

Social networks are not inherently positive in their effects. This has long been recognized in relation to the capacity of social networks to deny non-members access to the material and other resources monopolized by members. The shared knowledge and values characteristic of high-density social networks can be used to exclude others. Sibley (1995, p. 36) has suggested that this process may have a geographical expression by his comment that 'there is something approaching a conscience collective in some middle class North American suburbs and on some local authority housing estates in Britain, manifest in reactions to the mentally disabled, Gypsies and Bangladeshis, for example'. The type of social capital identified by Putnam (2000, pp. 22–3) as 'bonding' is, he recognizes, by its nature 'exclusive' and liable to reinforce social divisions; it thereby 'bolsters our narrower selves'. In the extreme this can be used for 'malevolent, antisocial purposes' as happens when it takes the form of 'sectarianism [and] ethnocentrism'. Simmel's examples of secret societies include 'a conspiracy' and 'a gang of swindlers' (Wolff, 1964, p. 346) and these serve to illustrate that highly integrated social networks pursuing their group interest do not always contribute to the wider social good.

A second sense in which social networks may be considered antisocial in their effects relates to their capacity to exercise undue control over their members. What Tebbutt (1995, p. 2) calls 'closed' social networks may, through an 'excessive degree of familiarity', allow 'a great deal of social pressure to be exerted over individual behaviour'. This point has been made about the potentially oppressive nature of social support. Oakley (1992, pp. 26–7) makes the observation in her study of the health of mothers that receiving social support 'may be experienced more as a burden than a benefit'. This is because much social support is conditional on the recipient behaving in ways approved of by those giving the support, as for example Duncan and Edwards (1999) found in their research on lone mothers. There is, in other words, a moral dimension to what passes between members of a network. Even where this is not spelt out explicitly, social support can still have the effect of reinforcing recipients' conformity to the norms of their group because of the sense of dependence and obligation that the receipt of assistance tends to engender.

The exclusivity of certain social networks and the unacceptable conditions attached to being a member of some others are both contributory factors to people becoming marginalized and socially isolated. Research in a wide variety of fields has shown that vulnerability to such marginalization is not evenly spread across the population. Social groups that are especially vulnerable to exclusion are homeless people (Hutson and Clapham, 1999), older people (see Scharf and Smith, in this volume), and the long-term unemployed (Morris, 1988), all of whom face particular challenges in maintaining social networks. Another group for whom this is the case is people with disabilities. Rowlands's (2001, p. 181) study of young adults with brain injury found that 'With time elapsing since injury social networks decrease and density increases, leading to the complaint of loneliness as the greatest subjective burden'. Parker (1993) reports similar findings in her study of the impact of disability on married couples' neighbourhood and friendship networks, while the term 'social death' has been applied to the situation of people with disabilities in residential care (Miller and Gwynne, 1972).

Giving social support can also be experienced as burdensome, as Oakley (1992) amongst others has noted, although people's sense of the personal costs to themselves of supporting others is not as much in evidence as might be expected. There are two particularly important reasons for this. One is that the performance of social support is shrouded in the language of duty, love and caring about, thus making the precise calculation of costs and benefits an inappropriate activity within the moral order of social networks. It is socially unacceptable, or at least disapproved of, for an individual to seek to withdraw from obligations on the grounds that he or she is giving more than he or she is receiving. The second reason is that such a calculation would be an enormously complex one to undertake with any degree of accuracy, for all the reasons noted above about the difficulties of specifying what passes between people in networks. Against this background, it is understandable how people can come to assume (rightly or wrongly) that their involvement in social networks is preferable to being excluded from them.

Social Networks are not Necessarily Antisocial

The challenge to the naïve equation of social networks with social benefit does not prevent recognition of the benefits that social networks have the potential to bring. Other things being equal, people with smaller social networks are more likely to be poorer and to have poorer health and general well-being than their better connected counterparts. Pescosolido's (2001, pp. 474, 483) general observation that 'Network ties can be helpful or harmful' is quite compatible with the point that 'others around us are important for our health and well-being'. Wilkinson's (1996, p. 182) survey of the extensive literature on variations in health leads him to the conclusion not only that there is a correlation between social capital and well-being, but that it is possible to identify a causal relationship, namely that 'lower social involvement in the community' will produce adverse health effects. Particular attention is paid by Wilkinson (1996, p. 191) to the adverse effects on people whose poverty acts as a barrier to social involvement. It is the case that 'the poorest areas suffer more crime and more of a wide range of social problems', and this can be linked to the lower levels of social cohesion found there than in middle class neighbourhoods.

The simple statement that 'Social networks help you stay healthy' (Putnam, 2000, p. 331) invites investigation of how this comes about. Putnam's (2000, p. 21) answer to this question is that 'Networks and the associated norms of reciprocity are generally good for those inside the network', giving as they do access to 'social capital'. His further argument is that 'bridging' social capital is particularly socially beneficial, helping people to 'get ahead' rather than simply 'getting by' (2000, p. 23). It does this by providing links into wider social networks that open up access to a more extensive range of information, material resources and social support than is available to people whose networks are limited to the stronger but more restricted 'bonding' type. Pertinent in this context is Hareven's (2000) view that families that retreat from the wider community into private, family-centred lifestyles do not benefit their members by doing so. She argues that 'The loss of the family's sociability as a result of its function as a refuge from the outside world has rendered it less flexible and less capable of handling internal, as well as external, crises'. The process of family privatization is at odds with what is required to keep up with economy and society as they 'have become more diversified over time' (Hareven, 2000, p. 308).

Hareven locates the origins of family privatization among the urban middle class of the nineteenth century and argues that this pattern has subsequently become more all-pervasive. This type of argument has also been advanced by Willmott (1986, p. 103), who in addition suggests that better-off groups have pioneered not only new family forms but also new forms of community involvement in which 'friendship networks ... and dispersed "interest communities" have become more dominant at the expense of local groupings'. His thesis is that increasing geographical and social mobility will open up opportunities for wider participation in these new informal networks, but his qualifying observation that 'class differences remain' is an important one. Subsequent research has confirmed that participation in community groups, voluntary associations and other dimensions of the informal relationships that make up civil society is skewed towards the middle classes (Black et al., 2002). This is not necessarily the outcome of a deliberate strategy, since the greater geographical mobility that is associated with middle class jobs means that middle class families are less likely than their working class counterparts to be immersed in local kinship networks. They are correspondingly more likely to be located in geographically extensive networks built up through their employment.

There are various suggestions that networks are becoming increasingly important in shaping people's life chances. Castells's (1996) analysis of *The Rise of the Network Society* advances this argument, but challenges the assumption that the emergence of ever-more global networks will automatically reduce social exclusion. At the local level, globalization can have the paradoxical impact of reinforcing existing networks such as those built upon family ties. Mitchell and Green's (2002, p. 19) study is one recent illustration of how 'although, on one level the world appears to be increasingly globalized, class, gender and locality continue to remain important and influential factors within individual actors' lives permeating personal relationships'. And on a more global level, networks are not necessarily experienced as liberating, as is indicated by Hochschild's (2001) use of the term 'chains' to describe the links between carers from poor countries and their rich country destinations. The challenge, as Hochschild concludes, is to find ways of managing these networks so that those who currently lose out as a result of their operation can join the ranks of beneficiaries.

The Promotion of Social Networks is an Intellectual Puzzle and a Political Challenge

The promotion of supportive social networks now occupies a prominent place on the political agenda. Policy-makers' interest in fostering 'social capital' is understandable in the context of governments' reluctance or inability to pursue more conventional programmes of redistribution of income and/or community building (Baron, Field and Schuller, 2000; Mulgan, 1997; Oppenheim, 1998a; Pierson and Smith, 2001). Questions remain, however, about precisely what it is about social networks that facilitates social inclusion, and about who is best placed to promote them. As Scott (2000, p. 3) has noted, relationships between people in networks 'cannot be reduced to the properties of the individual agents themselves', and the intellectual puzzle that this presents is that of identifying what it is about how people come together that enables them collectively to make the most of their individual skills and attributes. This is directly connected to the political challenge for governments of securing empowerment without resorting to compulsion. The investigation of these issues reveals a number of dilemmas and paradoxes that are by no means easy to resolve.

Granovetter's point that weak ties serve very important functions is among the best-known findings of network analysis. A key point that it illustrates is that 'social capital does not boil down to the volume of contacts because not all contacts have the same *value*' (Degenne and Forsé, 1999, p. 117, authors' emphasis). Its elaboration in Putnam's formulation relating to bridging and bonding forms of social capital highlights the enormous diversity of the routes by which such 'bridges' are developed, as would be expected of what are primarily informal relationships that are entered into for a whole range of reasons besides narrowly instrumental ones. Many of these connections arise in the course of the mundane interactions that make up everyday life, where trust is built up gradually as a by-product. There is no ready-made short-cut to the generation of trust, as governments have recognized through their incorporation of the tenet of contemporary community building, that it should be 'bottom-up' rather than 'top-down', that is, that it should be driven by agendas set by grassroots members rather than by officialdom. The record of government-driven programmes of community development is at best mixed (Taylor, this volume), and the history of projects failing to meet people's expectations has left a legacy of suspicion concerning governments' motives.

As a result of the recognition that governments are able to facilitate the development of social capital through the provision of a favourable environment for its growth but that they cannot directly supply social capital, attention has shifted to focus on the key elements of that environment. Government initiatives to make the social environment safer through crime reduction can be understood to be an important part of this strategy (Marlow and Pitts, 1998), although such developments necessarily take time to work their way through into tangible results in terms of social capital. It can also be noted that planning the housing element of the physical environment has an important part to play in influencing the levels of social capital found in particular neighbourhoods. The unintended consequence of post-war urban redevelopment programmes whereby housing improvement came at the cost of breaking up the established social networks of residents is now better appreciated, although the tension between giving priority to meeting the housing requirements of people most in need and preserving existing social networks remains a problem, as Foster's (1999) study of London's Docklands shows.

The growth of interest in social capital on the part of governments is the subject of competing interpretations. One is that it reflects belated recognition by policy-makers that top-down approaches are 'at odds with the dynamic fluidity of social and economic life' (Schuller, Baron and Field, 2000, p. 14). A rather different and more cynical view is that it is part of a general process of 'the state withdrawing from welfare and seeking ways of transferring responsibility for both delivery and financing of welfare to the market, family, community and individuals' (Taylor, 1995, p. 99). Taylor goes on to note that such cynicism is not wholly justified, but that policy-makers do face a knotty problem in findings ways of releasing people's energies without at the same time exploiting them. Governments continue to have an obligation to provide a social and economic environment that is favourable to the emergence of empowering social networks, even if the informal character of these networks means that they cannot be directly created through 'top-down' initiatives.

This problem is compounded by two further dilemmas, namely 'How to respect "difference" whilst organizing around common interests', and 'How to make local action relevant beyond the neighbourhood' (Taylor, 1995, pp. 108-9). The first of these issues leads to the recognition that members of social networks are rarely homogeneous. People brought together by a common concern to challenge social exclusion will not necessarily be seeking the same solution. The social exclusion of people with learning difficulties is not resolved by opening up their labour market opportunities, for example (Baron, Riddell and Wilkinson, 1998). Put another way, social inclusion does not have to entail social integration into a set of uniform practices, although the more diverse people's solutions to social exclusion are, the more likely it is that these outcomes will be unequal. The other dilemma is a variation on this theme, since there is a tension between local action and wider concerns. Area-based initiatives have the potential to tap into local community networks that are informed about the area's distinctive characteristics and needs, but the reinforcement of such networks may bring about more 'bonding' than 'bridging', to use Putnam's (2000) terms. Area-based policies are thus accompanied by the risk that the exclusion of 'outsiders' is reinforced, because of the priority that can be attached to the claims of local people, and the linked danger that people seeking to move on from their localities will find it harder to do so.

Conclusion

According to Mulgan and Briscoe (1997, p. 345), the 'society of networks' that we are entering has a completely different character to that of the industrial age. In place of 'organizations defined by their boundaries', the pattern that is emerging is one built around networks and 'connectedness'. Similar claims have been made about a similar transformation taking place in the realm of social relationships more generally as a result of globalization and related processes. We might be suspicious of such claims to a major qualitative shift in social life on two main grounds. One is that social networks have long been recognised as having vital importance in all areas of social and economic life, as Scott's (2002) survey of the literature reveals. Social networks, in themselves, are not new. The other ground for caution is that networks are not a substitute for formal organizations. Castells's (1996) 'network society' is very much the product of global capitalist organizations, as he notes. Nor is it the case that social networks have the capacity to replace governments and their agencies, as attempts to operationalize community care as care by the community have illustrated.

There are good grounds for treating the attention paid to social networks and social capital in recent years as part of the rediscovery of 'community' and 'civil society' that has accompanied the reaction to contemporary individualization and its attendant social problems. This is not to say that nothing has changed. Social networks are dynamic phenomena, and they have the potential to be powerful agents for change as well as for the reinforcement of existing patterns of social cohesion. The impact of family and neighbourhood networks has not always been conservative, as their roles in facilitating migration and in challenging governments over welfare provision reveal. New forms of social networks such as the women's movement and the disability movement that are not constrained by family loyalties or neighbourhood ties have at least as much potential to bring about change, if not more, and it is no coincidence that they have been at the forefront of challenging social exclusion. Social network analysis has the capacity to shed light on this process, and to inform judgements about its chances of success.

Chapter 3

Measuring Social Networks and Assessing their Benefits

James Lubben and Melanie Gironda

Social networks have gained increased respect and attention from a large and diverse group of scholars and practitioners. A growing body of social science and epidemiological evidence has established a link between social relationships and an array of mental and physical health outcomes, including mortality. As a result, a prestigious US national committee of scholars identified *Personal Ties* as one of the top ten priority areas for research investment that could lead to major improvements in health (National Research Council, 2001).

The upsurge of research on social networks spawned a profusion of measurement techniques but unfortunately most are not well documented. O'Reilly (1988) laments the inadequate clarity of definition and the general lack of attention and reporting of reliability and validity analyses of most social network assessment instruments. A common criticism is that many studies that examine social networks use instruments with unknown or unreported psychometric properties (Winemiller et al., 1993). Even when social support network instruments with acceptable psychometric proprieties are used, there are few examples of critical evaluation of these instruments that could suggest further refinements. These measurement deficiencies are most unfortunate given that the continued development of valid and reliable social network assessment instruments has become even more crucial to the appropriate practice of geriatrics and study of gerontology (Steiner et al., 1996; Glass et al., 1997).

The present chapter addresses these concerns by first reviewing the seminal literature accounting for the association between social networks and health. The chapter discusses specific challenges for measuring social networks. It then provides an example of a particular social network scale that has been used in over 100 studies, documenting its psychometric characteristics and offering a refined version of that scale. The analytic plan discussed could be employed to evaluate and refine other social and behavioural measures.

Importance of Social Ties to the Health and Well-being of Older Adults

Public heath experts posit that the association between social networks and health is now as strong as the epidemiological evidence linking smoking and health (House, Landis and Umberson, 1988). More specifically, inadequate social networks have been associated with both an increase in morbidity and an increase in mortality (Berkman, 1986; Berkman and Glass, 2000; Berkman and Syme, 1979; Blazer, 1982; Bosworth and Schaie, 1997; Ell, 1984; House et al., 1988; Hurwicz and Berkanovic, 1993; Kaplan et al., 1987; Rook, 1994; Seeman, 2001; Torres, McIntosh and Kubena, 1992; Zuckerman, Kasl and Ostfeld, 1984). Social scientists also report that social isolation is associated with increased symptoms of psychological distress or loneliness (Gironda and Lubben, 2003; Lin, Ye and Ensel, 1999; Mor-Barak, 1997; Thoits, 1995; Turner and Marino, 1994; Wenger, 1996a; Williams, Ware and Donald, 1983). Other scholars report an association between limited social integration and poor overall health and well-being (Chappell, 1991; Chappell and Badger, 1989; Cutrona and Russell, 1986; Krause, Herzog and Baker, 1992; Lubben, Weiler and Chi, 1989; Rook, 1994; Stuck et al., 1999). Others document a connection between social networks and adherence to desired health practices (Kelsey, Earp and Kirkley, 1997; Potts, Hurwicz and Goldstein, 1992). One recent study even suggested that people with fewer social ties are more susceptible to the common cold (Cohen, 2001; Cohen et al., 1997).

Although much of the social and behavioural science literature recounts the benefits of strong social networks, there is also evidence that negative aspects can be harmful. For example, conflictual interactions between family members, friends or neighbours may actually increase stress rather than reduce stress, thereby contributing to worse health (Seeman, 2001). There are also pivotal times when family members and friends may be too eager to offer help to an older adult and such support may prove detrimental. In a study of intergenerational support, Silverstein, Chen and Heller (1996) found that a threshold of support existed where support from children was beneficial up to a certain point, but too much support produced an increase in dependence and a reduction in well-being. Other researchers have found that some older adults may desire the perceived availability of family and peer contacts but not necessarily the actual contact (Mullins, Sheppard and Anderson, 1991).

A number of theories have been proposed to explain the link between social ties and health. One theory suggests possible direct biological effects of social ties on human physiology (Seeman et al., 2002). For example, strong social ties may serve to stimulate the immune system to ward off illnesses more effectively. Similarly a buffering effect theory suggests that strong social ties may reduce the susceptibility of an individual to stress-related illnesses (Cassel, 1976; Cobb, 1976; Krause et al., 1992; Krause and Jay, 1991; Mor-Barak and Miller, 1991; Thoits, 1982). A third theory suggests that social networks provide essential support needed during times of illness, thereby contributing to better adaptation and quicker recover time. Finally a fourth theory posits that social ties are instrumental in adherence to good health practices and the cessation of bad ones (Kelsey et al., 1997; Potts et al., 1992).

Challenges to Measurement

Due in part to the complexity of social relationship phenomena, there is a lack of agreement on definitions and preferred measures for social networks (Berkman, 1985; Ell, 1984; Heitzman and Kaplan, 1988; House et al., 1988; Lin et al., 1999; Lubben and Gironda, 1997; Lubben and Gironda, 2003; Vaux, 1988, Wenger, 1995; Wenger, 1996a). For example, this construct has been labelled as social bonds, social supports, social networks, social integration, social ties, meaningful social contacts, confidants, human companionships, reciprocity, guidance, information given, emotional support, and organizational involvement (Caplan, 1974; Cobb, 1976; Ell, 1984; Lowenthal and Haven, 1968; Lubben, 1988; Miller and Ingham, 1976). In one meta-analysis of social support research, Heitzman and Kaplan identified 23 different techniques for measuring social networks (1988).

Selecting the specific foci of social network assessment is another common challenge. Social support comes from a variety of sources, including family, friends and neighbours. It appears that family, friends and neighbours may serve different functions in older people's lives (Antonucci, 2001; Chappell, 1991). Having family support, for example, is often crucial in forestalling institutionalization (Felton and Berry, 1992; Hooyman and Kiyak, 1999). Spouses and children, particularly daughters, are often credited as primary caretakers providing in-home personal assistance to frail older persons, enabling them to remain within the community (Stone, Cafferata and Sangl, 1987). Immediate family members are usually the major source of help during illness and disability. Even within the family domain, variation in type of support is seen between spouse and child. Without such timely and dependable social support the likelihood of using extensive formal services and the risk for institutionalization is higher.

While family members often provide for most of the critical needs of an older person, a growing body of literature also testifies to the importance of having strong friendships in old age. Many scholars have noted how important friendships are to the psychological well-being of the elderly (Adams, 1986; Adams, 1987; Antonucci, 2001; Francis, 1991; Hooyman and Kiyak, 1999; Larson, Mannell and Zuzanek, 1986; Peters and Kaiser, 1985). Furthermore, in comparing the effects of satisfaction between family and friends, Crohan and Antonucci (1989) suggest that friendships are less likely to have negative effects on the well-being of mature adults while family relationships, on the other hand, can trigger negative effects when demands are too high. Carstensen (1992) followed a group of women and men for 34 years and found that even though interaction intensity with friends varied over the years, feelings of emotional satisfaction and closeness towards friends remained relatively stable.

When it comes to the need for immediate assistance, neighbours and proximal friends may prove to be an especially important source of support (Hooyman and Kiyak, 1999). Litwak (1985) suggests that for some tasks, such as responding quickly during illness or emergencies, friends and neighbours may be more accessible and readily available than family members who either live further away or who are away at work much of the day. Adams (1986) also notes that neighbours and near-by friends help when it is convenient to them and for predictable tasks, such as providing transportation, and thus relieve the family of some burdens in their care of the elderly. As individuals advance further in age, they become more neighbourhood-bound and neighbours have been shown to be important links to community services (Regnier, 1980). Also, natural helping networks in neighbourhoods often provide supportive and monitoring functions to community-dwelling older persons, especially those living alone, and even delay institutionalization (Balfour and Kaplan, 2002; Pynoos, Hade-Kaplan and Fleisher, 1984). The importance of friendship and neighbourhood-based helping networks is likely to increase as the proportion of older persons with adult children decreases (Gironda, Lubben and Atchison, 1999).

Social Network Measures

As House (2001) points out, we know that social isolation kills but we still do not know why and how it does its damage. An essential building block for such research is good measurement. Solomon (2000) states that geriatric assessment is the 'heart and soul' of geriatric practice. Much as for basic research, more attention must be given to developing such tools that are suitable for practice settings. Presently there is relatively little inquiry regarding social networks in geriatric assessment protocols. Researchers and practitioners often do not share the same priorities for assessment tools.

From applied research and clinical perspectives, there is growing pressure to develop short and efficient scales. Some elderly populations are unable to complete long questionnaires. Time constraints in most clinical practice settings also necessitate efficient and effective screening tools. Shorter scales require less time and energy for both the administrator and respondent. Thus parsimonious and effective screening tools are more acceptable to both elders as well as health care providers.

For more basic researchers, somewhat longer research instruments are highly desired. Having a larger number of items as well as better clarity of concepts generally contributes to a scale's reliability. Such instruments facilitate the appraisal and analyses of subtle differences in social networks. Rather than attempt to design a singular social network scale that fits all populations and all needs, a feat only remotely attainable, it seems more practical to design measurement instruments for specific populations along with clear intentions on how the instrument should be used (Mitchell and Trickett, 1980).

Reviewing the expanding array of social network assessment instruments is beyond the scope of this chapter. However two recently published resources should be referenced for those seeking to explore the growing list of instruments. Levin (2000) provides an updated overview of a wide array of measures noting their practical application. Cohen, Underwood and Gottlieb (2000) recently edited a guide to social support measurement and intervention for health and social scientists.

The description and critique of a commonly used scale provides a framework for further development and refinement of social network measures. The scale used for these analyses is the Lubben Social Network Scale (LSNS). More specifically, the authors examine the psychometric properties of the original LSNS (Lubben, 1988) and compare them with those from a recently developed revised version, the LSNS-R (Lubben and Gironda, 2003; Lubben, Gironda and Lee, 2003). The authors review the guiding principles used for the refinements incorporated in the LSNS-R.

Brief Description of the Lubben Social Network Scale (LSNS)

The original LSNS was developed as an adaptation of the Berkman-Syme Social Network Index (BSSNI; Berkman and Syme, 1979). Whereas the

LSNS was developed specifically for use among elderly populations, the BSSNI was initially developed for a study of an adult population that purposefully excluded older persons. The LSNS is based on items borrowed from questionnaires used in the original epidemiological study for which the BSSNI was constructed. However the LSNS excluded BSSNI items dealing with secondary social relationships (viz., group and church membership) because these organizational participation items showed limited variance when used with older populations, especially those having large numbers of frail elderly persons (Lubben, 1988). In contrast the LSNS provides an array of items dealing with the nature of relationships with family and friends, in response to the growing body of empirical evidence that the structure and functions of kinship and friendship networks are particularly salient to the health and well-being of older persons.

The LSNS has been used in more than 100 studies since it was first reported (Lubben, 1988). Low scores on the LSNS have been correlated with mortality (Ceria et al., 2001), all-cause hospitalization (Lubben et al., 1989; Mistry et al., 2001), physical health problems (Hurwicz and Berkanovic, 1993; Mor-Barak and Miller, 1991; Mor-Borak, Miller and Syme 1991), depression and other mental health problems (Chou and Chi, 1999; Dorfman et al., 1995; Lubben and Gironda, 1997; Okwumabua et al., 1997) and lack of adherence to good health practices (Potts et al., 1992). It has been used in an assortment of other applied settings (Luggen and Rini, 1995; Martire et al., 1999; Mor-Barak, 1997; Rubenstein, et al., 1994; Rubenstein, Lubben and Mintzer, 1994). Further, the LSNS has been employed in a variety of ways, including use as a control variable as well as an outcome variable in health and social science studies. It has been used as a screening tool for health risk appraisals and as a 'gold' standard to evaluate other social network assessment instruments (Pourat et al., 1999; Steiner et al., 1996; Stuck et al., 1999).

Four Guiding Principles used to Refine Original LSNS

The work to refine the LSNS had four guiding principles. One was to better distinguish between and specify the nature of family and friendship social networks. A second was to replace items in the original LSNS that have demonstrated limited response variance. A third guiding principle was to disaggregate 'double-barrelled' questions. The fourth was to produce a parsimonious social support network instrument to encourage and facilitate its use in research and practice settings where time constraints or other issues preclude using longer instruments.

In line with the first guiding principle, two questions that assessed the recipients and sources of respondents' confidant relationships were recast to distinguish between confidant relationships with family members and those with friends. These changes recognize that confidant relationships with family members may serve different functions than confidant relationships with friends (Keith, Hill, Goudy and Power, 1984).

With regard to the second guiding principle, it should be noted that social and behavioural measures are purposely designed to discriminate among groups for a given construct, and so lack of response variation within a given item limits a scale's ability to detect key underlying differences among respondents (DeVellis, 1991; Streiner and Norman, 1995). Thus, eliminating items with limited statistical variance generally increases a scale's overall sensitivity and specificity, and that in turn improves its effectiveness in measuring constructs of interest (DeVellis, 1991; McDowell and Newell, 1987).

Double-barrelled items are those in which two different questions are contained in one item. Such items often confuse respondents because they are not sure as to which aspect of the double-barrelled question they should respond (DeVellis, 1991, Streiner and Norman, 1995). Disaggregating double-barrelled questions not only helps respondents in answering, it allows researchers to determine the extent to which each part of the original question helps to define a particular construct.

From applied research and clinical perspectives, there is growing pressure to develop short and efficient scales. Some elderly populations are unable to complete long questionnaires, and time constraints in most clinical practice settings necessitate use of efficient and effective screening tools. Shorter scales require less time and energy of both the administrator and respondent. Thus parsimonious and effective screening tools are needed that are acceptable to elders, researchers, and health care providers as well.

Description of Refinement to Specific LSNS Items

Two items from the original LSNS scale ('Helps others with various tasks' and 'Living arrangements') were dropped because they demonstrated limited response variation among a number of sample groups including the present one. Furthermore neither of these items helps to distinguish between family networks and friendship networks.

The 'Helps others' item was originally included in the LSNS in part because social exchange theory suggests that a reciprocal social relationship is stronger than one that is unidirectional (Burgess and Huston, 1979; Jung, 1990). Thus, rather than only capturing what others do for the study respondent, it is desirable to include items that also assess what the older person does for other people, i.e., items should be included to assess reciprocity of social support within kinship and friendship networks. However in past studies the 'Helps Other' question generally demonstrated insufficient response variance with almost all respondents claiming that they extensively helped others. Thus this question was a good candidate for elimination or replacement.

The 'Living Arrangements' item has also not performed well over time. When the original LSNS was constructed, both living arrangements (usually in the form of 'lives alone') and marital status (in the form of 'not married', i.e., widowed, divorced, separated or never married) were common proxies for limited social support networks. It therefore seemed entirely appropriate at the time to include an item in the original LSNS that merged the two related constructs of living arrangements and marital status. However this item has been the worst performing item on the LSNS across different settings. Part of the problem has been scoring it, which is constrained by the limited number of response options available as well as by disagreements among scorers in assigning ordinal weights to specific response options.

Two items in the original LSNS are classic examples of 'double-barrelled' questions. One question asked, 'How many relatives do you feel close to? That is, how many of them do you feel at ease with, can talk to about private matters, or call on for help?'. A companion response set was asked regarding friends. These questions were each recast. One recasting asks, 'How many family members do you feel at ease with such that you can talk to them about private matters?' whereas the other half of the original question asks, 'How many family members do you feel close to such that you can call on them for help?'. The 'double-barrelled' question for friends was similarly recast. The first set of these substitute questions examines somewhat intangible or expressed support, whereas the other set taps into more tangible support, such as help with running an errand. Both types of support have been suggested as important aspects of social support networks (Litwak, 1985; Sauer and Coward, 1985).

The last refinement in inquiry addressed the two confidant items in the original LSNS. The items were recast to distinguish between confidant relationships with family members and those with friends. These changes recognize that confidant relationships with family members may serve different functions than confidant relationships with friends (Keith et al., 1984). Figure 3.1 summarizes these refinements to specific LSNS items.

Original LSNS items:
L1 Family: Number seen or heard from per month
L2 Family: Frequency of contact with family member most in contact
L3 Family: Number feel close to, talk about private matters, call on for help
L4 Friends: Number feel close to, talk about private matters, call on for help
L5 Friends: Number seen or heard from per month
L6 Friends: Frequency of contact with friend most in contact
L7 Confidant: Has someone to talk to when have important decision to make
L8 Confidant: Others talk to respondent when they have important decision to make
L9 Helps others
L10 Living arrangements

Step 1: Eliminate items with limited variation:
Items eliminated: L9 and L10

Step 2: Uncouple double-barrelled questions:
Items modified: L3 and L4 each split into two separate questions
  L3A Family: Number feel at ease with whom you can talk about private matters
  L3B Family: Number feel close to whom you can call on for help
  L4A Friends: Number feel at ease with whom you can talk about private matters
  L4B Friends: Number feel close to whom you can call on for help

Step 3: Distinguish target and source of confidant relationships:
Items modified: L7 and L8 each split into separate questions for family and friends
  L7A Family: Respondent functions as confidant to other family members
  L7B Friends: Respondent functions as confidant to friends
  L8A Family: Respondent has family confidant
L8B Friends: Respondent has friend who is a confidant

Figure 3.1   Refinements to LSNS items

Data Source

The data are from a survey of older white, non-Hispanic Americans in Los Angeles County, California, conducted between June and November 1993. A self-weighting, multistage probability sample was selected from 861 census tracts in the area in which the white, non-Hispanic population exceeded any other single racial or ethnic group. This sampling strategy insured a high level of homogeneity in the sample. The first three sampling stages were: 1) random selection of tracts; 2) random selection of blocks; and 3) random selection of households within selected blocks. Households were then contacted by telephone to determine the age and ethnicity of household members. All white, non-Hispanic persons aged 65 or over in each household were thus identified and then potential participants were randomly selected from this pool.

Of the 265 older persons thus selected, 76 per cent agreed to be interviewed, resulting in a final sample of 201. The sample included 130 women (65 per cent) and 71 men (35 per cent) and had a mean age of 75.3. Additional details on the sample are reported elsewhere (Moon, Lubben and Villa, 1998; Pourat, et al., 1999; Pourat et al., 2000).

Analytic Approaches

Reliability is a fundamental issue in psychological measurement (Nunnally, 1978). One important type of measurement reliability is internal consistency, i.e., the extent to which items within a scale relate to the latent variable being measured (DeVellis, 1991; Streiner and Norman, 1995). Cronbach's (1951) coefficient alpha was chosen to examine the internal consistency of the LSNS and modifications designed to improve upon the original version. The acceptable range of coefficient alpha values employed here was 0.70 to 0.90 (DeVellis, 1991; Nunnally, 1978) because assessment instruments with reliability scores higher than 0.90 are likely to suffer from excessive redundancy, whereas those with alpha less than 0.70 are likely to be unreliable (Streiner and Norman, 1995). A further test of item homogeneity used was the item-total test score correlation (DeVellis, 1991; Streiner and Norman, 1995). Here acceptable values of the item-total score correlation were 0.20 and greater (Streiner and Norman, 1995).

Principal component analysis looks for underlying (latent) components that account for most of the variance of a scale (Stevens, 1992). Principal component analysis with varimax rotation was used here to explore the component structure of various versions of the LSNS to see if the modified versions conformed in actuality to the hypothesized structure. Although more sophisticated methods exist to examine factor or latent variable structures, such as maximum likelihood factor analysis and confirmatory factor analysis, many scholars contend that principal component analysis is both adequate and yet more practical than more sophisticated techniques, as principal component analysis is mathematically easier to manage, easier to interpret, and yields results similar to those from maximum likelihood factor analysis (Nunnally, 1978; Stevens, 1992). The size of the sample used in the analyses discussed below is adequate to conduct principal component analysis according to general sample size guidelines (Guadagnoli and Velicer, 1988; Stevens, 1992).

Reliability Analyses

The Cronbach alpha value for the original 10-item LSNS scale administered to the present sample ($\alpha = 0.66$) is slightly lower than those previously reported (Lubben, 1988; Lubben and Gironda, 1997) and below the desired standard for internal consistency. As shown in Table 3.1, Cronbach alpha values increased in each subsequent step in the analysis, indicating that each successive modification contributed to improving the final product's internal consistency. Although the modification produced in Step 1 has two items less than the original LSNS, the alpha value is slightly higher than that for the original LSNS, suggesting that dropping items L9 and L10 was appropriate. Further, the greatly improved alpha value obtained for the variant produced in Step 2 indicates that disaggregating the two 'double-barrelled' questions (items L3 and L4) was quite beneficial. In final step changes the confidant items to distinguish between source and target confidant relationships with family members and those with friends had further increased internal consistency. This step demonstrates that the LSNS-R has very good reliability as measured by the Cronbach alpha and significantly improves upon the original LSNS in this regard.

Item-total Scale Correlations

Item-total scale correlational analysis yielded coefficients ranging from 0.27 to 0.75, indicating that LSNS-R items are sufficiently homogeneous and without excessive redundancy. All internal reliability coefficients fell within

Table 3.1   Cronbach's alpha value by product of each step of item refinements

Step in item refinement	α
Original LSNS; 10-item scale	.66
1 Items L9 and L10 dropped; 8-item scale results	.67
2 L3 and L4 split; 10-item scale results	.73
3 L7 and L8 split; 12-item scale (LSNS-R) results	.78

the acceptable range suggested by Steiner and Norman (1995). The correlation coefficient between the original LSNS and the LSNS-R was 0.68.

Factor Analyses

Principal component factor analyses were performed to explore for latent factors and to determine whether the final modified version has latent structural components corresponding to both kinship and friendship networks. The number of factors was determined by considering factors with Eigen values over one (Kaiser, 1960) and by identifying the elbow in the screen plot tests (Cattell, 1966). The factor loadings were subjected to varimax rotation.

Table 3.2 shows the rotated factor matrix for the original LSNS administered to the present sample. Although previous studies have reported three factors (Lubben, 1988; Lubben and Gironda, 1997), the rotated factor structure for the LSNS here showed a two-factor solution, with one factor consisting largely of family-related items and the other consisting primarily of items concerning friendships. However the family factor also incorporates items concerning confidant relationships and the 'helps others' item. Both confidant items clearly load onto the family factor in this step, but the 'living arrangements' item cross-loads on both the family and friend factors.

Principal component factor analysis of the LSNS-R (Table 3.3) revealed a single, clean family factor and two friendship factors. The friendship confidant items (L7B, L8B) and the frequency of contact with a friend item (L2) constitute one of the friendship factors, while the remaining friendship items make up a second friendship factor. The item on being able to talk to a friend about private matters (L4A) loads on both friendship factors.

Table 3.2   Original 10-item LSNS factor matrix

	Family factor	Friend factor
L3 Family: discuss private matters/call on for help	.72977	.12423
L8 Is confidant	.67426	.03773
L1 Family: number in contact	.66327	−.06391
L2 Family: contact frequency with a family member	.66292	−.07607
L9 Helps others	.57022	−.02692
L7 Has confidant	.53911	.20467
L4 Friends: discuss private matters/call on for help	.26056	.78075
L5 Friends: number in contact	.20716	.75203
L6 Friends: contact frequency with a friend	−.10817	.52249
L10 Living arrangements	−.34899	.44612

Table 3.3   LSNS-R factor matrix

	Family factor	Friend factor A	Friend factor B
L3B Family: call on for help	.75997	−.03523	.23273
L8A Family: has confidant	.74025	.08476	−.00240
L7A Family: is confidant	.73581	.24895	−.03842
L3A Family: discuss private matters	.73448	−.02925	.23203
L2 Family: contact frequency with a family member	.71338	.05138	−.14382
L1 Family: number in contact	.67122	−.15758	.15646
L8B Friends: has confidant	.04871	.88000	.12791
L7B Friends: is confidant	.19066	.84875	.11396
L6 Friends: contact frequency with a friend	−.14282	.54930	.18563
L5 Friends: number in contact	.09154	.05937	.84670
L4B Friends: call on for help	.08390	.27114	.76627
L4A Friends: discuss private matters	.09222	.49201	.60282

Conclusion

This chapter has briefly reviewed the growing body of evidence regarding social ties. As gerontologists and geriatricians begin to identify the means to increase active life expectancy, rather than mere life expectancy, it is likely that an older person's social support networks will prove to be even more essential. Although there are increasing opportunities to generate new knowledge in this important research area, improved social support network measures are essential. The present analyses should be viewed as part of an ongoing pursuit for well-constructed social integration scales that can be used in variety of research and practice settings.

The original LSNS was designed specifically for an elderly population. Although it has proven adaptable to a variety of settings, some deficiencies have been noted. The present chapter describes the LSNS-R that was designed to address these measurement problems. The refinements are theory driven and involved reworking items in the original LSNS so that the revised scale can better measure the distinct aspects of family and friendship networks (Lubben and Gironda, 2002).

Two other versions of the LSNS have been developed to respond to particular needs of practitioners and researchers. An abbreviated version of the LSNS-R has been developed (Lubben and Gironda, 2000). This six-item scale (the LSNS-6) can be especially suitable in practice settings as a screening tool for social isolation or for more general use in those research settings where longer social support network scales cannot be accommodated. For those social and behavioural researchers desiring more extensive inquiry into the nature of social relationships of the elderly, an 18-item version of the LSNS has also been developed (Lubben and Gironda, 2003; Pourat, et al., 1999; Pourat, et al., 2000). The major advantage of the LSNS-18 over the LSNS-R is that the former distinguishes friendship ties with neighbours from those with friends who do not live in close proximity to the respondent. Such distinctions are desirable for exploring a growing number of social and behavioural research questions regarding the functioning of social support networks.

In summary, scale development and validation are cumulative and ongoing processes. They require testing and retesting of instruments in various research and practice settings among diverse populations. Social integration scales must be tested on a variety of levels, using both psychometric and practical standards to assess their actual clinical usefulness. Future analysis of the scales should include an assessment of their sensitivity to various differences within and between groups, for example cultural and socio-demographic differences or levels of health and functional status that might affect response patterns. The present analysis offers an instrument that has been examined and refined over the past decade and this approach could be used to evaluate and refine other social support network measurement tools. Improved measures of social support networks are essential to better understanding the reported link between social integration and health.

Finally all health care workers must respond to the growing body of knowledge regarding the centrality of social ties to health and well-being of older adults. Geriatric practice protocols to regularly monitor social integration of older adult clientele need to be adopted. Treatment plans need to consider social interventions that could improve the quality of life as well as reduce the risk of mortality among older adults. Much as community health nurses are being urged to screen home health clients as well as assisted living residents for social isolation (Tremethick, 2001), other health care professionals should similarly adopt such practice protocols. Valid and reliable abbreviated instruments such as the LSNS-R can facilitate achieving this objective.

Chapter 4

Social Networks and Social Support in Later Life

Chris Phillipson

Introduction

The study of social relationships in later life has followed two main traditions. The first takes as its starting point the view that understanding the lives of older people requires them to be studied as 'members of families [and not] simply as individuals' (Townsend, 1957). Early work on this theme focused on the way in which the rise of the nuclear family might lead to the isolation of older people within the kinship network. This view was influenced by functionalist social theory, and in particular the work of Talcott Parsons (1943) in the USA. The argument here was that the nuclear family had become 'structurally isolated' and that the individual's responsibilities in adulthood were drawn to the family of procreation first, with those to parents, siblings and other relatives following behind (Allan and Crow, 2001). However, the 'rediscovery' of the extended family by researchers in the 1950s and 1960s (Litwak, 1960; Young and Willmott, 1957) identified the way in which family ties were still providing support or 'partial aid' to use Litwak's term, to groups such as elderly people. And later work exploring the 'generational' dimension of family life, highlighted the extent to which intergenerational flows – downwards as well as upwards – had retained their importance in advanced capitalist societies (Arber and Attias-Donfut, 2000; Bengston and Achenbaum, 1993).

Family relationships in their nuclear, extended and generational forms have thus far been the dominant approach to understanding relationships in later life. Research has examined the social world of older people as shaped by families in the first instance, friends and neighbours second, and voluntary and bureaucratic organizations a distant third (Shanas, 1979). A second approach, however, has been to take the wider social network, rather than family ties alone, as the main unit of analysis. In the case of gerontology, two factors contributed to this interest. First is the view that despite their importance, family relations comprise just one element in an increasingly varied range of relationships experienced by older people (Phillipson et al., 2001). Network analysis offers a new approach to understanding and measuring this diversity. A further influence came from those concerned with assessing the actual or potential support available to older people at risk. Here, network analysis was used to gain more detailed analysis of the different types of supportive ties operating within the community (Wenger, 1996b).

Given the increasing importance of the social network perspective within gerontology, this chapter has three main aims. First, the wider background to the interest in social networks is considered, with a review of some of the key studies and approaches in this area. Second, the chapter looks at the application of a network perspective to studies of later life and illustrates some of the findings that have emerged. Finally, we examine some of the problems encountered in the application of different network methods, and some priorities for future research.

Defining Social Networks

The idea of the social network has a long history within the social sciences, with its development in social anthropology from the early 1950s (Barnes, 1954; Mitchell, 1969). Subsequently, Bott's (1957) research on the impact of network structure on marital relations was important in spreading the influence of this approach (Bulmer, 1987; Crow and Allan, 1994; Scott, 1991). The application of the network idea has been extensive, varying from locality-based studies (Fischer, 1982; Wellman, 1979); research on the personal networks of parents and their children (Cochran et al., 1990); and studies of old adults (Antonucci and Akiyama, 1987a; Keating et al., 2003; Kendig, 1986; Knipscheer et al., 1995; Lang and Carstensen, 1994; Phillipson et al., 2001; Wenger, 1984, 1995). Allan (1996, pp. 126–7) suggests that:

> There can be no doubt that the concept of network has come to play a significant part in the study of informal relationships. Rather than just focusing on one type of tie – say, kinship, or neighbourship, or friendship – it provides a framework for appreciating the interplay of all these different relationships. Moreover, this framework is structural. Instead of simply allowing the characteristics of individual relationships to be assessed and compared, it allows for comparisons to be made between some of the collective properties of the set of relationships any individual (or family or other social unit) maintains.

In Britain, the best-known use of social network analysis within gerontology has come from Clare Wenger and her colleagues, who in a series of studies have explored the characteristics of social networks among the old in rural (Wenger, 1984, 2001), as well as urban settings (Wenger, 1995). Bowling (1994) has also used network methodology in studies of health issues in old age, in relation to both morbidity and mortality (see Bowling and Grundy, 1998, for a review of the latter). Phillipson et al. (2001) examined the social networks of older people in three urban areas of England, as part of a wider project examining the nature of family and community change over the postwar period.

As will be examined further below, in the gerontology field a threefold distinction has been made between social, support and care networks. Fast et al. (forthcoming) summarize this as follows:

> Individuals are embedded within webs of social relationships (the *social* network) ... which are said to have the potential to provide support and care ... In turn, *support* networks are the actualized potential of social networks that provide emotional and tangible aid ... *Care* networks are believed to be a further subset of support networks comprising individuals who provide emotional and instrumental assistance to seniors who need it specifically because of their physical or cognitive limitations (author's emphasis).

House and Kahn (1985), in an early review of different measures of social support, distinguish between the term social network as referring to the structures existing among a set of relationships (for example, their density, homogeneity and range); and social support as referring to the functional content of relationships (i.e. the types of help received by individuals). Bowling et al. (1991, p. 549) clarify this point with the following distinction:

> A social network is defined here as a set of linkages among an identified group of people, the characteristics of which have some explanatory power over the social behaviour of the people involved. It is the set of people with whom one maintains contact and has some form of social bond. Social support is defined as the interactive process in which emotional, instrumental, or financial aid is obtained from one's social network.

As a general summary, Antonucci (1985, p. 97) emphasizes the distinction between social networks as structures and social support as functional behaviours, noting that the critical research question with regard to both structure and function is that of: 'what is their effect on the support exchanged and how do they, either directly or indirectly, affect individual well-being?'.

A variety of approaches exist for measuring social networks, these reflecting the contribution of disciplines such as anthropology, psychology and sociology. Measures also vary in terms of whether the sole focus is on 'egocentric networks' (the set of direct ties which respondents have with significant others), or (as in many anthropological studies) on the question of the relationship between these significant others within the individual's network. In this review, the emphasis is on the former, this reflecting the bulk of sociological and psychological research to date. Van Sonderen et al. (1990) have usefully categorized three approaches to defining and measuring social networks, these labelled the exchange, affective and role-relation approaches. These different types will now be reviewed with examples from key research studies by way of illustration.

Exchanging Relationships

The exchange model has been used to examine those who perform different types of activities for the respondent, and how, or if, such support is reciprocated. It was originally developed by McCallister and Fischer (1978), and has been used in general population studies (Fischer, 1982) as well as in research on older people (Kendig, 1986; Wenger, 1984). The general approach of this measure is to ask the respondent to name those with whom they engage in valued interactions, assessed through questions such as: Who would care for your house if you went out of town? Whose advice would you consider in making an important decision? From whom could or would you borrow a large sum of money? Wenger (1984) used this methodology to assess the supportive potential of older people's relationships. Her 'supportive network' focused upon people with whom the individual had close ties or from whom she/he received regular help. Kendig et al. (1986) also used this approach to identify people with whom the respondent exchanged specific kinds of support. Questions covered the provision or receipt of a wide range of expressive and instrumental support, actual as well as potential.

The focus on exchanges between subjects has generated some useful empirical findings. In Claude Fischer's (1982) classic study *To Dwell Among Friends: Personal Networks in Town and City*, just over 1000 adults in the San Francisco area were interviewed. A particular focus of this research concerned the link between personal networks and systemic and structural factors. Of these, Fischer (1982, p. 251) found that educational level had the most consistent effect upon personal networks.

Other things being equal, the more educational credentials respondents had, the more socially active they were, the larger their networks, the more companionship they reported, the more intimate their relations, and the wider the geographic range of their ties. In general, *education by itself meant broader, deeper, and richer networks* (author's emphasis).

Fischer (1982) also found that household income made a sizeable difference in the networks reported, even with education held constant. People with more income included more non-kin in their networks, and were more likely to report adequate amounts of companionship and practical support than were the poor. A parallel finding in the field of ageing is that older adults who are relatively healthy tend to have more diversified support networks than those who are frail (Keating et al., 2002). Both findings would suggest that robust networks might often be least available to those who need them most.

Fischer (1982) also developed some important arguments about the impact of urban living on personal networks, suggesting that people in the city tended to 'disregard kin' in a way that was less true of those in rural areas. His argument was that urbanites had more alternatives – social as well as institutional – open to them when developing relationships. As a result, kin were less likely to feature so prominently in their daily lives. Fischer (1982, p. 83) concluded:

> This explanation is similar to the thesis of family breakdown but differs in subtle and important ways. [First] I am arguing that kinship involvement becomes selective concerning with whom and when people will be involved. Urban people, no less than rural people, can call upon kin ... but they have less occasion to do so. They can be more selective in deciding when to mobilize for which specific purposes. As a rural sociologist has put it: 'The very structure of urban society permits the individual to cultivate, with some impunity, the interpersonal relations he [or she] deems most important, whether they be with kin or friend.'

The study by Fischer also raised issues about the changing social construction of community, questioning, for example, the relationship between density and social support. The implication of this study was that: 'Local ties need not be superior ties' and that distant friends could be no less intimate than local ones (Bridge, 1995, p. 264). However, Fischer (1982) suggested that for low income households, maintaining what he termed 'the freight of distance' could produce insupportable costs. Thus, proximate contacts do have their uses: 'nearby associations are preferred when nearness is critical.

When proximity is less critical – and these are often situations involving most intimacy, sacrifice and faith – there is little or no preference for those nearby' (Fischer, 1982, p. 175; see, also, Phillipson et al., 2001).

Wenger et al.'s research (1989) on network structure led to the development of network typologies and the exploration of associations between network type and demographic and other outcome variables. Summarizing the results, Wenger (1996b, p. 289) reports that:

> The typologies show clear parallels ranging from close-knit, family-dependent to diffuse and fragmented. Differences between network types tend to be the result of marriage, fertility and migration patterns mediated by personality. The distribution of network types is affected by the patterns of these effects in a community or country. [The research demonstrates] network type to be related at the highest level of statistical significance to all demographic variables: morale, loneliness and isolation; patterns of self-help and mutual aid; use of formal services; and response to service intervention.

More recent work has focused on comparing the distribution of network types in urban and rural areas. Wenger (1995) reports on a comparison between Liverpool and rural communities in North Wales. The findings indicated the extent to which cultural, migration and socioeconomic factors interact to affect the formation of different types of support networks. An important finding in this study was the observation that, amongst the working class elderly in Liverpool, supportive networks had remained intact despite the experience of urban decline. Conversely, elderly residents of rural communities appeared to have less informal support available to them than their urban counterparts.

Intimate Ties

A second approach to studying networks focuses on the subjective dimension to social relations, with questions focusing on those who the respondent 'feels close to' or those with whom they have intimate ties. In the studies conducted by Kahn and Antonucci (1980), network structure is measured through collecting information about people who stand in different degrees of closeness to the individual (see also Pahl and Spencer in this volume). Data is collected by presenting the respondent with a diagram of three concentric circles with a smaller circle in the centre in which the word 'you' is written. Respondents are asked to place in the inner circle those persons who are 'so close and important' to them that they 'can't imagine life without them'. Those considered less close but still important are listed in the middle and outer circles. Respondents are then asked about a variety of support functions which network members provide or which they themselves provide (see Phillipson et al., 2001, for an application of this method to research on older people).

The approach developed by Kahn and Antonucci (1980) has generated a number of important research findings. A paper by Antonucci and Akiyama (1987a) reported on data from a representative US sample of men and women ranging in age from 50 to 95. The study reported that, compared with the oldest age groups (75–95), the 50–64 age group was 'more likely to have network members who are younger, who have been known a shorter period of time, who live closer and who are in contact more frequently'. A rather unexpected result was that there were no significant differences in network size by age (see Phillipson et al., 2001, for a similar finding). Additionally, a significant conclusion from this research was that support reciprocity continued to be an important feature in the daily lives of older people, this suggesting that 'reciprocity may play an as yet underestimated role in the well-being of people of all ages' (Antonucci and Akiyama, 1987a, p. 526).

Other research using the Kahn and Antonucci method has also clarified issues relating to the subjective dimension of relationships in old age. Lang and Cartsensen (1994), for example, found from their German sample that although overall network size was negatively related to age, the actual number of very close relationships did not decline. Indeed, their findings suggested that in old and very old age, emotional ties are maintained and become increasingly important as other relationships fall away. Very old (85 – 104) and old (70 – 84) subjects also reported comparable levels in the giving of emotional support. Lang and Carstensen (1994, p. 323) comment:

> Thus, [older people] continued to invest in their close relationships, not simply derive benefit from them. Granted the results we report are based on subject's self report, not observation, so we cannot know whether subjects actually gave the support they claimed. However, even if they did not, such reports could be seen as positive illusions ... that allow for the experience of subjective reciprocity in social relations.

Wellman and Wortley (1989), using a variation on the subjective approach, examined issues about the structure of support networks and their linkages with sociological debates regarding kinship and community. On the former, a crucial finding has been that networks tend to offer specialist rather than generalized support to individuals. As a consequence, Wellman and Wortley (1989, p. 274) argue that:

> There is no one kind social relationship called 'social support'. Rather, many different kinds of supportive resources flow through informal networks. Yet most network members provide only specialized aid. This means that the people at the center of these networks must obtain various kinds of aid from different network members ... people must search through their assortment of ties to find specific kinds of support.

At a macro-level, this research has also generated a number of hypotheses about changes to community organization and structure. For example, Wellman (1990) develops a model of thinking about communities as structures that enable people to draw upon different kinds of resources. In developing his framework, he distinguishes between 'community saved' and 'community liberated' perspectives. In the case of the former – epitomized it is argued in the writings of Young and Willmott (1957) and Gans (1962) – the vitality of kinship-based, mutual-aid communities, is emphasized. Such communities are seen to provide buffers against large-scale social forces, filling gaps in formal support systems by providing flexible, low-cost aid. In contrast to this, Wellman (1990, p. 218–19) suggests that network analysts now highlight the diverse, sparsely-knit nature of most personal communities (see, for example, Fischer, 1982). According to this view, communities are not merely havens from large-scale social forces, but active arrangements by which people and households reproduce. This 'Community liberated' model is seen 'to have the virtue of emphasizing the social ... basis of community and of showing how networks actively help people to engage with the outside world' (see, also, Bulmer, 1987; Crow and Allan, 1994). Wellman (1990, p. 219) concludes, however, that:

> communities are more apt to have mixed compositions and structures than to be purely Saved or Liberated. Within them, kin form a key cluster efficiently structured for communicating needs and coordinating support. This Saved cluster provides a haven from the demands of the outside world and many of the interpersonal bandages for domestic sores. Complementing this involuted group are strong and weak ties with friends, stretching outwards to connect a focal person to the diverse resources of other groups. These Liberated ties provide companionship in many arenas as well as entry points to new arenas ... To the extent to which both types of ties and structures are useful and complementary, then both are integral parts of a single personal community network.

Relationships and Roles

A third approach has been to define networks in terms of formal or prescribed categories. The approach here is to suggest that: 'By virtue of specific relationships with an individual, that is being related to the person or labelled by the person as a friend or co-worker, one would qualify as a member of his or her social network' (Antonucci, 1985, p. 961). The approach of defining the network in terms of formal role relations has been developed in a number of studies. Two such examples are, first, the research by Cochran et al. (1990), which looked at social networks among young children and their families; and second, the work by Knipscheer and colleagues (1995) in their major study of living arrangements among older people in the Netherlands (see also Dykstra in this volume).

In the study by Cochran et al. (1990) the interviewer began the interview by asking the parent (through a series of direct questions) for a list of individuals outside the immediate family 'who are important to you in one way or the other'. The word 'important' was clarified by a time frame ('people who you have contact with from time to time') and by examples of the kinds of exchanges that might characterize the relationship (e.g. 'when you need to borrow something'). The names were elicited from the parent – by role and context-related prompts; thus the interview began with neighbours and proceeded through relatives, workmates, school-mates, organizations and agencies, and other friends. The interview then continued with other questions relating to where each person named lived as well as more detailed information on the content of the relationship.

Knipscheer et al. (1995) used a modified version of the above procedure. Network members were identified in seven domains of the network: household members, children and their partners, other relatives, neighbours, persons from work or classes, members of organizations, and others (e.g. friends). A limit of 80 was set on the number of names to be mentioned, with information such as the type of relationship, sex, and contact frequency gathered for all identified network members. A key feature of this method is that it is possible, through the advance listing of potential network members, to gain a more complete picture of the older person's network. The Dutch study found that the 4,059 respondents who provided network data nominated a total of 54,522 network members (an average of 13.4, s.d. = 9.4). Of the relationships in the network (partner relationships excluded), 59.4 per cent were with kin. Children were nominated the most frequently, followed by sons- and daughters-in-law, brothers- and sisters-in-law, and siblings. Another important cluster of relations comprised cousins, nieces and nephews. Of non-kin relationships, neighbours were nominated most frequently, followed by friends, fellow members of organizations, acquaintances, and (former) work colleagues.

An important policy finding from the Dutch study was that the supportive network tended to be less robust in the case of very elderly people. The authors observed that:

> From the results emerges a somewhat worrying picture: the elderly who are more in need of support because they are older, lack a spouse, and experience more health problems are less likely to receive this support due to the lower support potential – of their proximate network ... it can be concluded that with the decline of important personal resources (age, health status, the presence of a partner), the proximate network also decreases in size as well as support potential (Knipscheer et al., 1995, p. 126).

This is clearly a major finding which needs testing in other social contexts, with clarification as well of the scope for modifying the networks of vulnerable older people within the community (see, also, Wenger, 1994).

Social Networks and Social Relationships in Old Age

At one level, the findings from network studies reinforce the message from family studies more generally: kin provide the bulk of intimate ties; primary or immediate kin are crucial for the provision of support; and older people are active as donors as well as recipients of aid to their network. This theme has been reported in a range of empirical work in different countries, for example Antonucci and Akiyama (USA) (1987a), Bonvalet, Gotman and Grafmeyer (France) (1999), Keating et al. (Canada) (2002, 2003), Knipsheer et al. (Netherlands) (1995), Phillipson et al. (England) (2001), Wellman (Canada) (1990), and Wenger (Wales) (1992).

Network studies, however, also provide important qualifications to this general picture. In the first place, the average number of intimate ties reported by older people (8.4 in Antonucci and Akiyama (1987a); 9.3 in Phillipson et al. (2001)) should be placed within the context of the small number of very close or important support providers or recipients (3.5 in Antonucci and Akiyama) and the significant proportion of older people reporting relatively small personal networks overall. For example, in the Phillipson et al. (2001) study, 30 per cent of those interviewed (n = 627) (men 65 and over; women 60 and over) reported social networks comprising five persons or less. Among respondents with very small networks, men appear somewhat more frequently than women: 5 per cent of men have networks of just one person or less, compared with 2 per cent of women. These figures are also confirmed in Canadian research by Keating et al. (2002, 2003). This reported that in relation to care networks (as defined above), these are predominantly small in size (in this study 40 per cent consisted of just one individual), female and kin dominated, mostly young to middle-aged and living in separate households from the care recipient.

Findings such as these raise issues about the vulnerability of networks to overload, and the difficulty individuals may face in spreading either the giving or receiving of care across a wide range of individuals. Moreover, many of these networks should more properly be viewed as 'couple' rather than 'family-centred'. As Jamieson (1998, p. 136) has argued: 'the historical shift from the "family" to the "good relationship" as *the* site of intimacy is the growing story of the couple relationship'. Older people (men especially) see their partner both as a confidant and the key provider of sustained help and support. This is almost certainly not a new development, but one that stands out more prominently in the lives of people studied in the late twentieth and early twenty-first century.

A second important finding concerns the specialist nature of the support provided by different network members. The argument here is that while extended family and generational ties are important, they reveal only part of the picture in respect of the nature of support given and received by older people. In reality, people place themselves within a complex range of relationships, using different ties for different purposes, but often with limited overlap among them. Wellman and Wortley (1990, p. 580) summarize the sociological basis of this in the following way:

> One segment of a network is composed of immediate kin whose relations are densely knit and broadly supportive, while other segments contain friends neighbours and workmates whose relations are sparsely knit, companionate, specialised in support, and connected with other social circles...Strong friendships as well as immediate kin provide much emotional aid and services, while siblings are often good companions. Yet friends and relatives usually are members of different clusters of relationships within these networks. The combination of kith and kin supplies both stable support from ascribed ties with immediate kin and adaptive support from achieved ties with friends, neighbours, co-workers, and other organisational ties.

Finally, network studies have identified the importance of non-kin ties in the lives of older people. Friends, for example, may be especially important in the networks of urban couples, in some cases substituting for children or other relatives (Fischer, 1982; see, also, Pahl and Spencer in this volume). This appears to be the case with the current cohort of older people and may become more prominent in later cohorts. Pahl and Spencer (1997) argue that in some instances friends may even be taking over from families as new 'families of choice' (see, also, Adams and Allan, 1998). They suggest that as the proportion of marriages that end in divorce increases and as men and women move geographically, and perhaps socially from their families of origin, so friends are drawn upon for support and security. Phillipson et al. (2001) reported that friends were the largest single group listed in respect of intimate ties among older people, and that in many instances they played a substantial role in the provision of emotional support. For the never-married, friends were listed as important sources of help (one in three would draw upon a friend for help with most areas of support). For those who were married, friends appeared to have a complementary role to partners and children (see, also, Keating et al., 2002).

Researching Social Networks: Problems and Potential

Despite the rich crop of studies emerging within the social network tradition, some critical concerns and issues need to be raised. This section will focus upon three main points: first, recognizing the strengths and weaknesses of particular approaches; second, developing links between quantitative and qualitative studies; third, identifying new areas for research.

The first issue is that more attention needs to be paid to the merits and/or difficulties with particular network perspectives, and these should be discussed more openly in research reports. Often in fact little may be said about network methodology, or why one method was chosen over others. But all have drawbacks as well as advantages, particularly in the way in which instruments include or exclude certain types of relationships. Some examples might be cited to illustrate this point. In relation to *exchange theory*, its value appears to reside in its ability to identify a spread of network members, together with a variety of supportive activities. On the other hand, this tells us very little about the strength of particular relationships (which may be more of an issue for some types of research than others) (Antonucci, 1985). Moreover, some variants of the exchange method adopt relatively strict criteria for assessing network characteristics, which may help to influence results. Wenger (1995), for example, has compared an urban community with her original rural sample, using an instrument comprising eight questions to assess the individuals network type. However, with just three of these focusing on community-wide relationships, there is the likelihood of a bias towards nominating kin within the network.

In the case of instruments that examine networks of *intimate ties*, these may be especially useful in measuring long-run as opposed to short-term relationships. Conversely, a disadvantage with this method is that definitions of 'closeness' and 'intimacy' are subject to wide variation in interpretation (reflecting class, ethnic and cultural differences) which may be difficult to control in any one study. Antonucci (1985, p. 97) herself makes the point that:

> To some 'close' might mean geographically close; to others, important might mean powerful or influential. Some respondents might feel that such terms as close and important should be reserved only for family members and thereby nominate a social network devoid of relatives or friends.

The *role relation* method also has a mix of advantages and disadvantages. This approach seems highly effective in capturing network diversity and the different tasks performed by individuals within the network. In addition, the types of questions used appear less vulnerable to the problems associated with the exchange and subjective methods noted above. However, there are at least two disadvantages that may affect some types of studies more than others. First, the approach makes *a priori* assumptions about network membership. The approach taken presents the respondent with a range of possible contacts, each occupying what are taken to be the main role categories in their universe. This fulfils the criteria of achieving adequate coverage of potential network members; it may, however, influence the selection of people chosen as members of the respondent's network. Second, as a method of data collection it is almost certainly more time-consuming than the other types discussed. This could present difficulties, for example, when interviewing people with serious health problems.

A second point to consider concerns the relationship between quantitative and qualitative data. Most studies tend to adopt the strategy of collecting either quantitative (see, for example, Antonucci and Akiyama (1987a), Knipscheer, (1995), Dykstra in this volume) or qualitative data (Francis, 1984; see Cattell; Pahl and Spencer; and Southerton, in this volume). But the value of linking both approaches is especially strong in the case of network methodology. Large samples may offer scope for developing meaningful analyses of issues relating to network size and density, as well producing typologies of network characteristics in terms of variables such as social and care support. But in the absence of qualitative data it may be difficult to establish with any precision the meaning of the relationships that are identified. Knowing that an individual has a 'large' or 'small' network is certainly important. But it is equally important to know something about the strength and quality of the ties involved. Eight relatively superficial ties may be less helpful than two or even one enduring relationship; qualitative data helps shed light on some of these issues. Equally, qualitative data has its own limitations in terms of ability to assess variations in the size and diversity of ties across different groups, as well as questions about the emotional and instrumental activities performed for and by individuals. These issues may be especially important to tackle for researchers seeking to evaluate the care potential of social networks.

Third, new areas for network research might also be explored. Network analysis has been especially fruitful in mapping issues relating to supportive ties in the community, and in documenting the wide range of relations in which older people are embedded. More could be done, however, to highlight the diversity of such relationships, and to move from the continuing preoccupation with kin (the chapters by Pahl and Spencer, and Cattell, in this volume indicate the potential for further work). There is also considerable scope for using network methods to aid understanding of the lives of minority ethnic groups. In some cases this may require adaptation of existing methods, particularly for non-English speaking groups. But network methods may be especially helpful for understanding the complexity of relationships among ethnic minority groups, especially where they maintain transnational relationships in addition to those maintained within national borders (Ho, 1991; Gardner, 2002). Another important issue concerns the extent to which networks change over time. Much research assumes that networks are relatively static, maintaining the same structure and composition for long periods of time. Yet some groups and individuals, subject to complex transitions associated with loss of work, ill-health or divorce, may experience significant change to their networks. From a policy perspective it would be helpful to have more information about the impact which this has, and to understand more about the precise way in which individuals experience and adapt to changes in their networks.

Finally, network analysis may be especially using in examining questions relating to social exclusion in old age (see Scharf and Smith in this volume). Network methods may, for example, provide a better understanding of the nature of isolation in old age, especially if data collection is extended to measure both the quality of social relationships and the nature of involvement in activities (political, social and cultural) within the community. Moreover, there is considerable scope for exploring how networks vary in respect of qualities such as trust and reciprocity (social capital as broadly defined by Putnam and others – see Perri 6 in this volume), elements which may be crucial to sustaining engagement with mainstream institutions. Researching social networks may thus be vital to the promotion of inclusion in later life, and the construction of policies to support this objective.

Conclusion

In the case of research in social gerontology, network analysis is still at a relatively early phase of development. To date, much work has focused on trying to improve our understanding of the type of support available to older people, and its impact on their health and well-being. This research has demonstrated, first, that a variety of ties are maintained well into late old age. Second, that elderly people contribute as well as receive support from their social network. Third, that some people may be isolated from their networks and that this can have major consequences for the quality of their daily life. These are certainly important themes but further research, on these and other topics must be carried out. Network analysis certainly has its limits. As Allan (1996, p. 127) reminds us this approach 'cannot fully answer questions about the sense of obligation and commitment we feel towards particular ties'. Nonetheless, we do need to know more about the wider set of relationships out of which the social world of older people is built and maintained. Developing and refining network techniques and perspectives will be a valuable aid to this task.

Chapter 5

Networks and Neighbourhoods: Children's Accounts of Friendship, Family and Place[1]

Virginia Morrow

Background

Children's and young people's friendship networks have been relatively under-explored by British sociologists working on social networks and the links with well-being. This chapter draws on data collected in a school-based study for the Health Education Authority (now Health Development Agency) that has explored the relevance of Putnam's (1993) concept of 'social capital' in relation to children and young people's well-being and health (see Morrow, 1999, 2001a). Putnam's conceptualization of social capital consists of the following features: trust, reciprocal support, civic engagement, community identity, and social networks; and the premise is that levels of social capital in a community have an important effect on people's well-being. For Putnam, social networks consist of *informal networks*, such as friendships and familial networks and spatial networks (people known in the neighbourhood); *voluntary networks*, that consist of activities such as involvement in sports, youth clubs, religious activities etc; and *formal community networks* linked to local government.

The protective functions of social networks are well documented for adults, the argument being that social support improves well-being through prevention of isolation, being understood, being valued, and obtaining help and advice when needed, that in turn have an effect on self-esteem, feelings of worth, and self-control (Cohen and Syme, 1985). However, very little research in the UK has explored this in relation to children. Most UK health-related research on children's friendships focuses on peer groups and has tended to see peer 'influence' in negative terms. The study of children's friendships has also been dominated by psychological approaches that tend to emphasize the importance of friendship for individual development and how this relates to adult sociability. As Pahl notes, 'Despite the very large literature generated by developmental and social psychologists, it does appear ... that friendship has successfully eluded their grasp' (Pahl, 2000, p. 142; see also Berndt, 1996; Erwin, 1998). Similarly, the literature on the sociology and anthropology of friendship is somewhat silent about children and young people's friendships (see, for example, Adams and Allan, 1998; Bell and Coleman, 1999; important exceptions are Griffiths, 1995; Hey, 1997; James, 1993). This chapter attempts to fill a gap in the research literature by exploring what a sociological approach to children's friendships might look like.

The research described in this chapter is based upon the paradigm proposed by the new sociology of childhood (see James and Prout, 1997). This suggests that we need to move beyond psychologically-based models that construct childhood as a period of socialization and development. Instead, we need to see children as active social agents who, at least at the micro-level, shape the structures and processes around them and whose social relationships are worthy of study in their own right. In other words, how do children themselves conceptualize 'friendship'? What do their descriptions of their social networks tell us about friendship? And how or why are these networks important for children in the here-and-now, rather than for their future? The chapter draws on empirical data from children, together with some recent sociological writing on friendship, and suggests that sets of social relationships with peers need to be seen in the context of wider relationships with family members, and location or neighbourhood.

Research Setting and Sample

Research was conducted in two schools in relatively deprived wards in 'Springtown', a town in southeast England, to match a study that had been conducted by Campbell et al. (1999) on the relationship between health and social capital in adults. One ward ('West Ward') consisted of 'suburban sprawl' on the outskirts of the town, with post-war housing and factories; the second ('Hill Ward') consisted of a mixture of industrial development, and Victorian, interwar and postwar housing development. The sample comprised 101 boys and girls in two age bands: 12–13 year olds (Year 8) and 14–15 year olds (Year 10). The children were drawn from mixed ability tutor groups with the exception of the Year 10 group in West School, who were in a mixed ability sociology class. In both schools, a significant proportion of children were from minority ethnic groups (West School 20 per cent; Hill School 35 per cent) and this was reflected in the children who participated in the research. In the West School sample, there were African-Caribbean and South Asian children; the Hill School sample included children from families who had originated in Greece, Cyprus, South Asia (i.e. Pakistan, Bangladesh, India); Jamaica and Turkey.

Methods

The research used a variety of qualitative methods:

(a) group discussions exploring the use of and perceptions of neighbourhoods; how the children would improve their neighbourhoods; and their community and institutional participation;

(b) written accounts of out-of-school activities; who was important to the children; definitions of 'friend'; social networks; descriptions of where they felt they belonged; and their future aspirations; one 14-year-old boy who preferred not to write volunteered to be interviewed;

(c) visual methods including map drawing and photographs taken by the participants of places that they defined as important. This generated 17 maps/drawings and 100 photographs.

Children chose their own pseudonyms. Group discussions were taped and transcribed.[2]

On the whole, there was a good deal of congruence between the two sites; where there were differences relating to age, gender, and ethnic background, these are discussed below. The remainder of this chapter draws on data from the project to explore the following themes: children's definitions of friendship, and the extent to which time, place, gender and ethnicity intersect to enable or constrain children's encounters and activities with their friends. It also explores ambiguities around friendship and the downside of falling out with friends. It briefly discusses familial relationships and networks, and describes children's aspirations for the future as well as the networks of information about jobs or further education they might draw upon. It also discusses examples where children have described their social networks becoming disrupted by moving house.

What is Friendship?

Children were asked to complete two sentences, 'What is a friend?' and 'What are friends for?' to elicit their definitions of friendship. These definitions were intended to provide some insight into children's beliefs and norms about friendship. Seventy children answered the questions, and nearly half of those responses (n = 33) contained the word 'trust' as an element of friendship. Other components included: emotional support, providing a sympathetic ear, respect, being there, providing advice, help, caring, sharing, reciprocity, someone to share secrets with, to have fun with (see Table 5.1).

Friendship and Time

Children often spend more time with their friends than they do with their families, especially as they get older. As Veronica, 15, put it: 'Why are my friends important? Because I spend nearly all of my time with them.' And Maria, 14, 'My friends are also very important to me because I spend so much of my life with them'. Daily activities were often structured around encounters with friends: Jody, 15, who lived in the ward bordering West Ward, described how:

> Mondays to Fridays are usually the same for me, get up and go to my best mate Shellie's house, then sometimes another one of my good mates Clare comes and then we all walk to school ... After school I usually go straight to Shellie's house and always find a way to scrounge a lift from someone. Once I get home I usually stay at home and do my homework – if I'm in the mood – or I go out and see my mates who live round the corner from me. On Fridays after school at about 7 o'clock me, Clare, Shellie [and two other girls] usually go out to meet new people or meet up with old/new friends. They usually end up staying at mine the night and we usually get in about 11.30 - 12.00. Saturdays I usually doss about down town with my mates. We always find something to do ... The kinds of things are dossing, parties, sleepovers, going town, going to activity places etc.

Shannon, 13, described how after school, she plays outside, goes to her friend's house 'or up the park with my sister. At the weekends I sometimes sleep over my friends'. Maria, 14, described how after school:

> I often ring my friends and talk on the phone for quite a while as well ... After eating I will either go round a friend's house, go to a local youth club, the cinema, or just stay in. My weekends are usually spent in the town centre with different friends. I sometimes go to the cinema, or bowling or just out.

Table 5.1   Examples of definitions of friendship

Year 10 girls

A friend: cares, shares, funny, friends are for sharing good times and having fun.

A friend is someone who is there for you and helps you get through bad times, i.e. family problems, boyfriends. Friends are for to have fun with and to help.

A friend is someone you can trust, someone who is loyal and is there when you need a friend. Friends are for companionship, support, help, trusting.

Year 10 boys

A friend is someone who helps you get along and someone who helps you out. Friends are to help you out and keep secrets and to trust.

A friend is someone who listens. Someone who cares. Friends are for doing stuff with and talking to.

A friend is someone you can trust and will always be there for you. Friends are for help and trust.

Year 8 girls

A best friend to me is someone who we can share secrets and talk about things together and go out together.

What is a friend? Help them out; never argue; care for; help, do favours; share; be friendly; someone you can share secrets with; you can trust.

What is a friend? A friend: hangs around with you; likes you; someone who looks out for you; sticks up for you.

Year 8 boys

What is a friend? Someone to have fun with, someone who looks after you, someone who protects you, a dog, person, dad, mum.

What is a friend: that plays with you, that liked you, helps you do things, animal, person.

What is a friend? Somebody who's there for you when you need them. A shoulder to cry on.

A friend is someone who sticks up with you, plays with you everyday.

Friends were also significant at school throughout the school day. For example, Kerry, 14, described how: 'In school when I am not in my lessons, I hang around with my best friend Sally and my friend, I walk to school with Becky. We normally just walk around having girly chats.' Isabelle, 15, reported: 'I have friends in school that are important to me and we talk all the time in school.' Teachers and schools have long recognized the centrality of friendship, and use friendship in various ways: some schools use the maintenance of friendship groups as a criteria for eligibility on the transition to secondary school from primary school; and in some schools, children from the same ethnic background might be clustered in class as a way of supporting each other.

Friendship and Place

As friends were central to many of the activities that children undertook outside school, it was not surprising that relationships with friends were depicted in the visual material that children produced. As noted, they were asked to photograph places, not people, but they found ways of incorporating friendships into these photos:

- 'This road is the most important road because it leads to my *friend*'s house' (Tom, 14);
- 'My old school: I often play football there with my *friend*s' (Bob, 14);
- 'This is our school playground, we hang around with our *friend*s there' (Wendy, Leila, Chloe);
- 'This is McDonalds. I always go there every week with my *friend*s' (Jennifer);
- 'Park. Where I used to go as a child and still go with my *friend*s now' (Maggie);
- 'School. Where we sit at lunch time' (Maria);
- 'I took this photo of my *friend*'s house, because she is my next door neighbour, and I hang around in and outside her house' (Gemma);
- 'Corner of a street where I meet my *friend*s' (Mary);
- '[High Road] area. Lots of my *friend*s live there' 'My *friend*'s house, I'm often in there, and there is a park behind the house' (Jagu).

In many cases, how children felt about where they lived seemed to depend on geographical proximity to their friends. As Maggie, 15, put it:

> I love my house and my area, because there are three parks near me, the town is a five minute walk away, the school is close and I can visit my friends without having to take a bus or walk miles. Most of my friends live in Hill Ward, or my area.

Not having friends living nearby was seen as a problem, and this seemed to be more marked in West School which was located in a quiet, sprawling, suburban locality with few facilities for young people. It was also mostly girls who described this, which could reflect constraints on girls' mobility. For example, Olanda, 14, described how:

> I'm fairly happy with where I live but would rather live in my old house ... this is because a lot of my close friends live up there. Usually I walk up there most days after school. It would be a lot less hassle if I lived up there near them.

Jade, 14, described 'I've known my best friend for about 10 years ... she is more like my sister. ... I live in West Ward and have done so for 10 years and [my best friend] lives across the road from me'. Rebecca, 13, described how she does not like her neighbourhood:

> It's boring, there's not many people of my age living round there. Because my best friend moved away she only lives 10 minutes away, but it's too much to walk every day there. I've been best friends with her all my life, and I've never broken up with her once. We do a lot of things together, she's coming on holiday with me this year as well, I can't wait.

Jody, 14, described how: 'It's a bit awkward because I live two miles away from the school and my mates live quite far away. At least I still have my old mates who live near me and I always make time for them'. In Hill School, some children did comment that they do not see their friends as often as they would like. For example, Tobi, 13, reported: 'During the week I don't go out much because all my friends live up in [Hill Ward] and I live down town'; and Amanda, 13, who lives outside Hill Ward, described how: 'There is nowhere around the area where I live to go in the evenings, and it is too far to go to my friend's house every night. So by the time I get there, I have to go soon after.' Paris, 13, who lived in Hill Ward, said (in discussion when asked 'How would you improve your area?') 'Have all my friends live next door to me.'

In a group discussion in Hill School, two boys said how much they liked their neighbourhoods. Wassef said:

> Yeah, but the thing is, he lives in a good place, in Hill Ward, because he's got all his mates there, it's got a community, and he [the other boy] lives just off town, he's got all the mates you can have, there, he's like the centre of attention where he lives.

Ajit, 15, described how:

> I don't like the area I live in, as many of my friends live far away from my area and I can't walk there, I would rather live in [another part of town] as more of my Indian friends live there.

Gender and Friendship

Allan (1989, p. 154) points out that gender differences in friendship in adulthood are quite well documented, though sometimes overstated, 'but in general, women seem more willing than men to talk through personal issues with their friends – men's sociability is framed around activities'. He notes this is usually explained by 'socialization and/or dominant notions of masculinity and femininity'. There were clear gender differences in children's definitions, but as Allan suggests for adults, these should not be exaggerated. (One difference was that girls tended to give more detail, so arguably we can find out more from girls about friendship than we can from boys, depending upon the methods used to elicit the data).

Girls' Friendships

Girls tended to describe 'close' friends, 'very close friends, 'oldest friends', 'best friends', even 'my most best friend', rather than groups of friends. The themes of uncritical support, trust, and 'being there' were frequently mentioned in girls' accounts of why their friends are important to them. Kellie, 12, described how:

> I have known Stacey for two years and she is my most best friend in the world, she is caring, I like her she is very kind and I can talk to her about my problems at school or at home.

Carly, 13, described how 'My best friend Angelina is important to me because I can tell her some secrets and she won't tell nobody else'. Isabelle, 15, described how she has friends she hangs around with who had already left school:

> They are really important to me because I can talk to them about arguments/ things that have upset me in school and they help because they are looking at the problem from the outside. They aren't all caught up in the situation.

Maggie, 15, described how 'Even though all of my friends are important to me, some are much more important than others, my very close friends or my oldest friends are most important because they've always been there to help and support me.' One girl, Dion, 13, wrote: 'My friends are important ... One of them is like my sister.'

Girls often use kin terms to describe the closeness of their friendship relationships – in a previous research study I undertook on children's definitions of family (Morrow, 1998), this was very clear. Danielle, 13, described how:

> My best friend, [girl] is important to me as she understands me for who I am and no matter what I go through she always sticks by me. She is very caring and loving to me and through being the only child I always feel that I have *an older sister because that is what she's like.*

Two other girls described close relationships, comparable to family relationships, with older female friends. For example, Janine, 13, described how:

> My next door neighbour is important to me because if I can't tell my mum something, I can always tell her. She is *like my second mum. Also ...[she] has twins, they're very special to me because they are like my brother and sister I will never have* [emphasis added].

Boys' Friendships

Boys tended to define friendship fairly briefly, and used notions of fun and having someone to go around with, though some boys reflected the importance of having someone to listen to them, who could be trusted, for example: 'A friend is a person who you can talk to and listens, and won't laugh or tell anyone about it. A friend is a person you can rely on' (Peter, 12). Three boys, two in West School and one in Hill School, and no girls, used the phrase '*a shoulder to cry on*' in their written definitions. Boys were more likely to list names of friends rather than to categorize them as 'best' friends, though there were exceptions to this. The assumption is often made that boys' friendships fulfil a different function to those of girls, that of active contributions, like sticking up for each other, and doing things together, and there were examples of this, in the descriptions of what they do outside school in terms of sport and other leisure activities. For example James, 14, wrote 'if I didn't have friends I wouldn't be able to do exciting things like go out to places with them like swimming etc'.

However, as noted, some boys described how their friends are important for them because they listened, were loyal and could be trusted: some described having known their friends for a long time. Bob, 14, wrote: 'My longest known friend is Dave. I have been friends with him since nursery school. He is a good friend and I value his opinion greatly.' Dave (who was in the same class) had written:

> My most important things is family, but in and around school, the most important thing to me is my friends. Some of my friends like Bob and Fred I have known for about nine or ten years ... A friend is someone who is there for you, when you need them most. They don't abandon you in times of need. Friends are for talking to, being there for them, giving them your support.

Joseph, 15, described how in the mornings, he would:

> ... call for my friend and go to school, evenings: go out with my friends and party, weekends: get up in the afternoon and then go out with friends. Mostly parks and down town. My friends and family are the most important people in my life. They're there for me when I need them. I trust them.

To some extent, boys are using a different language – of sticking up for each other, having fun together – but they also used the notion of uncritical support, in a similar way to girls. This could be partly related to the methods used. Children were providing freely written responses, and writing is (technically) a private matter – would boys have described the emotional significance of their friends if the question had been asked orally in group discussions, where pressures to behave 'like boys' might have constrained their responses?

Friendship and Ethnicity

Few children from minority ethnic groups attempted to complete the sentences defining friendship. Yet, from observation, and from their written accounts, friends were highly significant. For example, Jamel, 13, described how:

> I like to do a few things outside school such as playing basketball with my brother and with my friend; also I like to play cricket, football, I do these in our local community where they have recently built a basketball court ... To me I would say my family is important and will be for the rest of my life. I have a lot of friends who are good to me and I've known most of them since junior school and one or two from infants ... Friends: help you with school;

who will try to keep on a straight path; who you can have a conversation with; who will listen to your problems; who you can rely on; who stands by you. I feel I belong where I am now, I have good friends and a loving family.

Iftikhar, 13, described how:

When I am outside school I go out and play football with my mates or I stay in and play computer … my friends are important because you hang about with them, and if you don't have any friends, no one hangs about with you. I have known Paris and Fred since Infant school, and Henry since we started High School.

The following extract from an interview with Wasef suggests that for Muslim children, there may be practical constraints on participating in activities with friends:

I've got some friends that are Punjabi … I've got some white friends, too, but the white friends, they're allowed to come to my house more often than I'm allowed to theirs. They're allowed to go the [shopping] centre, and that, Miss, we have to get permission and we have to be in before like 8 o'clock, and that's just the lucky ones.

He then described how his dad is a shopkeeper, with many friends who were taxi drivers:

So they keep an eye out on you, so then you can't do nuffin. So even if you're going to your friend's house, that's all the way at the other end of [long main road], they'll say 'We saw your son, going all over there, with a group of white people', even if they see one or two white people, they'll exaggerate, and say, 'Oh, there was about 10–20 of them!'.

For Wasef, activities centred around friendship also clashed with his religious commitments:

At the weekend, you have to go to Mosque and that lot, and like once you've ruined the morning part of your weekend, you can't get it back. Now it all starts in the morning, and if you're gonna go and see your mates, that's 10 o'clock, you can't see them at 1, 2 o'clock. And we have to go Mosque after school, and all your mates are going everywhere else first, so it's going to be quite hard for us to go out, because my Mosque finishes at 6, so I have to go all up [to where his friends live] and I have to be back at 8, and in the wintertime it's even worse, 'cos it gets dark …

Wasef may have been reflecting how he had to negotiate relationships in three cultures: the context of school, which institutionalizes children in a particular way, dividing them by age and gender; in the culture of his family background; and in boys' culture outside school, from which he feels excluded, which is so different from his parents' values.

Mixed-gender Friendships

There were a few examples of mixed-gender friendship, and if children listed names of their friends, these usually included both boys' and girls' names. In only two cases was a close friendship with an opposite-gender friend explicitly described. This is Bart, 13:

> My friend Helen is important to me because I don't see any of my friends at the weekends and I can talk to her about things I don't have anyone to talk to about them. I have known Helen for a long time, for about four years. I know her because her mum is friends with my mum.

Amanda, 13, described how her 'very good friend Dave' is important to her, 'he understands me, listens to me. I have known him for eight years'. But these were exceptions. A (perhaps surprisingly) small number (six girls and one boy) of the older children mentioned a 'boyfriend' or 'girlfriend'.

Ambiguities of Friendship

As we have seen, some children described having known their friends for a long time. For others, however, friendship networks were dynamic, not static or fixed. For example, Beth, 13, described how 'I've just started hanging out with a new group of friends so I will be hanging around with them this summer holiday, going down town, cinema …'. As Pahl (2000) emphasizes, it is important to recognise that there are negative features to friendship relations. The downside of friendship is that when things go wrong, children can be quite badly hurt, despite school being a place for socializing and being with close friends, it was also a place where fights break out, and young people get physically and emotionally hurt. Mary, 12, said: 'I'm just having problems at the moment with this girl, she's getting all these Year 9s to beat us up for something we didn't even do, we didn't even know her until last year, so not

all friends are nice.' One Pakistani Kashmiri boy wrote about how he had lost
a friend, a relationship he had valued highly:

> I had one close friend but he doesn't want to know me now because I never
> treated him right. He was one in a million. Now he can't trust me, without
> him I don't want to have any friends. Life's a bitch. I treated him as my own
> brother now I feel alone and I will be until he is my best friend the way things
> were (Zishan, 15).

On the whole, though, children's accounts of friendship networks were
positive and inclusive, but even here there was some ambiguity. Some young
people described hierarchically arranged networks based on 'popularity' and
style, which led to exclusionary practices. 'Being part of the group' was clearly
crucial, and one discussion with older children focused on peer pressure (one
boy used this term and the others clearly related to it). Amy explained what
it meant:

> *Amy*: It's blending in with the rest of the group, if the rest of the group are
> wearing Nike trainers, you feel like you've gotta have Nike trainers, if the rest
> of the group are smoking, you feel like you've gotta smoke.
> *Gizmo*: Even with Nike trainers, as well, it's like oh they're the old model, this
> is the new model, you must have this, you haven't really got any free choice
> to wear what you want.

The groups and associations that matter to young people may consist of
clear hierarchies. Amy described it thus:

> *Amy*: You get class peer groups, you get like first class, like they're all popular,
> and if like say a third class person walked past 'em, they'd be jeering. They're
> exactly the same age, they know them, but in the street … you get some people
> who are so popular, everyone will be, often they're really horrible people as
> well, but everyone's like 'Oh, yeah, let's join their gang'. Then you get these
> other people, that nobody seems to like, and they're really nice people, and
> they walk past the other people, and they're like jeering at them. They've
> done nothing wrong.
> *Dave*: That's back to clothes, and stuff, again, though, innit?

This example illustrates the interrelationship between social capital and
symbolic capital – belonging to a particular 'class peer group' by having access
to the appropriate symbolic markers may provide a sense of belonging that

relates to well-being, but (paradoxically) may also set up habits (in this case, smoking) that may be damaging for future health.

And Family ...

Children's friend relationships need to be seen in the wider context of the close relationships they have with their families. It was clear that the quality of family relationships is very important to children's sense of well-being (see also Morrow, 1998). Sometimes it was hard to disentangle 'family-and-friends', though the following example sets this out quite clearly. Olanda, 14, described how she went to different people for support, depending on what the problem was about:

> My friends and family are important to me. Without my family I would have no-one to care for me and without my friends I would have nothing to do when I'm not at school. They are important to me because I care about my friends and family. I can talk to my family about some problems, for example problems at school or with friends and I can talk to my friends about things I can't tell my parents.

Parents, and especially mothers, were very important to both age groups. Virtually all the written comments the children made about their families (especially their mothers) were positive, and this appeared to be regardless of family structure. They were not asked a direct question about family structure but sometimes it was described in a matter-of-fact way:

> The most important people to me are my mother and my best mate. My mother because she always manages to cope with me and can manage to look after me and my brother on her own. My dad got divorced from my mum 5/6 years ago. I still occasionally see him, but not all the time (Jody, 14).

Brenda, 14, described how:

> The most important person in my life is my mum, she has brought me up the way I am. My dad hasn't brought me up because my mum and dad are divorced. My dad left when I was two years of age, I don't see him much. The other important family in my life are my two brothers [aged 23 and 19]. I also have a little sister ... she is 3 years old, sometimes she pulls your hair out till your bald, and other times she is a little sweetheart.

Cameron, 13, wrote: 'The most important person in my life is my mum. She understands me the most.' Asa May, 13, wrote:

> My mum is very important to me at the moment because she is due to have a baby at the start of July ... My dad is important because I don't live with him and I like to see him as much as I can.

Boys again were less expansive on the topic of family members but did convey the importance of parents. Harry, 13, wrote: 'My parents are very important to me as if I did not have them I would not be able to survive. Its not just about money, because they care for me and will always stand by my side.' And Dave, 14, wrote: 'My most important thing is my family.' Other comments included: 'My family [is important] because they're always there for you' (Shane, 14); 'My dad, mum and my family, because they love me, they trust me' (Imran, 15); and 'My parents [are important to me] because I love them, if it was not for them I would not be here. Family I love them and talk to them, play games and have fun with them' (Rock, 15).

Clearly, then, parents are important to young people's sense of well-being, not least because they are a source of emotional support just by 'being there' (see also Gillies, Ribbens McCarthy and Holland, 2000). However, in many cases, it was difficult to separate support provided by family members from that provided by friends.

Kinship Networks

Several children (a third of the sample) mentioned wider kin (usually grandparents), and some described a good deal of regular contact. Shenna, 12, described how:

> At weekends I do dancing at [a nearby secondary school, in Moss Hills] for 3 hours. Every other week on a Sunday I go to my dad's because my mum and dad are divorced. I go to my nan's every Saturday ...

Similarly, Sonia, 14, reported: 'My family and friends are important to me, especially my nephew and cousins, because they look up to me and I can look after them.' Paris, 13, drew his nan's house (in a different part of the same town) and wrote: 'At the weekends I go up to my nan's and I play with my friends, football, tennis, cricket.'

Familial networks appeared to be the main source of close relationships and support for children of Pakistani Kashmiri origin. This is not surprising, because the basic tenets of Islam emphasize the importance of family obligations and interdependence. Wassid, 15, described how 'In the weekends I go to my cousins and play with them at the [Park]. My family is most important to me and then my cousins and relatives. Because they're really close to me and they understand me.' Sabrina, 13, whose family is from Pakistan, wrote:

> The most important people in my life is my family. Although most of my family live in Pakistan, I still think they're really important to me. For example, I can't remember my gran or grandad, for eight years I haven't seen them. They still write letters to me and send me nice things from there.

So for Pakistani-Kashmiri children, family is clearly central, but the fact that so many white children maintain close ties with their family members, especially grandparents, contradicts the stereotypical idea than kin ties are no longer as central as they used to be as families have become more dispersed. Family members don't need to live round the corner to be important. On the whole, family relationships seem to give young people a context and a grounding for their lives in the sense of 'being there' in the background for them.

Aspirations and Networks: Family and Neighbourhood

Children were asked if they knew what they wanted to do when they left school and whether they already knew someone doing this kind of thing. Familial networks appeared to be the main source of information and guidance about jobs and future plans for education. Previous research has shown how (adult) individuals' economic chances are affected by their membership of a kin group (Grieco, 1987), and it seems likely that young people's first or subsequent jobs may be acquired through informal networks (see Morrow, 1994, on children's employment).

In West School, of the 39 children who said what they wanted to do, 20 (half of them) know someone who was already doing that kind of job. In 11 cases, these were relatives, or friends of relatives: for example 'My sister is a nanny and I want to be that as well' (Kellie, 12); 'I want to be a builder, my dad is a builder' (Stuart, 12) 'When I leave school, I hope to do A levels as this helps get jobs, my brother is at sixth form college, and it is a lot more free than school. After I wish to work with animals, which my cousin does and is very enjoyable' (Amy, 14); 'When I leave school, I hope to work in the field of law, possibly a barrister. My cousin is not a barrister but is a probation officer' (Dave, 14). Three children mentioned neighbours or people they know near where they live: 'When I leave school I want to go to college for a year to study Nursery Nursing. Then get a job in a nursery or playgroup. I know a lady around the corner from where I live who is a qualified Nursery Nurse' (Sandy, 15); 'I would like to do computer programming or do something to do with computers. I know someone who does work with computers and he lives across the road from us and he is a good friend of ours' (James, 14).

In Hill School, of the 39 children who said what they wanted to do, 26 (two-thirds) knew someone already doing this kind of thing. Fourteen mentioned relatives, or friends of relatives or relatives of friends; Tom, 15, described how 'I hope to be a painter and decorator when I leave school. My brother-in-law used to do this so I used to help him, that is why I'm interested in this work.' Ajit, 15, described how he hoped to 'go to college get an A Level, go to uni and get a degree in microelectronics and manage a company. My uncle in America has a printer chip company.' Jagu wrote:

> When I leave school I hope to go onto College and study A levels, which ones I don't know. I know quite a lot of people who go to College like my big brother and his friends and my friends' brothers.

Gemma wrote: 'When I leave school I want to be a hairdresser. My uncle in Scotland has his own hairdressing shop up there.'

As in West School, the neighbourhood was already a source of work for some children. Sabrina, 13, described in group discussion how:

> I just babysit, you know the girl opposite me, her auntie went to Pakistan, you see, and all the family did, apart from her grandad, so I used to babysit her every single day after school. That was when she was about three.

She also wrote:

> I want to be a nurse or a lawyer. The girl who I babysit, her mum's sister is a nurse. Or a lawyer because my sister's best friend's sister is a lawyer and is always getting certificates from her university. She is so clever.

Sabrina was the only child in Hill School who specifically mentioned someone in her neighbourhood as a source of information about work, though shared religious and cultural background may be the explanatory factor here rather than neighbourhood.

Disrupting Social Networks: Moving House

Moving house will obviously disrupt the social networks of parents and children, especially if it means a change of school (see also Nettleton et al., 1999). Mandy, 14, described how she had moved house several times within the town: 'I'm really happy where I live now but I want to move to (West Ward) so I can be closer to school, my friends, and my boyfriend'. Amy, 14 described how she lived in West Ward:

> … but for 10 years I lived in [adjacent ward]. In my old area I had *loads* of friends, you could just walk outside and there would be five or six people playing and you could just join in and everyone was welcome. I lived in a close so it was away from cars and so was safe. My old house was about three minutes away from my [school] so it was totally handy. My street now is not as fun because its mostly older people living there but in ways that is good, because it's nice and quiet for homework and relaxing. It is also good because it is just around the corner from the [local] shops. That is brilliant.

Mike, 14, had moved recently to a town a 20-minute drive away, but continued to attend West School. He explained:

> It's because at this school, I'm like really properly with my friends and everything, if I go to another school, I'm worried that I might not know no-one. I've got a good social life here, so I might as well keep it.

He explained that he stays in Springtown on Friday and Saturday nights, 'with my auntie, she lives where I used to live, so most of my friends live round that area'. For Tom, 14, moving house had been a positive experience, though how he felt about it was clearly due to a combination of factors:

> I used to live down town [near Hill Ward] but I never liked the area because it was noisy and trouble was there. West School is a fairer school than Hill School. Now that I go to West School, I have more friends and we go out on bikes, hang out at the local park, go bowling and play snooker. I never get bored and I can get on with my homework at home now because the atmosphere at home is a lot more better than when I was living with my stepmother and

brothers and sisters. That makes life easier for me now. My house is very nice as it is nice to live in.

Some children described having 'two homes' after their parents had divorced and this meant that had two networks of friends, one in each place. Sonia, 14, described how she had lived in Moss Hills, but she has 'two sets of friends, because I also have a home in (outskirts of London), with my dad for nearly six years'. In stark contrast to the negative conclusions that research has often made about the effects of parental separation on children, this is not *necessarily* seen negatively by the children themselves (see also Smart, Neale and Wade, 2001).

Sense of Belonging

Given the centrality of family and friendship that emerged so clearly from these data, it was not surprising that a sense of belonging appeared to derive from people and relationships. In Hill School, young people were asked to try to write about 'Where do you feel you belong?' if they had time. Twenty-five answered the question. See Table 5.2 for some examples of their responses. None described themselves as a 'Springtonian'.

A number of elements of social life appeared to be sources of a sense of belonging, but home, family and friends were the primary ones. As Rock, 15, put it: 'I think I belong in a community where I am treated right and a place that is warm and friendly'. However, as the section on moving house shows, place and neighbourhood are strong influences on how or whether young people can access the relationships that are so important to their sense of belonging.

Discussion

Thus friendship works in all sorts of ways. It is a complex and diverse relationship, often ambiguous. From children and young people's point of view, it was on the whole, a source of emotional support. Children's sources of a sense of belonging and identity appeared to reside in their informal social networks based on friendship and their kinship networks. 'Trust' was located in these relationships, and not generalizable to the wider community, and young people did not appear to exhibit a positive 'community' or 'civic'

Table 5.2   Where do you feel you belong? (School 2 only)

Boys	Girls
I belong somewhere bigger than Springtown, with more opportunities.	I feel most comfortable at home with my mum and dad because I can be myself and I don't feel like they are looking at me and judging me.
I feel I belong at home, at my friends, and my family's houses.	I feel I belong where I am. With my friends and family, at school and at home.
I feel I belong with my friends or at home.	I feel I belong where I am. With my friends and family.
I feel I belong where I am now I have good friends and a loving family.	I belong at home with my mum and my dad and my brothers and sister and my family.
I feel I belong at my school.	I feel I belong at home with my family and friends where I am now, but most of my family lives up Essex and Moss Hills.
I think I belong in a community where I am treated right and a place that is warm and friendly.	
I belong at home … in the back yard … in Pakistan.	I feel I belong in Cyprus, because most of my family live in Cyprus, and I hardly see them.
I feel I would belong in a school where there is more Indian or more people my religion as in this school I'm the only Hindu boy in Upper School, that is the reason why I've wanted to leave this school from Year 7.	I'm not really sure where I belong – maybe in my roots (Ireland) because I love Ireland … in all truths I really don't know where I belong but I intend to find out sometime in the near (or distant!) future.
	I feel I belong in London because that is where I was born in East London where some of my family are.

identity. They often seem to develop their own 'communities' in the face of a strongly-felt hostility from the adults around them (see Morrow, 2000). Yet friendship can operate in contradictory ways in terms of health behaviours.

As medical sociologists like Wilkinson (1996) have noted, it is friends with whom one shares cigarettes, alcohol, drugs and, in the case of these young people, visits to McDonalds. Simon, 14, wrote: 'During the night my friends and I go down [main road] and drink alcohol. Us teenagers don't go into any buildings, just walking on the street.' Zishan, 15 (quoted earlier), who regretted falling out with his friend, wrote 'I don't need friends because they pass their bad habits to you.'

Thus informal social networks based around friendship were central to children's everyday lives. Ethnic and religious background, and gender, interacted to inhibit or facilitate activities with friends. Friendship networks were dynamic, not static or fixed. Familial networks were important as a source of support and 'being there'. Wider kin were also important for a significant proportion of children, regardless of ethnic background, and were also perceived as a source of information about jobs in the future, as well as part-time work while at school. From children's perspectives, moving house disrupted their social networks, especially if it meant moving school too. Overall, a sense of belonging derived from relationships with family and friends, wherever they happened to be.

The neighbourhood may have been an influence on friendship networks, as it could be a source of friends and people to hang about with, and in a very small number of cases a source of information about jobs in the future. In the main, however, it appeared that young people thrived on tight, strong networks of trust and reciprocity. From their definitions of friendship, the link between friendship, trust and reciprocity were specific to individuals, rather than generalizable to their neighbourhoods. Formal community networks, so central to Putnam's conceptualization of social capital, did not seem to have much relevance to young people's daily lives; nor did the elements of trust, reciprocity, and community and civic engagement, at the neighbourhood level.

Elsewhere, I have argued that there are various limitations to using Putnam's conceptualization of 'social capital' in relation to the health of children and young people (Morrow, 2001c). These can be summarized as follows. First, there are methodological problems related to trying to research some of the components of social capital. For example, what is meant by the concept 'community'? What do we mean by trust, and how do you 'measure' it? Social capital is a catch-all category that incorporates a number of features of social life which may or may not have relevance to young people's daily experiences. The data gathered in the research reported in this chapter suggest that a range of practical, environmental and economic constraints were felt by young people, so it might be more helpful to think in terms of 'social resources' rather than 'capital'. A second and related problem is that there is a danger that broader structural elements of social life are ignored in research that focuses solely on local community issues and specific neighbourhoods. A third problem lies in the different ways in which academic researchers and policy makers use the concept of social capital – the first as a way of exploring social relationships; and the latter as if it is a buildable, measurable 'thing'. However, it is also important to acknowledge that using social capital as a research tool or heuristic device has enabled social policy research to focus on the processes and practices of people's everyday lives rather than on 'outcomes'.

At the beginning of his recent book *On Friendship*, Pahl claims that 'In contemporary Western society, we chose our friends to form part of our private life' (2000, p. 13). The examples given in this chapter allow us to see how choice is constrained for children and young people by the institutions and structures of their everyday lives, such as their families, and their schools. These influence their friendship patterns. Moreover the 'private' world of friendship spills over into the public sphere in school where children's days are not only patterned by the structure of the school timetables, but also by their all-important encounters with their friends in the playground and between lessons. An analysis of children's experiences lends support to Allan's (1989) suggestion that relationships conventionally depicted as voluntary, informal and personal are in reality highly constrained and context-specific. But overall Pahl's observation that modern conceptions of friendship are concerned with fidelity, solidarity and trust seems particularly pertinent to children's descriptions of the quality of their friendships. A sociological approach to children's friendships, then, demonstrates the importance of these relationships for children's quality of life and well-being in the here and now rather than for their individual development and social relationships. It demonstrates how friendship is patterned by social structural factors, and suggests that children's friendships need to be seen in the wider context of other relationships they have with family members and with the physical environment.

Notes

1   The author would like to thank the children and young people who participated in the research project, and the staff of their schools, who enabled the research to take place. She also gratefully acknowledges funding from the former Health Education Authority and the Eleanor Rathbone Trust.
2   The methodology used in this study is discussed in more detail in Morrow (2001b).

Chapter 6

Capturing Personal Communities[1]

Ray Pahl and Liz Spencer

Changing patterns of family formation, the supposed break-up of close-knit communities, the decline of stable full-time employment, and reduced rates of civic involvement have led some politicians, policy makers and social commentators (Etzioni, 1993a; 1996; Putnam, 1995a) to fear a 'collapse of community', with people becoming increasingly individualistic, isolated, and lacking in public responsibility. Rather than subscribing too readily to the assumption that social cohesion is under threat, however, we believe that it is important to take a close look at the micro-social world of personal relationships, and at the nature of informal social ties. Our particular interest is in the role of friends and friend-like relationships in providing a form of social glue.

There have been many different approaches to mapping the micro-social worlds in which people live out their personal lives. Traditionally, most sociologists and social anthropologists focus on kinship, leaving friends a relatively minor role, (with the notable exception of Allan, 1979; 1989; 1996; see also Pahl, 2000). Others have singled out friends or neighbours for specific analysis but definitional problems often create practical difficulties (Bulmer, 1986; Willmott, 1987). A strong research tradition has focused on studying social networks, but there is often a confusion between, on the one hand, a map of all possible social linkages, sometimes running into hundreds of people and an actual network star, centred on ego, where all or most of the named people have some known connection with each other.

Within a network, some connections will clearly be more significant than others. Whether one is concerned with the ego-centred star of relationships or more complex social networks, some ties will be more effective or salient than others. Some parts of a network may be more readily mobilized for specific purposes and such a grouping has been termed an 'action set' (Mayer, 1966). Split networks may reoccur when, for example, migrants move from one country or from one part of a country to another. The migrant may have two tightly knit networks in the two locations with only his or her social link to bring the two worlds together. This might happen, typically, with students who may have a 'home' world based on family and school friends in one place and a 'university' world of fellow students.

In an attempt to discover the meaning and significance of friends and friendship in people's micro-social worlds, we were wary of using the established methodologies of those concerned with social networks. This was partly because, however sophisticated some of these studies appear to be, they are frequently concerned with easily measurable attributes such as, firstly, the *structural* features of networks, such as their size, the physical distance between members and the density of their connections. Secondly, they focus on *interactional* features such as how frequently people make contact with each other through visits, letters, telephone, email and so on. Gathering such information is time consuming but it does have the advantage of being amenable to statistical and mathematical analysis of considerable subtlety and rigour (Wellman and Berkowitz, 1988).

It is, perhaps, understandable that the actual *content* of the relationships in social networks often gets neglected. There will evidently be qualitative differences between particular ties that may be of the greatest significance. Thus, interactional information about contacts between siblings, for example, can say nothing about their significance. Siblings can be life-long enemies based on childhood experiences or quarrels about inheritance or they can be the closest possible soul mates. The fact that an individual has one or more siblings in his or her social network provides very limited social understanding of the micro-social world in question. Despite its early promise, particularly in social anthropology (Mitchell, 1969), the early enthusiasm of practitioners gave way to disappointment and frustration so that Boissevain (1979, p. 393) somewhat scathingly remarked: 'Networks are compared with regard to density, size and even composition, much in the same way butterfly collectors compare the colouring, wingspan and number of spots on their favourite species'.

Our problem in attempting to re-think the contemporary salience and significance of friends and friendship was compounded by the fact that there was no clear agreement on what precisely the term 'friend' meant (Davis and Todd, 1985; Leyton, 1974). Some people might refer to their spouse or partner as their 'best friend', whilst others would refer to an old school friend, who is rarely seen, in similar terms. Likewise some people would wish to include all those whom they know well enough to address by their given names (often over-familiarly used after one fleeting meeting), whereas others might be more discriminating and refer to a small, selected band of individuals as their friends. Thus, simply adding up all those persons an individual designates as 'friend' could be misleading and would not tackle the issue of the content and quality of the relationship.

For our purposes, in order to understand the social role of friends and friend-like relationships it was vital that we adopted a research method which would enable us to study the content of friendship in some detail. For this reason, we chose a qualitative approach involving a series of in-depth individual interviews. In addition to this, our interest in *friend-like* relationships as well as friendship, more conventionally understood, meant that we needed to look at a range of personal ties, not just at those designated as friends. Consequently, we decided to focus on *personal communities*, that is people's 'intimate and active ties with friends, neighbours and work mates as well as kin' (Wellman, 1990, p. 195; see also Hirsch, 1981; Wellman, 1988), and to ground our exploration of friendship within this context.

Evolving a Method

Generating Personal Communities

Our initial concern was how to generate these personal communities given that people would probably not think of their everyday social relationships in such a way. We began with the assumption that it might be possible to collect information about an individual's micro-social world and map the whole universe of a person's social relationships, and then categorise these in discussion with the participant into meaningful clusters. We considered, for example, asking people to list the entire contents of their address book, but our pilot phase happened to be in the weeks running up to Christmas so we arranged a few pilot interviews in which we asked people to list those to whom they sent Christmas cards. Of course, we had no intention of using this strategy in the main study, since the sending of Christmas cards is too culturally specific, but this simple exercise provided us with some interesting lessons. Firstly, people recognized that their Christmas card list included contacts who varied enormously in terms of the importance of the relationship and its role in their lives. Secondly, although people found it illuminating to discuss these different relationships, the exercise was immensely time consuming. Exploring and comparing systematically the content of up to 100 different relationships from 'very good friends', to 'friends at the office', to various fossilized links with social worlds long since left, together with all familial links bound along a continuum from love to duty, was daunting and unmanageable within the context of a single interview. Thirdly, we found that it was difficult to keep tabs on who our participants were talking about and we needed some way of recording and displaying the names of the people being discussed. We concluded that we needed to: limit the number of relationships to those which were considered significant; generate the list in advance so that the interview could be spent exploring and contrasting different kind of relationships; and find a way of visually representing people's personal community.

In order to generate members of a personal community, we considered the three main strategies used in network studies: the role relationship approach in which people are asked about the people they know in particular contexts; the social exchange approach in which people are asked to nominate those to whom they would turn in specified situations; and the affective ties approach in which people include those with whom they feel they have a special or close relationship (see Phillipson in this volume). In practice, we included all three strategies. In generating an initial list, we used an affective approach, but then subsequently included both an exchange and a modified version of the role relationship approach to make sure we had not excluded other significant relationships.

Having chosen a method for generating personal communities, we then had to decide how to present the study to our participants. Because we were interested in friend-like relationships as well as friends and were concerned not to make people feel they *ought* to have friends, we decided not to prejudge the issue by asking about friends specifically. Instead, we asked our participants to list people whom they considered were 'important to you now'. We made it clear that such people 'could include a partner, family, friends, neighbours, people you work with and so on'. We did not emphasize in any way in our initial approach that we were primarily interested in friends and friendship. By leaving the participants free to decide those who were important to them at the time of the interview we were better placed to see the relative significance of each category. We chose those words carefully, rejecting adjectives such as 'close' (emotionally or geographically), 'helpful' and so on.

In order to save time during the interview and to give people a chance to reflect on their personal community, we decided to ask participants to generate their list in advance. A week or so before people were interviewed we sent a letter and 20 sticky labels, asking people to list the names of people who were important to them.[2] We made it clear that they should only use the number of labels they needed, that they were not obliged to use all the labels, but that if they wanted to write more than one name on a label they could do so. Our aim was for people to use the labels as flexibly as possible as we wanted to avoid conveying any expectations about how many names people *should* include. Apart from the name of the 'important' people we also asked participants to give details of their age and occupation (if appropriate), how far away (in miles) they lived, and how the relationship was designated, for example family member, friend, colleague, neighbour and so on. At the beginning of the interview we explored the criteria people had used when deciding who to include.

The next stage in representing personal communities involved asking participants to arrange their labels on a map. This map[3] consisted of a large piece of paper with five concentric rings (see Figure 6.1). We asked participants to imagine themselves in the centre, and then to place their labels – again in terms of the 'importance' of the relationship – in an appropriate place in relation to the centre. They were encouraged to use only as many of the rings as they wished, and were also able to place labels straddling across two rings. We were at pains not to hurry participants at this stage, allowing them time to compare and contrast their relationships, and to reconsider placements, sometimes rearranging labels as the map began to take shape.

Throughout this process we asked participants to talk us through their decisions so that their considerations, justifications and prevarications could be recorded on tape.

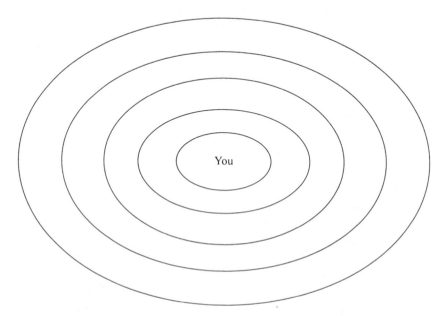

Figure 6.1　　A personal community map

Participants were able to add further names at other stages in the interview. For example, once the map had been drawn up, we asked them whether there were 'any other important people' in their lives who should be added for the sake of completeness. We also used some exchange-based questions to see if other relationships might be mentioned, asking to whom participants would turn in a range of situations. Finally, although we were interested in the current composition of people's communities and had asked about 'people who are important to you now', we were also concerned to discover how the situation had changed over the life course, since evidently the social convoy (see Antonucci, 1985; Antonucci and Akiyama, 1995) of significant others can change through marriage, social and geographical mobility, divorce and so on. Given the constraints of time, we could not conduct long and elaborate life histories for our participants, however desirable in principle that might be. Instead, we worked through significant periods of their lives such as school/ college, employment before marriage or cohabitation, the period with pre-school children, other work experiences, after divorce, on retirement and so on. For each phase we asked who were the most important people in their lives at that time and, if they did not already appear or were not subsequently included on the personal community map, on what grounds these people had been excluded. This enabled us to explore faded, forgotten, and fossilized relationships, as well as those that had been consciously dumped.

Having generated and mapped personal communities in this way, there was one further aspect of their structure we wished to explore, namely the extent to which members of a community were linked. We therefore asked participants to draw a line between those on the map who already knew each other, and those who were friends with each other, and in this way mini-social networks appeared.

Exploring Content

Our aims, however, were not simply to describe the *structure* of people's personal communities, we also wished to explore the *content* of relationships, particularly friendships, in considerable detail. The nature of different ties was explored in a number of ways throughout the interview. Firstly, when participants explained why they had included certain people, and why they had placed them in particular positions on the map, they were making comparisons in terms of the quality of a relationship and the nature of the tie. Then, once participants were happy with the map of their personal community, we went on to explore the nature of their friendships. We asked what the participant meant by the term 'friend', 'best friend' and any other term that had been introduced when describing different relationships. Having established what people understood by these terms at a *general, abstract* level, we then went on to look at *actual* friendships. However, we knew that we would not be able to examine every relationship where participants had included a large number of friends, and we therefore adopted three complementary strategies. First, using an exchange approach we posed a number of situations, such as wanting to have fun, looking for a job, being in financial difficulty, falling ill, being bereaved, and experiencing difficulties in a personal relationship, and asked to whom participants would turn in such a situation. This enabled us to see how people distinguished between friends in terms of the kind of help and support they might provide; it also enabled us to see the extent to which family members and friends were seen to play distinctive or overlapping roles. This approach has been used in many studies, but we wanted to go much further. So we adopted a second strategy which was to select names from each of the rings, chosen to represent different kinds of friendship, and ask participants to elaborate on the nature of the social relationships concerned and how they differed from those in other rings. Again, the subtlety of judgements was revealed: participants were often operating in a complex, multi-dimensional way and their placing of people involved many kinds of 'importance', as we discuss in detail below. Finally, we asked participants 'Is there anything you get from friends that you don't get from family?' and conversely, 'Is there anything you get from family that you don't get from friends?', inviting them to illustrate their views by comparing particular relationships.

Capturing Personal Communities in Practice: The Method Reviewed

Having described our method in some detail, we now report on our experience of using it in a small-scale, qualitative study.

Design and Conduct of the Study

Between May 1999 and June 2000 we conducted in-depth face-to-face interviews in two separate phases, analyzing the first round interviews before proceeding to the second stage. We were anxious to avoid a 'home counties' bias, which would certainly have been more convenient from our base at the University of Essex. Locations included North West England – focused largely in Greater Manchester but stretching down as far as the Potteries

– mid-Wales, Inner London and East Anglia. An initial purposive sample was drawn up to include as broad a cross section of participants as was possible within our financial constraints. Participants were chosen taking into account age (from 18–75), sex, social-economic background, stage in the life course, marital status, geographical mobility, ethnic background, and geographical location. This initial sample was contacted using the services of a professional recruitment agency. In the second stage, a range of sampling strategies was used. Iterative sampling was employed to identify and recruit under-represented groups such as unemployed people, people in manual occupations, and people who were living alone, as well as to ensure that our sample included people with non-heterosexual sexual orientations. We also snowballed from the initial sample according to types of friendship. Finally, extreme case sampling was used in order to explore and illustrate certain experiences in depth: we selected young care leavers and people with mental health problems who might be at risk of exclusion and who might have restricted friendship repertoires. In all, a total of 60 in-depth interviews were conducted ranging in length from one-and-a-half to three hours.

All interviews were tape-recorded and transcribed. These transcripts were then indexed thematically, using a structured framework drawn up using themes identified through a preliminary reading of the transcripts and categories from our own conceptual model of the issues we wanted to explore more systematically. Once all the transcripts had been indexed, the material was summarized, retaining the 'feel' of the participants' own language, and displayed in matrix form in a series of thematic charts. These thematic charts contained summaries of all participants' views on each key issue or concept (see Ritchie and Spencer, 1994; Ritchie, Spencer and O'Connell, 2003). However, we also produced individual charts for each participant's personal community on which were logged all the factual information about each member, such as age, occupation, and length of the relationship, as well as details of the relationship such as its development over time, the nature of the interaction, and frequency of contact. Exemplary quotations were either logged or transferred to relevant charts.

All the transcripts were treated in the same way. This is an important point. Very often qualitative studies are criticized for spattering cases or quotations through the text to support the author's argument. The reader has little means of judging how these cases or quotations relate to the body of data as a whole. Have particularly apposite quotations been chosen highly selectively to back up the author's position? Are they used to add a little 'local colour'? Or do they represent a perspective or position which has emerged from careful analysis of

Table 6.1   Profile of the sample

	Men	Women	Total
Age range			
18–39	9	12	21
40–55	9	13	22
56–75	10	7	17
Marital status/children			
Single, never married, no children	5	6	11
Married, living as married, no children	2	3	5
Married, living as married, children at home	7	9	16
Lone parents, children at home	2	3	5
Married, living as married, children left home	8	8	16
Single, divorced, separated, widowed, children left home	4	3	7
Social class			
Unskilled manual	4	7	11
Skilled manual	7	5	12
Intermediate	8	15	23
Professional managerial	9	5	14
Ethnic background			
White British	24	26	50
White Irish	1	1	2
Black British (Caribbean)	1	4	5
Black British (African)	1	1	2
Black British (Central American)	1	0	1
Sexual orientation			
Heterosexual	24	30	54
Non-heterosexual	4	2	6

the data, chosen from a number of possible cases. By seeing all the material on a series of charts, reflecting the complete sample, it is much less easy to be swayed by a particularly memorable turn of phrase, which may reflect a position at odds with what a more balanced appraisal of all the material would suggest.

Evaluation of the Method

Although we had deliberately avoided instructions as to the number of 'important people' who should be included, one of our initial concerns was that, by issuing 20 labels we had implicitly suggested that personal communities should be of a certain size, or that we wanted participants to restrict themselves to a maximum of 20 people. In practice, we feel that the flexibility we encouraged, stressing that people should use no more labels than they wished, and that they could put more than one name on each label, worked very well, as evidenced by the wide range in the number of labels used and in the size of personal communities. At one extreme, just five labels were used, one for each person; at the other extreme 41 names were included by making multiple entries on many of the 20 labels. Nevertheless, there were people (three out of 60 in our study) who claimed they would have liked more labels. Interestingly, however, only one of these added more than two or three names during the course of the interview. In some cases, participants initially included only a few friends as they had used most of their labels for family members, but during the course of the interview asked to add as many as 13 friends. On the other hand, there were those (two in our study), who confessed that they had 'scraped the barrel', including some names simply because they felt they should use most of the labels. Because this was a qualitative study, however, we were able to accommodate additional members of a personal community and to identify cases where names had been added as 'fillers'.

We were also keen to evaluate the way in which people interpreted the instruction to include 'people who are important to you now'. It was clear when participants chose who to include on their list and where to place them on the map, they were involved in a complex balancing of different criteria, and that this was possibly the first time that they had considered their personal community in such detail. We found that 'importance' was being interpreted according to three rather different kinds of criteria (see Table 6.2). Furthermore, we found that these criteria were not necessarily applied in the same way to family as they were to friends.

When deciding who was important to them, one of the first things people considered was whether or not there was a family connection. In the case of 'close family' there was generally a strong emotional attachment and no equivocation about whether or not to include them, examples being spouse or partner, children, grandchildren, parents, a favourite sibling and so on. In rare cases in our study, however, people chose to exclude their parents, particular siblings, and even some of their own children or grandchildren because of difficulties in the relationship, estrangement after an acrimonious divorce, a feeling of being let down, or simply a sense that they were not important in the other's life. Whether or not extended family members were included varied enormously. Whilst some participants excluded these kin unless there was a special relationship, others included aunts, uncles, nephews and nieces and various in-laws because of strong normative or cultural pressures that 'family should be important'.

Table 6.2   Criteria for determining 'importance'

Categorical criteria	Whether family or not
Intrinsic criteria	the qualities of the relationship: – the strength of the emotional tie – the extent of dependability and support – the degree of trust and confiding – the sense of being known and accepted
Extrinsic criteria	the context of the relationship: – the duration of the tie and sense of continuity – the frequency of contact – the sense of involvement or presence – the sense of 'having things in common'

The second major factor people took into account when deciding who is important in their lives was, not surprisingly, the intrinsic quality of the relationship. This was particularly the case with friends. Those who were liked or loved, and those who could be trusted and relied upon for practical help and support were likely to be given a more central place. Interestingly, dependability and helpfulness were more often used to distinguish *between* friendships, rather than as an invariable criterion for inclusion in a personal community; some unreliable but fun friends could still be considered sufficiently important to be placed on the map, albeit not in the centre. Friends were also not necessarily excluded because of a lack of intimacy but close confidants were consistently seen as the more important relationships and given a more central place on the map. Finally, being known and accepted '*for who you are*' was another indicator of importance and a highly valued aspect of friendship: 'They've seen the very worst side of you and like you in spite of it ....You don't have to put up with any pretence at all, they know you as you truly are.' As discussed above, however, loving and liking are not always applied to family, some of whom can gain a place on the map simply because they are family.

There were also extrinsic factors which helped to determine the importance of, mainly, non-kin relationships. Frequency of contact, for example, which may bring a detailed familiarity with the day-to-day content of the other's life, was a key element of some relationships. In other cases, however, it was the duration of the friendship which was valued; a sense of continuity had deepened and strengthened the tie so that it was possible to 'pick up where you left off', despite minimal contact. Unsurprisingly people were also included if they had things in common, shared values or felt they were on the same wavelength.

However, whilst this was considered almost a *sine qua non* of friendship, it was seen as an unexpected bonus in family relationships.

Our exploration of the criteria people used to determine 'importance' suggests to us that people's personal community maps represent something more complex and multi-faceted than some kind of social distance scale. For example, where siblings or parents were placed some distance from the centre, this could mean that participants felt less affectionate towards or less compatible with these kin, but not that they felt less *socially close*. Where friends were placed in outer circles, this often reflected the fact that these were more light-hearted or companionable rather than confiding friendships, but again did not *necessarily* imply greater *social* distance.

The Diversity of Personal Communities

Having reviewed the efficacy of our method, we now turn to some of our main findings. One of the first things which struck us was the sheer diversity of personal communities among the 60 people included in our study. For example, in terms of structural features, these communities varied in size, in the balance between friends and family, and in the centrality of friends and family on the map. As we discussed earlier, participants nominated from just five to more than 40 people who were considered 'important to them now'. The number of family members ranged from two to 32, with larger family contingents comprising three generations or a wide range of extended family; the number of friends ranged from just one to 24, with large friendship groups partly boosted by the inclusion of more casual, non-intimate friendships. At one extreme, there were personal communities which contained four times as many family members as friends; at the other extreme, there were cases where friends outnumbered family by as much as ten to one. While some personal community maps contained only family members in the first two rings, others gave friends a central place alongside immediate family. We consider the centrality given to friends in some personal communities, even by those who are very close to their family, an important justification for our study.

In order to make sense of this diversity, however, we need to look at the *content* of relationships as well as the *structure* of personal communities. Because of our interest in friends and friend-like relationships, we concentrated our analysis on the articulation of friend and family ties. Partners played an important role in all types of personal community, but were particularly crucial in one type. Neighbours and work colleagues, on the other hand, unless they were also designated friends, were usually placed in the outer rings of people's maps and played only a minor role.

Table 6.3   Types of personal community

Type of personal community	Key characteristics
Friend-like	Friends included in the central ring
	Friends outnumber family and play wide range of roles
	Importance of friends reflected on map
	Strong feeling of choice of relationships combined with sense of responsibility towards those considered important – both family and friends
Friend-dependent	Family only in the central ring, or in first 2 rings
	Friendships outnumber family
	Friends play wide range of roles
	Strong normative importance of family displaces the true importance of friends
Family-dependent	Family only in the central ring, or in first 2 rings
	Family outnumber friends
	Broad range of family relationships, some ambivalent
	Friends play specialized companionable, fun role
	Map reflects major importance of family
Family-like	Same as above except that friendships split between 'close' core and then more casual ties
	Strong normative importance of family means importance of core friends not reflected on map
Partner-dependent	Partner and family only in centre of map
	Heavy reliance on partner for most forms of support
	Friends play specialized companionable, fun role
	Map reflects centrality of partner and specialized role of friends

We found five main patterns in the way in which friends and family relationships were mapped (see Table 6.3). Each of these personal communities varied in terms of the emphasis placed on friendship and family, and the degree to which the map reflected the quality of different relationships. People with *friend-like* personal communities nominated more friends than family as 'important', had a wide range of different types of friends, and placed heavy emphasis on the importance of friendship. This was directly reflected in the way they mapped their personal community, with long-term, confiding and multi-faceted friendships being placed in the central ring, and more light-hearted or casual friendships further from the centre. Only 'close' immediate family were given a central place; other family members were placed further out or excluded altogether. There was a strong element of choice in both family and friend-based relationships, combined with a sense of commitment to those considered important.

> I mean with them it's about sort of unconditional acceptance, isn't it, really? … they get on your nerves, don't they, but you know, it doesn't change the way you feel. You don't wake up one morning and think: 'I don't love them any more'.

These personal communities most closely resemble the 'families of choice' described by Weeks, Heaphy and Donovan (2001), and were found among men and women in our study who had moved geographically, and were from professional or intermediate service backgrounds.[4] Figure 6.2 shows an example of a friend-like personal community.

People with *friend-dependent* personal communities also nominated more friends than family, had a broad repertoire of types of friend, and relied on friends for a wide range of social support. However, they also placed a heavy emphasis on the importance of family, and this strong sense of family influenced the way they constructed their map. Friends, even very close ties, were not placed in the central ring which was reserved for family members, usually a partner and children. Again, this kind of personal community was found among men and women who were geographically mobile from professional, managerial or service backgrounds. Figure 6.3 shows an example of a *friend-dependent* personal community.

In *family-dependent* personal communities, family rather than friends are in the majority and are relied on for a wide range of social support. Friends, by contrast, play a highly specialized role, usually confined to sociability and fun, and are placed in the outer circles of the map. Family relationships vary a great deal, but nevertheless kin are given a central position on the map – regardless of the closeness of the tie – because family relationships are seen as the most important. Figure 6.4 shows an example of this type of personal community.

Family-like personal communities are also characterized by a strong emphasis on family, and family members also outnumber friends in the

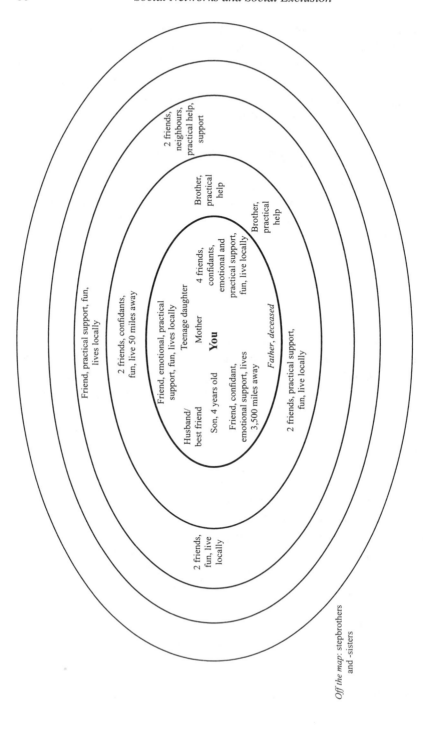

Off the map: stepbrothers
and -sisters

Figure 6.2   Example of a friend-like personal community

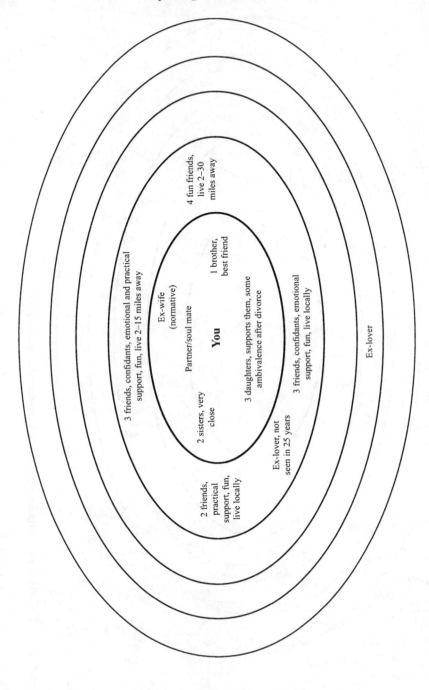

Figure 6.3   Example of a friend-dependent personal community

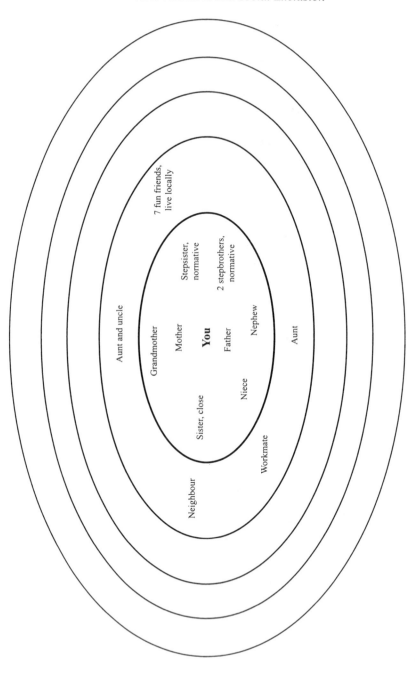

Figure 6.4   Example of a family-dependent personal community

personal community. People with this kind of personal community tend to have a small core of confiding or supportive friends who play a key role in social support, and then sometimes a broader group of more light-hearted friendships. This distinction between core and more casual friends, however, is not reflected in the map because family ties are seen as most important and take a central place, regardless of how close or supportive they are.

> Your family come first ... because it's your blood, your family, you know, who better can you trust more than your family? ... those friends that I've written down there believe it or not I could trust those friends with my life ... but they've still got to be out there [on the map]. And I think if they were to be standing here tonight they would be happy to be there. Because they know they're not the immediate family and the cousins, they know they're in the next line which is friends.

There were two quite different profiles for people in our study with this kind of personal community. Either they had lived for most of their lives in the same local community and came from traditional working-class backgrounds, or they came from professional and managerial backgrounds but belonged to particular religious or ethnic groups which stressed the importance of family life. One participant felt that a strong sense of family came from a number of cultural influences:

> Mother was Nigerian, Ghanaian and Irish ... father was Syrian ... I think this family thing is a Ghanaian, Nigerian and a Syrian thing ... all three – even though Syria is in a different part of the world, they seem to have a lot in common as far as the family unit is concerned.

Figure 6.5 shows an example of this kind of personal community.

Finally, we identified a kind of personal community which was *partner-dependent*. Although family members were given a central place on the map, relationships were not necessarily close and partners provided most of the social support. As with *family-dependent* personal communities, friends played a specialized, sociable role. Figure 6.6 shows an example of a partner-dependent personal community.

Of course, this classification of personal communities relates to the present – who is important to you *now*. But, following Antonucci (1985), we were also interested in the way an individual's significant others may change through the life course, with the role of kin and friends altering at different stages, and consequently adopted her concept of a *social convoy*. Personal communities

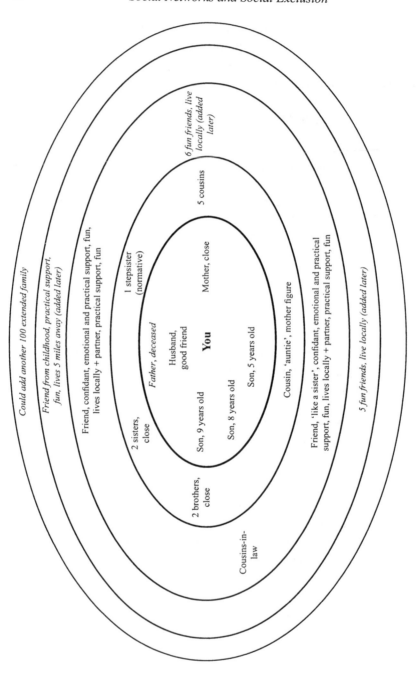

Could add another 100 extended family

Friend from childhood, practical support, fun, lives 5 miles away (added later)

Friend, confidant, emotional and practical support, fun, lives locally + partner, practical support, fun

1 stepsister (normative)

2 sisters, close

Father, deceased

Husband, good friend

You

Mother, close

Son, 9 years old

Son, 8 years old

Son, 5 years old

2 brothers, close

Cousin, 'auntie', mother figure

Cousins-in-law

Friend, 'like a sister', confidant, emotional and practical support, fun, lives locally + partner, practical support, fun

5 cousins

6 fun friends, live locally (added later)

5 fun friends, live locally (added later)

Figure 6.5   Example of a family-dependent personal community

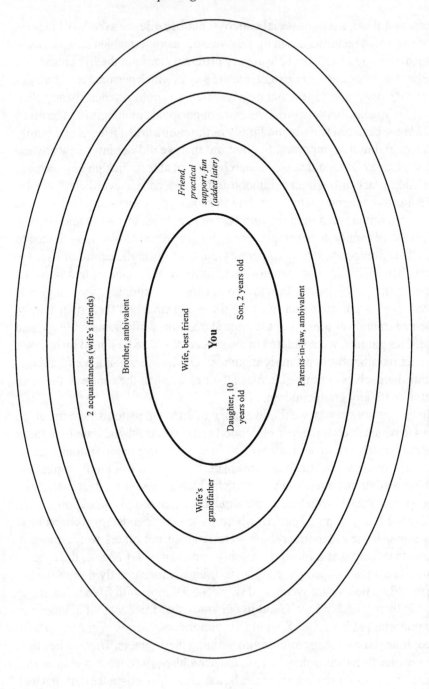

Figure 6.6   Example of a partner-dependent personal community

reflect, as it were, slices of social convoys, but because we asked participants about important relationships in the past, and our sample enabled us to compare personal communities of people at very different stages in the life course, we have been able to gain some insight into the way in which personal communities can change over time.[5] From our own research we could not identify any clear patterns of change in the *overall structure* of personal communities in terms of the *balance* between friends and family or the *centrality* of friends and family on the map, but it is important to point out that we did not interview anyone below the age of 18, so that our research was not able to pick up key changes which take place throughout childhood and adolescence. Nevertheless, we did find patterns of change *within this overall structure*, in terms of *which* kin and friends are important and in the *addition of new types* of family and friends. In the case of family, for example, young single people in our study tended to place their immediate family of parents and siblings in the centre of the map unless there had been some major breakdown of relations, as had been the case with the young people brought up in care. Unsurprisingly, when people moved away from their family of origin and established their own family, these new members took over the central position while some siblings, and sometimes parents, were situated in the second circle, to be joined by in-laws, and later possibly by step-family members. On the other hand, we found that parents themselves continued to place their children in the centre of the map, together with any grandchildren.

In the case of friends, we found a range of different patterns in terms of the extent to which friends made in childhood and early adulthood remain within a personal community. In one pattern these friendships are retained throughout the life course and few new friendships are made through work or family formation. At the other extreme, there can be complete changeover of friends at each major stage as new friends who '*are in the same boat*' are added and old ones fade. Finally, we found a mixed pattern where some new friendships were made at each stage, some older friendships were retained but others were gradually lost, so that there was a blend of stability and change. Of course, the amount of time and attention people can give to friends varies greatly during the life course. When people are young and single, socializing with friends is a major focus in their lives, and we found in our study that frequency of contact was very important at this stage. Keeping up with friends, however, can be difficult if people are busy raising children and building their careers. This is a key time when earlier friendships may be lost. Once children have left home or during the early years of retirement, there can be a friendship renaissance during which people may make new friends or pick up again with old established ones.

Finally, in addition to the composition and nature of relationships within personal communities, we were also interested in the degree to which 'mini-social networks' were contained within them. As Table 6.4 shows, we identified a wide range of patterns in terms of the extent to which friends were known to each other and to members of the participant's immediate family. At one extreme, there were very dense personal communities with a strong network of friends and family; at the other were more disparate patterns with few connections between members of a personal community. The most common pattern in our own study was for distinct clusters of friends to know each other, and for some friends to be known to family members.

Table 6.4   Patterns of density in personal communities

	Most friends are known to immediate family	Some friends are known to immediate family	Few friends are known to immediate family
Most friends know and are friends with each other	Dense		
Most friends know but are not friends with each other			
Clusters of friends know each other and are friends			
Few friends know each other			Disparate

Where at least some family and friends know each other, this can be in a variety of contexts, most commonly where the people live in the same area. The pattern, however, appears to vary at different stages in the life course. For example, among some of the young single people in our study, long-standing friends were known to parents and siblings because they had lived in the same neighbourhood and the friends had visited each other's houses as children. Parents and their children may be friendly with other families as '*family friends*' so that different generations know each other. Finally, where people treat some of their friends as quasi family, or alternatively treat some family members as friends, they include both family and friends in social '*get togethers*'.

> There's none of these people in this whole thing that haven't eaten in my house, or stayed here ... the others ... all except Rose because she lives so far away,

have certainly been here at any type of function that we've had ... They all know each other, yes ... so they all certainly, for instance, have been invited to my 40th last year.

By contrast, where few if any friends are known to family members, this tends to occur when there has been social or geographical mobility, where childhood friends have fallen away or when close family members have died or distanced themselves on account of previous feuds or disagreements.

This diversity in clustering and links between friends, and between friends and family, adds substance to our contention that personal communities are emphatically not the same as social networks, even though networks (certainly in most cases for the family) are, generally, an important part of them.

Conclusions

In this chapter we have described a method through which maps of personal communities may be constructed. We have also proposed a preliminary typology of personal communities, based on the balance between friends and family and the extent to which they play distinct or overlapping roles.

We are making no claim that personal communities are a peculiarly modern or late-modern phenomenon, which replace the communities of fate of 'traditional' society (Giddens, 1991). It would be slightly ludicrous to imagine that at some hypothetical benchmark in the past personal communities did not exist. Such detailed historical evidence as is available (largely based on diaries) for the seventeenth and eighteenth centuries provides clear examples of personal communities at that time (Macfarlane, 1970; Tadmor, 2001). It would be hard to imagine a time in recorded history when people did not live in structured micro-social worlds. It is, of course, likely that there was a greater congruence in the past between geographical, occupational and personal communities. But whether or not that was so is not our concern.

Of greater importance for us is to consider the implications of what may or may not have always been there for current sociological and public policy concerns. Our elucidation of our participants' personal communities helped them to recognize something they already 'knew', but to see it in a different way: they become conscious of the processes of which they formed a part. In particular, they became aware of the roles played by friends and family in providing different kinds of social support. However, the recognition of the salience and significance of personal communities experienced by individual participants also has wider implications.

As we suggested in our opening paragraph, there are many commentators and opinion formers who voice concern about the growth of individualization (Beck and Beck-Gernsheim, 2001), the collapse of 'community' – often very loosely defined, if at all – and the so-called 'decline' of the family (Abbott and Wallace, 1992; Berger and Berger, 1983; Davies, 1993; Dennis and Erdus, 1992; Etzioni, 1993b). Sometimes the debate becomes highly moralistic (e.g. Bellah et al., 1985) and there is a fear that society is now less cohesive, stable or in a vague sense 'good'. Part of the reason for this somewhat depressing perspective, which admittedly has been common amongst sociologists since Durkheim and Simmel, if not also amongst the political economists of the eighteenth century (Pahl, 1991) is that commentators have been focusing on the wrong indicators. Those concerned with a loss of community find it hard not to focus on specific geographical milieux, documenting, for example, declining communal activities in urban neighbourhoods. Others have documented the decline in membership of certain local clubs and institutions, as well as other indicators such as a decline in trades union or political party membership (Hall, 1999; Putnam, 1995a). It may be that an overall decline does involve some loss of civic responsibility. People may find it more rewarding to join choral societies or angling clubs or they may use the Internet to unite them with like-minded people. This is not the place to discuss in any detail the debates on 'social capital'. Suffice to say that counting differing or declining membership figures reveals nothing about the nature of interactions in people's micro-social worlds. Another indicator, frequently used in large-scale social surveys, attempts to document changing patterns of interaction by focusing typically on frequency of contact. Thus, for example, less frequent contact with parents by adult offspring is often taken to imply a weakening of family ties.

The important policy implication of our study is that many of the problems described by commentators using inappropriate indicators may look very different when viewed through the lens of personal communities. Thus, we found that people have widely different personal communities which offer varying levels of support, some supplied by family, some by friends, some by professional agencies and some in which it is shared. We suggest that personal communities at least allow us to consider the nature of people's micro-social worlds without leaping to gloomy conclusions as those looking through other lenses seem so prone to do. Through our recognition of the amount of suffusion between friends and families in different kinds of personal communities and the degree to which they play a range of overlapping roles, we can describe degrees of robustness in personal communities that those with a more limited focus miss. If subsequent research confirms our view that personal communities are, indeed, communities and not simply, crude resources for a self-centred individualism, then the implications for public policy could be great. As we develop our ideas we hope we may do something to dispel the gloom generated by some of the more vocal Jeremiahs by helping to change the perspective within which the somewhat hackneyed topics of 'community' and 'family life' are viewed.

Notes

1   For a more extended account of the issues raised in this chapter, see the forthcoming book by Spencer and Pahl on personal communities. This research was funded by the ESRC Grant No. R000 23 7836.
2   We were guided by the experience of Fischer (1982) who provided empirical support for choosing the limit of up to 20 people.
3   This mapping method has been used by a number of researchers, including those working on historical records (Macfarlane, 1970). For a recent example see Phillipson et al., 2001.
4   Pressure of space does not allow us to explore these patterns further. See our forthcoming book on personal communities.
5   Disentangling cohort from life course effects is a perennial problem; something we discuss in more detail in our forthcoming book.

Chapter 7

Cultural Capital, Social Networks and Social Contexts: Cultural Orientations Toward Spare Time Practices in a New Town

Dale Southerton

Introduction

Social networks are important. They are a resource that offer sources of information (about education, jobs, etc), access to places or social groups, and provide material and emotional support (Portes, 1998). Networks are often regarded to be class-based in the sense that people tend to socialize and come into contact most with people of a similar class position (Allan, 1989). This is not to say that those in the middle classes do not have contact with the working class (or vice versa), but to say that class has a bearing on the formation of networks. Given that social networks are a resource, it follows that they might play an important role in the reproduction of social class. This is the position taken by theorists such as Bourdieu (1984), who describes networks as one of three critical resources, metaphorically described as 'capital', which represent and reproduce class differences. These three forms of capital are economic (wealth), cultural (knowledge and education) and social (networks). However, theories which address the impacts of processes like globalization, economic restructuring and the centrality of market modes of provisioning bring into question the continued significance of class as a basis for shaping the life-styles, identities, practices and values of social agents (see for example, Bauman, 1988; Beck, 1991; Featherstone, 1991; Giddens, 1991).

This chapter examines the role that social networks played in shaping the cultural orientations, as represented in spare time practices, of working and professional middle class people living in a New Town. It demonstrates that respondents, grouped according to volumes of economic and cultural capital, differed systematically in their orientations toward spare time practices. This lends support to theories that an individual's amount of cultural capital, and therefore their class, has significant impact on their cultural orientations. However, intra-group variations in the types and significance of practices engaged in, casts doubt on the degree to which cultural capital alone shapes orientations toward cultural practices. This is because impressions of 'competent conduct' in the particular contexts that certain practices took place were central to the significance attached to those practices and, more importantly, whether specific types of practices were preferred in the first place. Crucially, interpretations of 'competence' were influenced by type of networks (friends, family or acquaintances) engaged in and their shared understandings of the practice itself. In conclusion, it is argued that cultural capital and social networks are resources that together shape cultural orientations and reproduce class-based differentiation. Cultural capital influenced the practices and types of networks that respondents engaged in, while networks acted to legitimate particular modes of engagement in different contexts of interaction by generating normative understandings of competent conduct in those practices.

Consumption, Capital and Networks

Bourdieu (1984) identifies three important resources that constrain and structure dispositions toward consumption. Such dispositions are reproduced to constitute differential tastes which emanate from the pursuit of the conduct of a life which is subjectively acceptable in the context of objectively given circumstances (Harvey et al., 2001). These objective constraints are found in the volumes of economic, cultural and social capital possessed by individuals.

Economic capital refers to flows of money and material wealth, can be measured according to indices of affluence, and can be converted into cultural capital through its capacity to provide access to cultural goods and services. This is because cultural capital is a resource of knowledge which has direct implications for tastes and cultural preferences, and is embodied in demeanour. Much of its analytic use has referred to the knowledge that individuals have of particular practices of consumption, hence levels of educational attainment have become the proxy for high or low volumes of this resource. It can be converted into economic capital by exchanging cultural knowledge for material advantage.

Bourdieu's definition of social capital makes this resource the most difficult to conceptualize: 'the sum of resources, actual or virtual, that accrue to an individual or group by virtue of possessing a durable network of more or less institutionalized relationships of mutual acquaintance and recognition.' (Bourdieu and Wacquant, 1992, p. 119) In this definition, social capital is presented as a resource deployed for personal advantage in a variety of contexts (Warde and Tampubolon, 2002), although what this personal advantage might actually be is left rather vague. Conversions of social capital into economic gain are most obvious in relation to favour, for example in the job market, a private monetary loan between friends and the informal provision of services.

Insight into how social capital might be converted into cultural capital can be found in some studies which look at these capitals in isolation from one another. The first explanation treats social networks as valuable sources of information about cultural practices. The starting point is Granovetter's (1973) 'strength of weak ties' argument, in which having weak connections within many networks was more advantageous for finding employment than having 'strong connections' within a few. A similar distinction is also found in Putnam's (2000) analysis of 'bridging' (weak ties) and 'bonding' (strong ties) capital, the former being a resource which increases the potential for information transmission within inclusive networks, the latter referring to dense and exclusive networks which offer high degrees of trust, solidarity and reciprocity between network members. Approaching 'social capital' in terms of the strength of network ties presents the possibility that many 'weak ties' might convert into cultural capital through the sharing of diverse knowledge about cultural practices, or that strong ties increase depth of knowledge in specific practices.

Peterson and Kern's (1996) account of 'omnivorousness' presents a possible explanation of how cultural capital could be converted into social capital. The omnivore thesis suggests that high cultural capital relates more to a broad range of knowledge about many cultural practices and less to significant depths of knowledge about a few. If those with high cultural capital are 'omnivorous', it seems reasonable to speculate that participation in a diversity of cultural practices increases the potential breadth of an individual's networks and subsequently generates more 'weak ties'. Such a claim is partially supported by Bellah et al. (1985) and Fischer (1982). Both accounts of American urban networks emphasize the principle of 'homophily' (a general tendency for people to 'seek out' and prefer the company of those 'like themselves') in their claims that individuals develop ties within 'life-style enclaves' centred around particular cultural practices. Speculatively, omnivorousness might therefore generate network multiplicity (having specific networks for specific cultural practices), meaning that those with high cultural capital should exhibit both diversity of cultural orientations and network ties. The latter would provide a rich source of information about 'other' cultural activities because network contacts would also hold omnivorous orientations.

None of these explanations take sufficient account of the processes through which networks are formed and how interpersonal relationships, such as friendships, develop. While networks are likely to be influenced by pre-existing cultural orientations through the principle of homophily, they may also present an opportunity to challenge and change such orientations. In relation to friendships, Allan (1989, p. 60) explains how: 'throughout social life, friends are important in reinforcing, moulding, and, on occasion, challenging each other's identities, no matter how conventional or esoteric their content'. Allan identifies humour as an essential mechanism in this process, along with the basic premise that friendships are equal and contain no material gain for either side, only sociable reciprocity. Lamont (1992) focuses on social and geographical mobility to explain how the formation of new 'friendships' challenged her respondents' 'assumptions' about various cultural orientations and forced them to 'learn' new modes of engagement in a wider variety of social contexts. In this way, the formation of networks has the potential to increase stocks of cultural capital by broadening and deepening cultural knowledge.

Taking a cue from such studies, this chapter examines the impact that social networks had on respondents' cultural orientations toward spare time practices, in order to explore how networks affect the accumulation and deployment of cultural capital in daily life. After describing the methods used in this study, the chapter describes the orientations toward sociable spare time practices of those interviewed for this research. This is followed by a discussion of respondents' narratives of network formation and their interpretation of who constituted 'friends'. Together, this analysis demonstrates how cultural capital shaped cultural orientations toward spare time practices and, because of homophily, affected the types of social networks formed. This was important because different types of networks not only generated different interpersonal relationships within networks but also generated particular forms of contextual competence necessary for participation in many spare time practices. Networks and the contexts in which they interacted had a direct bearing on the process through which cultural capital shaped cultural orientations and illustrates how volumes of cultural capital are reproduced. Before tackling spare time and social networks, it is first necessary to introduce the town of study.

The Place of Study and the Research Sample

The research was conducted in a New Town called Yate, located on the fringe of a large city in Southern England. Being a New Town, Yate's population grew rapidly from 3,000 in 1961 to reach 35,000 by 1991 (the majority of new houses were built in the 1970s and 1980s), and as a result many residents have experienced geographical mobility away from their natal localities. Like many New Towns, Yate also has high levels of home ownership (88 per cent of all households). These two features present a town with core mechanisms identified by theories of privatism – a process whereby residential immigration and high levels of home ownership replace household participation in collective practices with privatised home and family centred orientations toward everyday social life (Pahl, 1984; Saunders, 1990).

Two further features of Yate are worth noting. On the one hand, the socio-demographic profile of its residents is one of homogeneity. Not only were the majority home owners, only 1 per cent were classified as ethnic minorities, 50 per cent of the population aged above 16 were married, and 38 per cent of households had dependants (Census, 1991). On the other hand, socioeconomic status divided the town according to area of residency – north Yate being the most expensive area. In 1991, 32 per cent of north Yate heads of household were classified as professional or managerial and 27 per cent were manual workers. This compares with 17 per cent of south Yate heads of households being classified as professional or managerial and 45 per cent manual workers (Census, 1991).

Employing a 'conversational approach' (Douglas, 1985), in-depth semi-structured interviews were themed around perceptions of neighbourhood, spare time interests, social networks, and consumption of kitchens. Interviews were conducted with men, women and couples from 35 households, 15 from south and 20 from north Yate.[1] All respondents were white, owner occupiers, living as married, and aged between 23 and 68. Respondents varied systematically in their volumes of economic and cultural capital,[2] producing three groups who, in almost all cases, comprised residents from three neighbourhood areas.

Living in two south Yate streets were Bowland Road respondents. They had low economic and cultural capital and most heads of households were semi-skilled and skilled manual workers. Having moved to Yate during its first phase of development, all but two had lived in south Yate for over 15 years. Cartmel Street in north Yate housed the second group. They had low cultural but marginally higher economic capital than the Bowland group. All heads of households were skilled manual workers and all had moved to the Town within the previous five years. Lonsdale Avenue respondents, who lived in the two most prestigious streets in north Yate, formed the third group. All were professionals and had high levels of economic and cultural capital. This group could be further divided between 'established' and 'newcomers' according to length of residence within the Town (above or below five years).

Sociable Spare Time Practices in a New Town

To avoid potentially restrictive interpretations of leisure – 'an actively pursued recreational activity' (Rojek, 1995) – the term 'spare time' was used. Respondents described spare time as being that outside of paid and domestic labour. For the purposes of this chapter, discussion centres on those interests in which the potential for forming networks through sociability was strongest: entertaining at home; eating out; and membership of clubs, associations and societies. The data address both personal interests and those shared between couples.

Entertaining at Home

Bowland respondents did not entertain others at home, except for 'special occasions' involving the extended family. This was in stark contrast to Lonsdale and Cartmel respondents, although the frequency and contexts of sociability were discussed in very different ways. Cartmel respondents described 'conventional' dinner parties involving one other couple: 'It's very rare that we have more than one couple over at any one dinner party. Mind you, that's probably because I'm not sure some of them would get on so well with some of the others' (Stephanie). Such dinner parties also followed rather conventional formats. Angela explained how: 'I always do [cook] something which I wouldn't normally and we get out the best glasses, cutlery and that … It's always bring a bottle, that sort of thing … It's the same for whoever we invite.'

Lonsdale respondents, by contrast, listed a diversity of home-based sociability, ranging from regular coffee mornings to eating-in events. While the conventional two couple, 'bring a bottle of wine' (Sylvia), dinner party was frequent, this did not always involve 'best glasses' and 'cutlery' or cooking 'special' meals. Judith explained how: 'Sometimes we go the whole hog, other times we slap in a pizza, get an expensive bottle of plonk and eat off our laps. Depends who's coming and what mood we're all in.' Other dining arrangements included the very popular 'safari parties' enjoyed by five respondents. Initiated after the Genery link (a twin-town project with a Ghanaian Town), 'safari parties' were street based events held approximately once a month. They involved street members cooking one 'exotic' dish, non-street participants provided the drinks, and the group travelled between each others' houses sampling the dishes.

For both Cartmel and Lonsdale respondents, the home was a space of sociability within partners' mutual networks. While Cartmel respondents lacked Lonsdale's diversity of practices and frequency of network interaction within homes, they nevertheless presented favoured home-based interests that involved a variety of other people. Bowland respondents did not describe the home as a space of sociability but one of personal relaxation.

Eating and Drinking Out

'Eating out' divisions followed the same pattern as did 'eating in'. Bowland respondents enjoyed eating out but the activity was infrequent and largely restricted to special family occasions. By contrast, five Cartmel partners named eating out as their favourite spare time activity, favoured because it was a joint interest. Most ate out on average once a month and, again, this involved the company of one other couple (but not always the same couple). Eating out, as opposed to 'in', was preferred because restaurants offered 'neutral territory' (Patricia) and required 'less effort' (Anthony) with regards to food preparation and cleaning dishes. This contrasted with Lonsdale respondents who described the importance of both eating in and out. For them, eating in offered a more 'intimate' (Charlotte) context in which to potentially form closer bonds within networks, while eating out served as an opportunity for new culinary experiences and the chance to 'get out' (Barbara) with other couples. Like eating in, eating out was not restricted to the company of one other couple at each event.

Ten Bowland respondents described regular visits (once a week or more) to the pub as a favoured spare time practice, two being women who accompanied their partner. This contrasted with only one man from the Cartmel group and four men from Lonsdale. Others did visit pubs but not with any regularity. It was not just the number of people who regularly visited pubs but the form of sociability that took place which differentiated the groups. Neither Bowland nor Cartmel respondents described pub visits as arranged in order to meet with others, although regular visits to the same pub resulted in 'recognized faces' (Jack) and 'general chatting' (Patrick). By contrast, the four Lonsdale respondents explained how pub visits were always pre-arranged: 'Actually it all started when they [his wife and her friend] suggested we went for a drink after a curry at our house one Friday night, and we go most Fridays now' (James). In this case, four women had established friendships through coffee mornings which quickly expanded to an eating-in event and then to regular Friday evening visits to a pub by their husbands. As Tracey explained, 'It helps if they [the husbands] get on, otherwise only the women get to know each other'. While each of the other three cases presented different stories of how pub visits became regular, all cases featured pre-arranged visits with the same person(s).

Clubs, Associations and Societies (CAS)

Membership of CAS presented the most significant difference between the groups. Table 7.1 shows how both the number and type of CAS membership reported by at least one adult in each household varied between the groups. 'Clubs' referred to a sport or recreational activity in which formal membership and payment of fees was required. 'Associations' referred to voluntary organizations which required regular involvement and commitment rather than monetary exchange for access. Finally, 'societies' also did not require membership fees but did involve strict selection criteria, whether by application, election or nomination from existing members.

Table 7.1   Number of households that reported at least one membership of a club, association or society

	Bowland	Cartmel	Lonsdale
No. of households	13	8	14
Clubs	4	1	7
Associations	0	2	12
Societies	0	0	6

Bowland respondents only mentioned membership of a club, and only one (Robert, a skittles player) participated with any regularity. As for drinking out, the activity was regarded as a personal practice not dependant on the presence of specified others. Martin, a local Ramblers club member described his participation as: 'I just go along when I've the time and when I feel like it.' Consequently, network interaction was limited: 'I might chat to 'em and say hello if I see 'em in the street, but like, not all of us go for the social side as it were.' Martin's case is interesting because he highlighted an instrumental orientation toward club membership, the benefit for him being organized walks which 'motivate me to go places I wouldn't go on my own'. Bob was equally instrumental in his cricket club membership: 'I joined to get a reduced ticket to hear Ian Botham at an after-diner speech.'

CAS membership as a means to pursuing a spare time interest rather than to purposefully develop network ties was also apparent in Cartmel narratives. Andrew, a member of a 'cheap' local golf club, reported no contact with other members: 'I just use the facilities and that's it. In and out, no fuss. I bet the regulars would never even recognise me in the street.' On occasion he would invite others to play golf with him – 'When my brother's down we might have a round and I gave Justin from work a game once' – but he stated: 'On the whole I like playing on my own, I'm not competitive and I like getting on with it, I don't need someone to hold my hand.'

The other two Cartmel respondents were members of associations. John described his school governor role as a means of finding out what happens at his son's school and qualified that: 'It takes up little time, one hour a month at most ... I have nothing to do with the others outside the meetings.' Margaret, on the other hand, felt her membership to the Women's Institute might have begun as 'something constructive to fill my time' but had become 'my main contact with the outside world'. For her, association membership was largely motivated by sociability even though 'I don't see the others outside of the WI except for if I bump into them at the shops'.

Table 7.2 provides an indication of the volume and range of Lonsdale CAS memberships, with only one couple abstaining from any form of membership. The number and frequency of engagement within these activities, in addition to their various eating events, demonstrated the extent of these respondents' network interactions. Unlike the other two groups, Lonsdale respondents joined CAS with the specific intention of initiating network contact. Barbara, who at the time of interview had recently moved to Yate, explained such a network initiation strategy:

> Once we'd settled in the house we got that blue book out, you know the one that comes through the door, and trailed it for groups to join. I fancied the tree planting group so joined and Alex joined the swimming club ... You have to make the effort in a new place because you can't expect others to do it for you.

Table 7.2 Regular involvement and significant engagement within clubs, associations and societies for all Lonsdale respondents interviewed

Respondent/s	Clubs	Associations	Societies
Tom and Sylvia	Golf; cricket; hockey	Genery link	
Charlotte		Parent governor; trade association; mothers' group	Amateur dramatics
Anne	Ramblers	Church group; Genery link	
Peter and Elizabeth		Church group	
Tracey		Mothers' group; baby-sitting circle	
Alex and Barbara	Swimming	Mothers' group; baby-sitting circle	Local environmental group; music group
James and Michelle	Hockey	Trade association	
Beatrice		Genery link; Salzenberg link; church group; mothers' group	Cancer support; Rotary and 'Piggies'
Danny and Linda			
Colin	Football; hockey	Church group; play-schemes	Music group
Judith	Hockey; swimming	Genery link; Salzenberg; mothers' group; baby-sitting circle	Music group
Juliet	Fitness club		
Mark and Rose	Hockey	Church group; Genery link	
Katherine		Mothers' group; baby-sitting circle	Morris dancing

Like other forms of sociable activity, Lonsdale respondents presented regular and pre-arranged interaction within specified networks, using CAS as mechanisms for meeting people and developing network ties. This was important because CAS membership often led respondents to join other CAS as a consequence of forming new network contacts. Beatrice explained: 'Obviously the Genery link came from the Rotary Club but it's all the same people, you know, we got into the Rotary Club through Jenny and John who we met at the church group'. Indeed, all respondents described how some of those invited to share eating events were initially met at a CAS.

Summary

Lonsdale respondents narrated the greatest diversity of spare time practices and described network formation and sociability as critical components of those activities. By contrast, Bowland and, to a lesser extent, Cartmel respondents described privatised orientations toward spare time practices, the formation of networks through such practices being viewed as a by-product of the activity rather than as a purpose for engaging in that activity. This indicates a similarity in orientation that might result from the comparatively low volumes of cultural capital held by the respondents in these two groups. On these terms, cultural capital could be regarded as patterning orientations and, in doing so, impacts on the type of networks formed and shapes the normative modes of interaction within the contexts that practices were conducted. However, intra-group variations were apparent. For example, Cartmel, like Lonsdale, respondents used their homes to entertain others whereas Bowland respondents rarely entertained at home.

Given the relatively low expense of entertaining at home, it seems unlikely that marginal differences in the volume of economic capital between the Bowland and Cartmel groups explain this difference. An alternative explanation highlights the impacts of geographical mobility on the type of spare time practices engaged in. Like Lonsdale newcomers, Cartmel respondents had recently moved to Yate from distant localities. Consequently, such respondents had less time in which to develop extensive networks, and this might have affected their orientations toward spare time practices. Partial support for such a claim is found in the tendency for Cartmel and Lonsdale respondents to socialize as couples, which contrasts with Bowland descriptions of largely individual participation in sociable spare time practices (Bowland couples had many shared interests but they centred around private activities such as television watching, gardening and walking the dog). Lack of network integration as a result of recent geographical mobility might, therefore, shed light on the intra-group differences between those who shared volumes of cultural capital and held similar orientations toward spare time practices but engaged in different activities.

Spare Time Practices, Networks and Contexts of Interaction

To further examine whether cultural capital and/or geographical mobility explain the group-based differences of spare time practices, it is necessary to look in greater detail at the type of networks formed, the modes of network interaction, and the contexts within which shared understandings of competent conduct in spare time practices were developed. This is because the potential affect of geographical mobility on cultural orientations is a line of enquiry based on the impact that social networks have on participation in spare time practices.

'Keeping Themselves to Themselves' – Bowland Networks

Bowland respondents narrated two types of networks – ascribed kinship and acquaintances. Family members were regarded as close ties, largely because they represented a reliable source of material and emotional support: 'We'd always go to our brothers or sisters first if we needed any help or anything … We're always there for one another even if we're not getting on at that particular time' (Susan). Consequently, family members were named as their most significant social contacts, even if they did not particularly like them: 'Yeah, we see 'em quite a bit. Saying that I don't like my brother much but I tolerate him for Sandy's sake … I would say they're friends though' (Claire). Describing family as 'friends' illustrated that for this group friends were 'given' rather than interpersonal ties that required purposive cultivation. Friendship was not described as something that could be acquired, and this was the reason given when reporting no sociability with work colleagues: 'I work with them but I could work with anyone, it doesn't mean we're friends' (Simon).

Neighbours and acquaintances formed through sociable spare time practices were also not described as friends because these network ties reflected co-presence rather than sociability: 'Our neighbours are our neighbours, we're friendly in as much as we'll help each other out in trouble but we're not friends' (Wendy). Even when respondents described regular and committed practices the networks formed were not counted as friendships. Arthur and Joan, who went dancing every Saturday night, were a typical case: 'We're our own people, when we go out we like to go out what time we like, to come away when we're ready because if you start going with people and arranging when to pick 'em up, and you've gotta stay.' (Arthur)

Neighbours, acquaintances, and possibly work colleagues increased their total number of network members but engagement within such networks was a case of 'chance' rather than arrangement. Given this, and Bowland orientations toward independent engagement in spare time practices, it was not surprising that the networks formed were characterized as 'weak ties'. It was not the case that Bowland respondents were 'unsociable', more that they held orientations which separated network formation from practices pursued for personal interest. Indeed, distinguishing acquaintances formed through spare time practices from 'friendship' acted as a source of competent conduct. As Robert explained:

> It's a case of whoever turns up plays, it's never the same team. Saying that, I go because its better than just propping-up the bar and there's always the same old faces even if their not playing … it's not cliquey or anything, just a bunch of blokes having a few drinks and some of 'em playing skittles.

Sheila shared this sentiment and described her interest in line dancing as a means of maintaining fitness, and admitted: 'We all get on and that but I wouldn't say any are friends, they're a good laugh and all that but no, we just do the dancing'. For Bowland respondents, competent conduct in the contexts of spare time practices was captured by the statement: 'People keep themselves to themselves' (Vera). As an example of homophily, networks formed through shared practices appeared to share the same normative understandings of competent conduct, which amounted to avoidance of complicated interpersonal relationships.

The Scripted Interactions of Cartmel Networks

Cartmel respondents also described brothers and sisters as 'friends'. Sarah was a typical case: 'I speak to my sister regularly, at least once a fortnight and she's come down now and then … she'd always be there though. You know, blood's thicker than water.' Not all Cartmel respondents shared Sarah's degree of family connection and for others family was mostly described as a dependable source of practical support. Similarity with Bowland respondents was also clear in attitudes toward work-based networks, all stating that they did not socialize with work colleagues.

Neighbours were described as 'friendly rather than friends' (Nicola), although interaction was more frequent than in Bowland Road: 'We'll always say hello and occasionally stop and chat' (Margaret). Angela described her next-door neighbour as a regular point of contact: 'Yeah we'll chat over the fence and at Christmas maybe they'll come round for a drink.' Recognizing neighbours as acquaintances was significant, particularly as the other couples with whom Cartmel respondents socialized were afforded the same status. Stephanie stated: 'We have lots of people who might come for a meal or whatever but true friends I think I've got about five, who I would at anytime of day or night phone, who I would do anything for and they would me.' This perception of 'friends' as those who shared a deep-rooted personal bond generated clear distinctions between their network ties. In all cases, 'friends' were those left behind when they had moved to Yate and whom they no longer had significant face-to-face contact.

The term acquaintance best captures those networks formed after respondents had moved to Yate. Children and mothers played a critical role in the formation of such networks. Stephanie explained: 'Most come from the school gates, you get chatting and then you might see them in the shops or park and it goes from there'. Anthony described a similar process: 'A few of us played rounders over the green last Sunday … just a few kids and their Dads … You never know, we might be going for a meal with some of them in a few months.'

Initiating contact through shared circumstances (such as having young children), rather than shared cultural orientations, helps explain why Cartmel respondents described dinner guests as acquaintances rather than friends with whom shared orientations were known. As Anthony hinted, meals were the favoured mode of developing initial contact into sociability. This is significant because much network interaction took place in restaurants, which present participants with a formal script regarding contextual practices (Finkelstein, 1989). Such 'scripts' were also employed when entertaining at home. Angela, for whom use of best cutlery and china at dinner parties was important, outlined the etiquette:

> We'd expect them to bring a half decent bottle of wine, not the cheap stuff … and yeah, to dress smart, not in jeans or anything like that … and like I will tell them what is on the menu, if you like, and try and give them a choice, like for starter.

Despite different practices, the formal reciprocity (of wine exchanges) and scripted contextual norms held similar implications for engagement in types of social networks as did the privatised orientations toward interaction of Bowland respondents. The network ties remained weak not simply because interaction with the same people was infrequent, but also because by following scripted contextual norms, the chances of not 'fitting-in' were reduced. Consequently, as for Bowland respondents, interpersonal relationships did not develop beyond the notion of acquaintance because interaction remained relatively impersonal. This was hinted at by Stephanie's statement regarding dinner guests not being 'true friends'. John was more forthright: 'Yeah, we get to know them but it's more like polite conversation than, you know, like openly talking … Well, I don't mean like guarded or anything but just, you just don't really know each other that well.' Such networks neither challenged respondents' existing cultural orientations nor did they provide new cultural experiences that might increase volumes of cultural capital because the contexts and modes of interaction remained restricted and predictable.

The 'Contextual Competence' of Lonsdale Networks

Given the comparatively diverse range of cultural practices engaged in by Lonsdale respondents, it was not surprising that they described a range of network types – including acquaintances, friends and close friends. For this group, friendship was not associated with interpersonal ties that revolved around obligation. Tom was one of six Lonsdale respondents to declare: 'You can choose your friends, not your family', although some did name family members as 'friends' due to shared cultural orientations. As this suggests, 'friends' were regarded as those who shared cultural orientations and co-participated in the same spare time practices. 'Friend' was not used in the same sense that Bowland and Cartmel respondents applied the term acquaintance to describe their networks. Lonsdale respondents also used the term acquaintance with reference to those who co-participated in spare time practices but with whom no interaction took place beyond that practice. Friendships, by contrast, were cultivated through interactions that took place in a variety of contexts, whether through participation in CAS, eating events or neighbourhood activities. Barbara and Alex, who were newcomers to the area, explained:

> *Barbara*: This street is brilliant … When we're at home in the daytime we will meet up at least once a week for coffee.
> *Alex*: We're also all determined to work at it, we're all determined to say 'Well let's get into the routine of going to the pub once a month or something like that and make the effort, do something different.

It was Barbara who previously stated that joining CAS was also partially motivated by attempts at initiating network contact, and Alex's intent to forge closer interpersonal ties within newly formed networks demonstrated how Lonsdale respondents actively sought to develop acquaintances into friendships. For 'established' residents, this process had already occurred. James and Michelle outlined the process:

> *James*: Actually you knew 'um first, and we saw them once in Tesco's and said we were going for a drink after ... And they said 'We'll see you in there' and it went on from there.
>
> *Michelle*: Yeah. I knew Sue from netball. But we hit it off didn't we? Like you say, it's never a problem over who gets the drinks in, it's just sort of automatic ...
>
> *James*: That's right ... We're of similar interests and mind and we both respect each other's views. And oddly enough, they aren't much different. I mean not just politics or the royal family and that. But like, we like the same things when we go out, like for a meal we all like three courses, you know spread over the night with cheese and that, port, after. We just like the same things ... going to the same sort of places.

James and Michelle illustrate the process whereby similar spare time practices can, in time, move an acquaintanceship toward a 'close friendship'. However, common practice was not enough to develop such an interpersonal bond. Rather, this process required that a number of criteria regarding tacitly shared cultural orientations were negotiated during the course of interaction. This was illustrated by shared interests being qualified by specific 'ways of engaging' those interests that were mutual to all parties within the friendship.

Lonsdale newcomers had yet to develop such 'close friendships'. They used the term 'close friend' but, in a similar way to how Cartmel respondents employed the term 'friend', to describe interpersonal relationships with people living in their previous residential locality and with whom they had limited social contact. Instead, Lonsdale newcomers described local friends through an emphasis on shared competence in formal contextual norms. Mark stated that:

> The Hockey Club doesn't have so many set rules, but there are expected ways of behaviour, no standing on top of tables or things like that. And I don't like the kind of people who don't respect such expectations and rules of behaviour. Nor do any of my friends there, which is why it doesn't ever happen.

Emphasis on formal contextual norms of conduct shares a certain similarity with the scripted modes of interaction that Cartmel respondents used to describe their acquaintance networks. The critical difference between these two newcomer groups was that Lonsdale respondents described friends as those who shared an interest in producing 'friendships', in addition to acquaintances who simply shared spare time interests and followed scripted rules of conduct. Given the range of practices in which Lonsdale newcomers participated, they were in a better position (than Cartmel respondents) to find others with whom tacitly shared cultural orientations could be found and developed.

Despite the differences between the types of network ties formed through participation in spare time practices, all Lonsdale respondents placed significant emphasis on developing strong ties from weak network connections. To some extent, this could represent a form of instrumentalism in network engagement. However, seeking 'stronger ties' in the form of 'friends' and 'close friends' was presented largely as an end in itself – to generate forms of sociability dependant on close interpersonal bonds. Yet, such networks did provide Lonsdale respondents with the resource of access to information regarding a diversity of cultural activities and, more importantly, nuanced understandings of competent modes of conduct in a range of contexts in which such practices took place.

Summary

As the discussion of their sociable spare time practices indicated, Lonsdale respondents engaged in a wider range of cultural activities than did low cultural capital respondents, and did so with the intention of developing friendships. On the one hand, by opening more avenues of network contact, high cultural capital increased the range of weak network ties that could be formed. Moreover, cultural capital, by shaping orientations toward competent conduct of practices and interpretations of the importance of different network types (family, friends, neighbours, acquaintances), also played a role in whether interpersonal relationships developed from weak to strong ties. In this sense, high cultural capital and the resulting cultural orientations toward a diversity of practices were converted into social capital.

On the other hand, variety of network types and modes of interaction can be regarded as crucial mechanisms in the reproduction of cultural capital. In the case of established respondents, 'strong ties' brought with them a confident grasp of 'nuanced' contextual codes of conduct and generated competence in the pursuit of practices that affirmed their sense of 'refined' cultural tastes, while weak ties (acquaintances) provided information and access to other cultural practices. Lonsdale newcomers had yet to develop the strong network ties exhibited by their established counterparts, and as such talked about friendship ties in ways not dissimilar from how Cartmel respondents described acquaintances. The difference between these two newcomer groups was largely one of diversity in cultural practices and an emphasis among Lonsdale newcomers upon shared orientations (such as Mark's account of behaviour in public spaces) rather than upon shared circumstance (such as Cartmel accounts of networks emerging around children). In this way, Lonsdale newcomers' greater emphasis on establishing 'stronger' ties (developing acquaintanceships into friendships) placed them in a better position from which to utilize diverse forms of cultural knowledge and competent conduct in different practices that a variety of network types offer.

Conclusion: Cultural Capital, Social Networks and Orientations toward Spare Time Practices

Respondents' volumes of economic and cultural capital had a significant effect on their orientations toward practices. Those with low cultural capital engaged in a relatively small number of spare time practices, held privatised orientations towards their conduct and, in the case of Bowland respondents, preferred to participate independently from others or, in the case of Cartmel respondents, to socialize with a small number of acquaintances in private spaces. Significantly, for these respondents it was the practice itself which attracted participation rather than the opportunity to forge ties within networks. This was clearest in Bowland descriptions of CAS membership, but also found in Cartmel accounts of eating events where the formal scripting of practices appeared more important than did the company. By contrast, those with high cultural capital engaged in a broad range of cultural interests from which various forms of social interaction within a variety of networks took place. They used private and public space with equal enthusiasm and forged networks that had both weak and strong ties. For these respondents, practices were conducted for the intrinsic properties of the activity as well as to initiate and generate network connections.

The relationship between cultural capital and spare time orientations was, however, not static nor a one-dimensional process. If it were, the small differences between those with similar volumes of cultural capital would amount to little more than arbitrary variation. Rather, intra-capital group variations were patterned according to respondents' length of residence in the town. For example, the Bowland and Cartmel groups might have shared a comparatively narrow range of interests that were characterized by privatised forms of engagement and the production of 'weak' network ties, but the groups did differ with respect to the types of interaction within those networks and this affected the relative weight of significance attached to specific practices. In both cases, practices described as being of greatest personal interest were those that involved interaction with others, despite enjoyment of the practice not depending on the participation of specific others. In the Bowland case, preference was for engaging with others by 'chance' and led to a favouring of 'recreational activities' in public space, safe in the knowledge that within such contexts 'there's always someone to chat to' (Arthur). For Cartmel respondents, being relative newcomers to the town limited the range of 'acquaintance' networks from which to draw, and made them more receptive to forging new acquaintances. As a result, they favoured spare time practices that facilitated the best conditions upon which to engage and produce weak network ties – namely formally scripted eating events.

All Lonsdale respondents described a broad range of similar spare time interests. In this respect, their cultural orientations exhibited many features of omnivorousness through their emphasis on diverse knowledge of, and participation in, cultural practices. However, established respondents drew from their 'strong' network ties to reveal nuanced understandings of competent conduct in such practices and, in doing so, their cultural orientations moved beyond a little knowledge of many cultural practices to a little knowledge about many and significant 'know how' in a specified few.

Cultural orientations toward spare time practices might reflect differential volumes of cultural capital (as measured through education as a source of cultural knowledge) but social networks play a significant role in the process through which cultural capital shapes orientations, because networks are a resource that impact on normative understandings of cultural practices. In other words, cultural capital might impact on 'knowledge' regarding a diversity of practices, but social networks impact on 'know how' and understandings of competent conduct in the pursuit of those practices. In this way, social networks are a resource that could be equated with the concept of social capital in that they offer sources of tacit understandings about 'how to' competently participate in cultural activities. In this process, volumes of cultural capital are reproduced because social networks act to constrain orientations toward practices. At one level, this was demonstrated by the relationship between volumes of cultural capital and orientations towards the formation of new networks (whether acquaintances or friends). More significantly, the principle of homophily indicates that by forming network ties within particular practices and according to shared normative understandings of competent conduct, the type of networks formed are likely to reproduce similar orientations toward that practice. Social networks do, however, offer the potential for increasing volumes of cultural capital through the provision of knowledge regarding other cultural activities and 'know how' regarding appropriate conduct in a variety of contexts. In this research, only those who already had high cultural capital inadvertently utilized their networks in such a way. Their cultural orientations toward participating in a diversity of spare time practices and toward initiating new network contacts exposed them, and offered access, to new practices and different norms of conduct within them. In sum, social networks reproduce cultural capital by legitimating orientations, but also act as a resource that, in particular circumstances, can increase individual volumes of cultural capital through the accumulation of knowledge and 'know how'. In Yate, those with high cultural capital and established within 'friendship' networks were best placed to utilize this resource.

Notes

1   Interviews were conducted with 13 couples, 12 women alone and ten men alone. The distribution of couples, men and women was representative across the three groups.

2   Economic capital was measured according to household income, number of cars and house value at the time of interview. Cultural capital was measured according to educational attainment, high cultural capital referring to those with a university degree.

Chapter 8

Diversity in Partnership Histories: Implications for Older Adults' Social Integration[1]

Pearl A. Dykstra

Studies of changes in the life course show a trend, beginning in the late 1960s and early 1970s, toward increasing diversity in people's lives (Buchmann, 1989; Liefbroer and Dykstra, 2000; McLaughlin et al., 1988; Modell, 1989; Ravanera, 1998). There is less and less uniformity in the ages at which major life transitions are made and in the sequences in which they occur. There is also greater variation in the range of familial and occupational roles. Family roles and obligations, in particular, are increasingly detached from chronological age (Held, 1986). The process of decreasing uniformity is a reversal of an earlier trend toward increasing standardization (Kohli, 1986; Kohli and Rein, 1991; Kuijsten, 1999).

The studies reporting increasing diversity in people's lives have focused on the early stages of the life course, looking at trends in home-leaving, labour market entry, first union formation, the birth of children, and so forth. Little work has been done on the later stages of the life course (George, 1996). Old age is a 'socially unstructured' period of life (Hagestad and Neugarten, 1985), meaning there are few social expectations about the roles for older adults to fulfil, and few institutionalized mechanisms that impose order in life. This may be one of the reasons why there have been few studies of late-life transitions. Nevertheless, old age is definitely not 'uneventful', as attested by experiences such as becoming a grandparent or a greatgrandparent, losing a spouse, losing a child, outliving friends and siblings, remarrying, adult children returning to the parental home, moving house, entering a residential care facility, re-entering the educational system, taking on a new paid job, and so forth.

With its focus on old age, this chapter addresses a phase in life that has been neglected in life course research. As yet, there is little knowledge about the degree of diversity in older people's lives (Dannefer, 1996). I will be examining the diversity in older adults' marital and relationship histories, considering two questions. Firstly, how much diversity in past and current partnerships is there? Is there evidence, for example, that serial monogamy is replacing marriage-for-life or that older adults are engaging in forms of partnership other than marriage? Secondly, what are the implications of diversity in partnership histories for older adults' social embeddedness? Marriage has been seen (from Durkheim onwards) as an avenue toward social integration. An open question is whether this is equally the case for second marriages or for so-called 'new' forms of partnership.

Historical Change

One might wonder about the relevance of looking at the diversity in the marital and relationship histories of current older adults, arguing that little diversity is to be expected. Current cohorts of older adults grew up at a time when life options were narrowly defined. Reasonably clear-cut expectations existed about the 'normal expectable' life course (Hagestad and Neugarten, 1985; Hareven, 1981; Neugarten, 1969). Marriage and launching a family were part of the shared expectations, as was a gender-based division of tasks in marriage with wives devoting themselves to homemaking and husbands investing in paid jobs so they could maintain their families. Marriage was a bond for life, and unmarried cohabitation – whether with a partner of the same or of the opposite sex – was virtually unthinkable. In line with this consideration, previous research shows that the early life marriage and childbearing patterns of current cohorts of older adults are characterized by the greatest uniformity ever (Cherlin, 1980; Liefbroer and Dykstra, 2000; Uhlenberg, 1993). The men and women in these cohorts have the highest marriage rates, the lowest mean age at marriage, and the lowest rates of childlessness in history. The rise in unmarried cohabitation, non-marital childbearing, childlessness, and divorce occurred *after* they reached middle age.

    The changes in demographic patterns of the last decades in western society are manifestations of both structural economic and autonomous ideational change (Lesthaeghe and Surkeyn, 1986). The rise in the standard of living and the expansion of the welfare state have enabled and encouraged people to organize their lives with a degree of financial and social independence that did not exist previously. The increases in economic security have been accompanied by an ideational shift. A more fatalistic view of life was characteristic of the time when current older adults were young: life events 'happened' or were determined by the needs and preferences of other family members (Hareven, 1977). This more fatalistic view has been replaced by the notion that what transpires in life is largely of one's own making. Recent decades have witnessed a growing emphasis on individualism, with the notion of being captain of one's biography: people are expected to take their lives into their own hands (Beck and Beck-Gernsheim, 1996). In the private domain, people can (and as Beck and Beck-Gernsheim argue, 'must') choose the living arrangement that suits them best: to live alone, with friends, 'apart together' as a couple, in a consensual union or in marriage. As Allan, Hawker and Crow (2001) write: 'marriage and the standard nuclear model of family structure and domestic organization become less a matter of routine, constrained practice and more a matter of lifestyle choice' (p. 825).

In this chapter, I use life history data from Dutch older adults born between 1900 and 1940. It goes without saying that evidence that their marital and relationship patterns were affected by the ideational changes of the last few decades can emerge only for the middle and later parts of their lives.

Source of Data

This chapter is based on data from the 1992 Dutch survey titled 'Living Arrangements and Social Networks of Older Adults' (NESTOR-LSN). Interviews were held with 4,494 men and women aged 55–89 (birth cohorts 1903–37). Respondents were obtained by drawing samples from the population registers of 11 municipalities in three regions of the Netherlands: the city of Amsterdam and two rural communities in the western part of the country, one city and four rural communities in the northeastern part, and one city and two rural communities in the south. The regions and municipalities were selected to make the sample as representative as possible for the Dutch population above the age of 55. To facilitate comparisons across age groups and between males and females, the sample was stratified according to sex and year of birth, and approximately equal numbers of men and women within each five-year cohort from 55 to 89 were drawn from the population registers. Older adults in private households as well as institutions were included in the sample. The overall response rate was 61.7 per cent, which is comparable to response rates for the general population in the Netherlands in surveys conducted by the Dutch Central Bureau of Statistics (de Heer, 1992). More detailed information on data collection and non-response can be found in Broese van Groenou et al. (1995).

Respondents were interviewed in their homes using CAPI (computer assisted personal interviewing) techniques. On average, the interviews lasted an hour and 37 minutes. Questions were posed on a wide variety of topics, including life histories, social networks, supportive exchanges, organizational memberships, and physical and psychological well-being. The analyses are based on the 4,076 respondents for whom full partnership history data are available.

In the NESTOR-LSN survey, information was collected on the start and end of each marital or non-marital relationship insofar it involved an intimate partner with whom the respondent had ever or currently was sharing a household. In addition, among those who were not living with a partner at the time of the interview, questions were asked about the possible existence of an intimate partner who was residing elsewhere – a so-called 'LAT-relationship' (living apart together).

Partnership History

Results underscore the dominance of marriage in the cohorts under investigation: 93.4 per cent of the sample had ever married.[2] At the time of the interview, men were more likely be ever married than women, 94.3 per cent versus 92.7 per cent. Living with an intimate partner outside of marriage (consensual union) had occurred sporadically. An analysis of partnership histories before the age of 30 shows that 0.5 per cent of the sample had lived with their partner before marriage. Those who lived in a consensual union at any point in life without ever marrying amounted to 1.0 per cent of the sample; men and women living with a same-sex partner are included in this figure. Clearly, unmarried cohabitation in early adulthood was not an option for those born between 1900 and 1940. Taking both marriage and consensual unions together shows that 5.4 per cent of the sample had never lived with an intimate partner at any point in life, either inside or outside of marriage. Few respondents reported homosexual unions: 0.4 per cent had either lived with a same-sex partner in the past or had a same-sex partner (consensual union or LAT-relationship) at the time of the interview.

What happened to the marriages? Results show that 10.0 per cent of the ever-married had ever divorced; some for a second or third time. As regards the years in which the divorces occurred, two clusters are visible: one around the years 1947–50, and a bigger one around 1972–74. The first indicates higher rates of divorce after the Second World War. Marriages that had remained intact throughout the war were nevertheless dissolved a few years afterwards, a pattern described previously by the Netherlands Central Bureau of Statistics

(NCBS, 1976). The second reflects the liberalized divorce laws. In 1971 the procedures for obtaining a divorce were simplified, resulting, along with other factors such as changing attitudes toward marriage and the declining role of the church (NCBS, 1994), in an increase in the number of dissolved marriages. One should note that the mean duration of marriage before divorce in the NESTOR-LSN sample was close to 20 years. The majority of the marriages that ended in divorce did so after a relatively lengthy period of time. In the divorce patterns we have evidence that older adults' lives were touched by the changing normative climate of the late 1960s and the early 1970s in which marriage became a negotiable relationship rather than a contract for life. Concomitant changes in legislation facilitated the termination of unhappy marriages.

At the time of the interview, widowhood was not (yet) a collective experience: 25.3 per cent of the ever-married had lost one or more spouse by death. Women (36.3 per cent) were more likely to ever have lost a spouse than men (12.1 per cent). This finding does not come as a surprise given that men tend to have shorter lives than women (Vaupel, 1997), and that they tend to marry women who are younger than they are (Bozon, 1991; Smeenk, 1998). For the majority (62.1 per cent), widowhood had come relatively early, defined as before the age of 70 for men, and before the age of 65 for women. The relatively low age at widowhood is of course typical for the sample under investigation with its 55–89 age-range. Most (66.5 per cent of the ever-married) were still in their first marriage, ageing with their spouse. Widowhood becomes a more common experience at highly advanced ages.

The majority of the widowed had remained single: only 15.8 per cent had remarried and 5.1 per cent had started living with a partner outside of marriage. Serial monogamy was more characteristic of the divorced: 38.9 per cent had remarried and 8.6 per cent had started living with a partner outside of marriage. Of course the second partnerships were not necessarily still intact at the time of the interview. The higher likelihood of repartnering following divorce than following widowhood is strongly linked to the age at which people became single. Divorce tends to occur earlier in the life course than widowhood. Research has consistently shown that the likelihood of remarriage declines with age (Uhlenberg and Chew, 1986; van Hoorn et al, 2001). Analyses of Dutch data show, however, that age does not fully account for the higher propensity to remarry following divorce than following widowhood (van Hoorn, et al., 2001). Uhlenberg and Chew (1986), citing Glick and Norton (1977), also note that, controlling for age, remarriage rates have always been higher for the divorced than the widowed in the United States.

In the NESTOR-LSN sample, men were more likely to repartner than women, a pattern that is consistently observed in the literature (Uhlenberg and Chew, 1986; van Hoorn et al., 2001). Whereas 44.9 per cent of divorced men had remarried and 11.6 per cent had entered consensual unions, 34.0 per cent of divorced women had remarried and 7.8 per cent had entered consensual unions. Among widowers, 29.2 per cent remarried and 10.9 per cent entered consensual unions. Among widows, the figures are 9.5 per cent and 3.0 per cent respectively. Note again, that the second partnerships were not necessarily intact at the time of the interview. One explanation for men's higher propensity to repartner is that they can draw upon a larger pool of potential mates. There are more single women than single men (particularly at older ages), and whereas it is socially acceptable for men to choose younger partners, women's choices are generally restricted to men who are senior in years. A more social psychological explanation is that men are more motivated to remarry given that marriage tends to be more beneficial to men than women (Antonucci, 1994; Bernard, 1972; Gove, Style and Hughes, 1990; Thompson and Walker, 1989).

Current Partnerships

To what extent do older adults' current partnerships show evidence of 'new' arrangements, which are governed less by social convention and presumably more by choice and mutual reward? Table 8.1 provides an indication of the extent to which the NESTOR-LSN sample members were involved in 'new' forms of partnership, such as consensual unions and LAT-relationships at the time of the interview. It provides a breakdown of the respondents' legal marital status by their partner status. Five partner status categories are distinguished: (a) sharing a household with one's spouse; (b) living in a separate household from one's spouse; (c) living with one's non-marital partner (consensual union); (d) living in a separate household from one's non-marital partner (LAT-relationship), and (e) not involved in a partner relationship (single).

Among those who were legally never-married (6.6 per cent of the sample), 11.8 per cent were partnered. 'Partnered' means they were either in a consensual union or a LAT-relationship. A higher percentage of never-married men than of never-married women were partnered: 13.7 per cent versus 9.0 per cent. Among those who were legally divorced (6.2 per cent of the sample), 29.6 per cent were partnered, while this was the case for 7.2 per cent of the legally widowed (who constitute 21.4 per cent of the sample). Here again, the findings show

Table 8.1   Older adults' marital status by partner status (percentages weighted)

	Spouse in household	Spouse outside of household	Consensual union	Living apart together	Single
Men (n = 1999)					
Never-married	–	–	9.8	3.9	86.3
Divorced	–	–	19.1	27.6	53.3
Widowed	–	–	11.3	12.0	76.7
Married	98.5	1.5	–	–	–
Women (n = 2077)					
Never-married	–	–	5.4	3.6	91.0
Divorced	–	–	8.2	8.8	83.0
Widowed	–	–	1.5	2.4	96.1
Married	97.8	2.2	–	–	–

that unmarried men were more likely to be involved in a partner relationship than their female counterparts: 47.6 per cent of divorced men versus 17.0 per cent of divorced women, and 23.3 per cent of widowers versus 17.0 per cent of widows were partnered. As regards the legally married (65.8 per cent of the sample), Table 8.1 shows that not all were living with their spouse. Reasons were that either the spouse or the respondent had entered residential care or that the spouses had separated without legally going through a divorce. Among the married, 1.8 per cent were not living with their spouses; this was less often so for married men (1.5 per cent) than for married women (2.2 per cent).

The data in Table 8.1 illustrate that older adults' partner status is more complex than their legal marital status suggests. Those who are unmarried are not always single, partners who live together are not always married, and partners can belong to different households even if they are married. Keilman's (1988) observation that people's legal marital status is no longer an accurate indicator of their actual living arrangement can be extended to older cohorts. Nevertheless, if one looks at the group of older adults as a whole, the percentage with experience in 'new' arrangements is quite small. At the time of the interview, 1.5 per cent of the respondents were in a consensual union (with a partner of the same or opposite sex), and 2.2 per cent were engaged in a LAT-relationship. The percentages would be somewhat higher if those who previously were in a consensual union or LAT-relationship but were not at the time of the interview were also considered.

Implications

The partnership data clearly show that diversity in life styles is not restricted to younger cohorts: a pattern of divorce and remarriage is also seen among older adults, as are forms of intimate relationships other than marriage. Now this fact has been established, the question arises: What are the implications? I ask this question because 'marriage matters', to adopt Waite's (1995) terminology. Research has consistently shown that the married enjoy better health, live longer, have more and better sex, are better integrated socially, have greater wealth and better outcomes for children than the unmarried. We do not know, however, whether the benefits of marriage extend to second and third marriages. Neither do we know what is happening to older adults in non-marital relationships such as consensual unions and LAT-relationships. Most research tends to bunch first and subsequent marriages together (Karney and Bradbury, 1995), while older adults' involvement in 'new' partnerships has generally been ignored (Cooney and Dunne, 2001; de Jong Gierveld, 2000). Moreover, research has tended to focus on current marital status, thereby overlooking important events in older adults' pasts (Cooney and Dunne, 2001; Wister and Dykstra, 2000). To understand older adults' well-being, not only their current partnership status but also their partnership histories should be considered (Peters and Liefbroer, 1997).

In what follows I examine implications of increasing partnership diversity for older adults' social integration. In particular, I explore the links between older adults' partnership history and loneliness. Loneliness is distinct from social isolation, which is the absence or lack of enduring ties with others. Loneliness is a subjective state, involving the way in which people perceive and experience their circumstances. Feelings of loneliness arise when there is an unwanted discrepancy between the relationships a person has and the relationships he or she wants (de Jong Gierveld, 1998). The discrepancy can pertain to the number of relationships (having fewer ties than desired) or the quality (existing relationships do not reach the desired level of closeness). By looking at different types of partnerships (first and subsequent marriages, consensual unions, LAT-relationships) and marital histories (never married, ever divorced, ever widowed, remarried), this analysis elaborates on previous research which has tended to look only at the presence versus the absence of partner relationships.

Type of Partnership

There are several reasons why marriage generally provides protection against loneliness. One pertains to the exclusivity of the bond. In marriage – if it is a happy relationship – needs for intimate attachment are fulfilled (Weiss, 1973). The spouse serves as confidant, companion, personal coach, sex partner and helpmate. Another is the embedment in a wider social circle (Stueve and Gerson, 1977). Many social engagements are organized on a couple-companionate basis, and being a member of a couple facilitates participation in social activities. Marriage also provides access to a wider pool of associates: not only in-laws, but also the friends and acquaintances of the spouse. Marriage often marks the start of one's own family. Children, in turn, often serve as bridges to contacts in the neighborhood, schools and clubs.

Many of the provisions of marriage also pertain to non-formalized partnerships. Given that consensual unions and LAT-relationships provide *emotional gratification*, sexual satisfaction and companionship, they should also serve to protect against loneliness. Nevertheless, there are reasons to believe there might be differences in loneliness by partnership type. Consensual unions and LAT-relationships are not publicly affirmed and socially sanctioned in the way marriage is. Marriage is marked by a *ritual ceremony* which is often celebrated in the church, and involves the respective networks of the couple and their families. The act of marrying serves to integrate the couple into a wider social group. Comparable celebrations do not exist for consensual unions and LAT-relationships, and for that reason people in these types of relationships might be more prone to social isolation. Of course this observation is valid primarily for the integration in family, church and community circles. Those in consensual unions and LAT-relationships might place greater emphasis on self-selected ties such as friends, and not be socially isolated at all.

Consensual unions and LAT-relationships are not as 'inevitably binding' (to use the terminology of Allan et al., 2001) as marriage is. The absence of a *legal* framework means there are fewer barriers to leave the relationship. Not surprisingly, research shows that consensual unions are more prone to dissolution than marriages (Manting, 1994; Teachman, Thomas and Paasch, 1991). Note, however, that these findings are based on younger adults. Relevant to the current discussion is that 'new' partnerships might be more selective than marriage, with a lower proportion of individuals who feel trapped in their relationships. Assuming that the feeling of being caught in an unhappy situation leads to loneliness, we should find, at the aggregate level, higher levels of loneliness among the married than among those in 'new' partnerships.

In marriage, women are said to do most of the relationship work. Wives tend to be more open to their husband's affective needs than vice versa (Antonucci and Akiyama, 1987b; Lowenthal and Haven, 1968; Rubin, 1983) and wives often function as the social secretaries, organizing and managing the social agenda of the couple (Rosenthal, 1985). Presumably then, men are more likely to find emotional fulfilment in marriage than are women. In 'new' partnerships there is less *gender asymmetry* than in marriage. Partners in consensual unions have a more egalitarian division of tasks (Batalova and Cohen, 2002; Blumstein and Schwartz, 1983). They strive to be economically independent from one another and emphasize nontraditional family roles (Clarkberg, Stolzenberg and Waite, 1995; Lesthaeghe and Moors, 2002), characteristics which apply to partners in LAT-relationships as well (de Jong Gierveld, 2000). These considerations suggest that one is more likely to find gender differences in loneliness among the married, with men being less lonely than women, than among those in 'new' partnerships.

So far, in discussing differences between marriages and 'new' partnerships, I have not taken into consideration that virtually all of the 'new' partnerships of the older adults under investigation were formed after the dissolution of their first marriage. Neither have I considered differences between first and second marriages. A second partnership tends to be a more complex transition than marrying for the first time. Viewed from the perspective of the individual's life history, more emotional baggage is carried to the relationship – the feelings, both positive and negative, surrounding the loss of a loved one or the disruption of an intimate relationship. From a social network perspective, a second partnership means that previously separate family networks are brought together, resulting in an expansion of ties requiring the negotiation of respective loyalties, responsibilities and obligations. Whether a second partnership provides the same kind of protection against loneliness as the first remains an open question. The lives of older adults in second partnerships may not be as tightly enmeshed as they are in first partnerships, perhaps resulting in lower levels of commitment. Their shared life generally has a shorter history, and is more likely to be troubled by conflicting obligations – to children from the respective first marriages in particular. Interestingly, one of the reasons put forward by older adults for preferring a LAT-relationship over marriage, is that it better enables them to continue to have close relationships with their children (de Jong Gierveld, 2000). They do not wish their children to feel obligated to the new partner, and not marrying is perceived as a safeguard against imposing on the children.

What do the previous considerations tell us about possible differences in loneliness between older adults in first and subsequent marriages? Under the assumption that the provisions of second marriages, such as *emotional gratification*, companionship and sexual satisfaction, are similar to those in first marriages, there should be no differences in loneliness. However, remarriage is likely to result in an *expansion* of the social network, and thus provide greater opportunities for socializing, the exchange of support, and developing a sense of belonging. On the basis of this consideration, one would expect to find higher levels of loneliness among those in first marriages than among the remarried. Alternatively, the complex of biological and stepfamily ties may be the source of insecurity about allegiances and *conflicting loyalties*, resulting in a sense of detachment. On the basis of this consideration, one would expect to find lower levels of loneliness among those in first marriages than among the remarried.

As the previous discussion reveals, straightforward predictions about differences in loneliness by partnership type cannot be made. Some characteristics of 'new' partnerships, such as the lack of ritual ceremony to publicly celebrate the relationship, suggest they provide poorer protection against loneliness than marriage. Other characteristics, such as the lower likelihood of feeling trapped due to the absence of legal barriers against leaving unhappy relationships, suggest they provide greater protection against loneliness. There are also competing predictions for differences in loneliness between those in first marriages and subsequent marriages. The notion of remarriage resulting in an expansion of the social network suggests lower levels of loneliness among the remarried than among those in first marriages. However, the notion of remarriage producing conflicting loyalties suggests higher levels of loneliness among the remarried compared to those in first marriages. The possibility of no differences in loneliness by partnership type also exists. The underlying assumption is that the emotional gratification derived from partnerships is not affected by the form the relationships take or the context in which they are maintained. Table 8.2 provides a summary of the mechanisms that have been suggested, and describes the differences in loneliness associated with them.

Marital History

In addition to the type of partnership, older adults' marital history should be considered to gain a better understanding of conditions contributing to loneliness.[3] A focus on marital history draws attention to stability (never marrying, still in the first marriage) versus change (divorce, widowhood,

Table 8.2   Predicted differences in loneliness by type of partnership and marital history

Mechanism	Level of loneliness
Type of partnership	
Emotional gratification	Marriage = 'new' partnership
	First marriage = subsequent marriage
Ritual and ceremony	Marriage < 'new' partnership
Legal framework	Marriage > 'new' partnership
Gender asymmetry	In 'new' partnership: men = women
	In marriage: men < women
Expansion social network	First marriage > subsequent marriage
Conflicting loyalties	First marriage < subsequent marriage
Gender socialization	Outside marriage: men > women
Marital history	
Stability	Never-married, first marriage < divorced, widowed
Nature of loss	Divorced < widowed
Disruption social network	Divorced > widowed
Normal expectable life	Divorced > widowed

remarriage). In taking older adults' marital history into account, one can address the question of whether undergoing a transition in marital status is more consequential for well-being than the mere presence or absence of a spouse (Chipperfield and Havens, 2001; Peters and Liefbroer, 1997).

Among those without a partner, the marital history tells us why they are single. Have they never married? Are they widowed or divorced? The lives of the never-married are characterized by greater *stability* than are the lives of those who experienced divorce or widowhood. They are long accustomed to being on their own and to fending for themselves. Research findings consistently show that never-married older adults tend to be less lonely than formerly married singles (Dykstra, 1995; Essex and Nam, 1987; Peters and Liefbroer, 1997). One explanation is that they have had fewer experiences of grief, anger, disappointment and desolation (Gubrium, 1974). Another is that in the course of their lives, the never-married have become highly self-reliant (de Jong Gierveld, 1969). Yet another is that the never-married have developed more intensive relationships with siblings, friends and colleagues (Dykstra, 1993). Men and women in first marriages have also known greater stability in their marital career than have those who experienced a marital disruption. For that reason one should find lower levels of loneliness among the former than among the latter.

The loss of partner support is common to divorce and widowhood. In that sense, both transitions contribute to a higher likelihood of psychological problems (Gove and Shin, 1989). However, there are also differences between the two transitions as regards the nature of the *losses* suffered. Divorce marks the end of a relationship that no longer brings pleasure and is the source of conflict. Widowhood often means the end of a longstanding relationship that was characterized by feelings of affection and warmth. It is not unlikely that the loss is felt more deeply in the latter case. For that reason, widowhood might be associated with higher levels of loneliness than divorce.

However, there are also reasons for predicting higher levels of loneliness after divorce than after widowhood. Problems of blame and failure often come into play in the event of divorce. Whereas in the event of bereavement friends and family actively join forces – at least during the period of mourning – to help, comfort and assist the person who has suffered the loss (Stevens, 1989), in the event of a marital break up they feel pressured to take sides for one of the partners (Broese van Groenou, 1991; Milardo, 1987; Rands, 1988). That is why divorce leads to greater disruptions in the social network than does widowhood. Another reason why divorce may be more consequential than widowhood pertains to socially-shared expectations about the life course. Divorce is not part of the 'normal expectable' life script (Neugarten, 1969); widowhood – at least in late life – is. People who enter into an exclusive partnership do not expect it to be dissolved by divorce, whereas with advancing age, the loss of the partner by death becomes part of the expectations for the further course of life. Deviations from the *normal expectable* life script tend to have negative consequences (de Jong Gierveld and Dykstra, 1994). Those experiencing unexpected transitions are in a deviant position relative to peers, a situation accompanied by feelings of marginalization and social exclusion.

In summary (see Table 8.2), the prediction is for lower levels of loneliness among the never-married and those in first marriages compared to the formerly married because the lives of the former are characterized by greater stability, not having experienced the upsets in their social networks and the emotional pain that comes with the break up of a marriage. There are competing predictions regarding differences in loneliness among the formerly married. Under the assumption that the loss of the intimate attachment is more severely felt among the widowed than among the divorced, the prediction is for higher levels of loneliness among the former than among the latter. The opposite prediction follows from the notion that divorce leads to greater disruptions in the social network and requires a greater reorganization of one's life than widowhood does.

Previous research has shown that men tend to be poorer equipped relationally to living on their own, and to be more devastated by the loss of the spouse than women (Stevens, 1995). Presumably, men's *socialization* brings them to rely heavily on an exclusive partner relationship for the fulfilment of their emotional and social needs, while women's socialization brings them to seek fulfilment in a wider circle of relationships (Chodorow, 1978; Gilligan, 1982). Outside of marriage, men are expected to be more vulnerable to loneliness than women. This pattern should be observed across all groups of singles, regardless of marital history.

Method

Measures

Loneliness In the NESTOR-LSN survey, loneliness was measured by means of the scale developed by de Jong Gierveld and Kamphuis (1985). This instrument consists of six negatively formulated items and five positively formulated items, none of which uses the word 'loneliness'. Examples of scale items are: 'I often feel rejected', and 'There are plenty of people I can lean on when I have problems'. The answer categories are 'no' (score 1), 'more or less' (score 2) and 'yes' (score 3). The scores on the positive items have been reversed. The loneliness score is the sum of the item scores, and ranges from 11 (no loneliness) to 33 (severe loneliness).

Type of partnership and marital history Five categories of partnered respondents were distinguished: in a first marriage, remarried after divorce, remarried after widowhood, in a consensual union and in a LAT-relationship. Those who were unpartnered were distinguished on the basis of their partnership history: never in a union (whether in or outside of marriage), single after divorce (including the separation of a consensual union), and single after widowhood (including the loss of a cohabitant). The most recent type of union dissolution was used to categorize respondents who experienced both divorce and widowhood. Given their small number ($n = 16$), respondents who were or had been in a homosexual relationship were excluded from the analyses. The same goes for the 46 married respondents who were not residing with their spouses at the time of the interview (e.g. because the respondent or the spouse had been admitted to a nursing home or a residential facility for the elderly).

Social relationships As described earlier, differences in loneliness by partnership type and marital history can possibly be traced to differences in the number, range and quality of social relationships. Several measures of social relationships were introduced in the analyses. The first is network size. Members of the social network were identified through a so-called 'domain contact approach' (see van Tilburg, 1995, for details). Seven relationship domains were specified: household members; children and their partners; other kin; neighbours; colleagues; organizational contacts; and 'others'. For each domain, the respondent was requested to specify the names of those with whom they were 'in touch regularly' and who were 'important' to them. The definitions of 'regular contact' and 'important' were left to the respondents. Only people above the age of 18 were eligible as network members. The partner was excluded from the computation of network size to increase the comparability between singles and respondents with a partner. The size of the social networks ranges from zero to 71. A second measure assesses the quality of the social network: it is the mean of the emotional support received and given across all the relationships in the social network (i.e. sharing personal experiences and feelings) and of the instrumental support received and given across all the relationships in the social network (i.e. helping with daily chores in and around the house, such as meal preparation, house cleaning, transportation, small repairs and filling in forms). Scores range from zero (no support) to three (high mean support). A third measure assesses the quality of the partner relationship. It is the mean of the emotional support and instrumental support exchanged with the partner, with scores ranging from zero (no support) to three (high mean support). Men and women without a partner were assigned the mean score obtained for their partnered counterparts. A measure assessing the frequency of contact with children was also included. It is a dichotomous variable contrasting those who had weekly contact with at least one child with those who interacted with their children less often. Older adults without living children were identified via a separate variable. Finally, several measures for community involvement were used: the active membership of voluntary organizations (no/yes), active participation in volunteer work (no/yes) and weekly attendance at religious services (no/yes).

Controls Age, health and socioeconomic status served as control variables. The analyses included three assessments of health. The first is an indicator of functional capacity: the sum-score of the responses to four items enquiring into difficulties in performing personal activities of daily living (ADL) (walking up and down stairs, walking for five minutes without resting, getting up from and sitting down in a chair, dressing and undressing). Scale scores range from four (no ADL-capacity) to 20 (full ADL-capacity). The second is an indicator of vision: the ability to read and the ability to see at a distance, taking into account the possible use of glasses. Scores range from two (poor vision) to eight (good vision). The third is an indicator of the ability to hear the other person in a private conversation, taking into account the possible use of a hearing aid, with scores ranging from one (not at all) to four (good hearing). The first indicator of socioeconomic status is educational attainment, as measured by the number of years to attain a certain level of schooling, ranging from five (incomplete elementary education) to 18 (university education). The second is monthly net household income. Income categories were converted into an interval scale by assigning the median income value for each income category to individuals in that grouping. In order to make the household incomes of those who live alone comparable to those of older adults co-residing with a spouse, a family equivalence factor was used. The monthly incomes of the married were multiplied by a factor of 0.7 in accordance with research conducted by Schiepers (1988). One should note that these data provide only an approximation of differences in household income. The missing cases for household income were recoded using mean substitution for the sex/marital history groups.

Descriptive information on the explanatory variables incorporated in the analyses is provided in Table 8.3.

Differences in Loneliness

Table 8.4 shows differences in loneliness for the various groups of partnered and unpartnered older adults. Not surprisingly, the results show lower levels of loneliness, on average, for the partnered as opposed to the unpartnered. Among partnered men and women, differences by type of partner relationship emerge. Remarried men and women, and those in consensual unions and LAT-relationships tend to be more lonely than those in first marriages. There are no gender differences in loneliness among those in first marriages. The same holds for those who remarried after divorce and those in consensual unions. Widowed men who remarried tend to be less lonely than their female counterparts, whereas men in LAT-relationships tend to be more lonely than their female counterparts. Among single men, there are no differences in loneliness by marital history. Whether men are formerly married or never married seems to make no difference for their level of loneliness. A different picture emerges among single women, where the relatively low levels of the

Table 8.3   Descriptive characteristics of the men (n = 1894) and women (n = 1983) in the sample (unweighted data)

	Men	Women	t
Age (54–89)	72.6	71.8	2.5 *
Functional capacity (4–20)	18.9	18.4	6.1 ***
Vision (2–8)	7.6	7.4	7.4 ***
Hearing (1–4)	3.7	3.8	-3.6 ***
Education (5–18 years)	9.3	7.9	13.6 ***
Income (€510–2610)	915	818	8.1 ***
Network size (0–71)	12.7	13.0	–0.9
Mean network support (0–3)	1.0	1.1	–4.5 ***
Mean partner support (0–3)	2.6	2.5	–3.5 ***
Weekly contact children (no/yes)	75.5	76.9	–1.0
Childless (no/yes)	12.9	15.7	–2.0 **
Active member voluntary association (no/yes)	53.3	50.5	1.8
Works as volunteer (no/yes)	30.2	22.7	5.4 ***
Weekly church attendance (no/yes)	35.0	41.0	–3.5 **

* p < .05; ** p < .01; *** p < .001.

Table 8.4   Mean loneliness scores of partnered and unpartnered older adults by marital history

	Men		Women		t
	n	M	n	M	
Partnered					
First marriage	1,279	13.4	881	13.4	.1
Remarried after divorce	59	15.3	27	15.4	–.1
Remarried after widowhood	65	13.5	21	16.1	-2.4 *
Consensual union	46	14.9	19	14.5	.3
LAT-relationship	48	15.4	27	13.5	2.1 *
F	8.7 ***				4.0 **
Unpartnered					
Never-married	91	17.1	116	14.4	4.1 ***
Divorced	46	17.6	101	16.4	1.1
Widowed	260	17.6	791	16.2	3.9 ***
F	.3				5.8 **

* p < .05; ** p < .01; *** p < .001.

never-married stand out. On average, never married men are more lonely than never married women, and widowers are more lonely than widows. However, there are no gender differences in loneliness among the divorced.

A step-wise regression analysis was carried out (a) to disentangle the effects of type of partner relationship and marital history, and (b) to find out to what extent they might be attributable to differences in network characteristics, quality of the partner relationship, relationships with children and community involvement. The analysis was carried out separately for men and women. Not only do men's and women's marital histories differ (with men being less likely to lose a spouse to death than women, and formerly married men more likely to enter a new partnership than their female counterparts), but the determinants might also differ by gender. In Model 1, the type of partner relationship was entered into the regression analysis, distinguishing those in first marriages from those who have remarried, are in consensual unions, are in LAT-relationships or are single. Model 2 incorporated marital history characteristics, distinguishing those with stable marital statuses over the course of their lives (the never-married and those in first marriages) from those who experienced either divorce or widowhood. Model 3 introduced characteristics of older adults' social relationships. Controls for age, health and socioeconomic status were incorporated at each step.

The Model 1 results show (see Table 8.5) that the loneliness of remarried men does not differ from that of men in first marriages. Among women, the pattern is different: the remarried tend to be more lonely than those in first marriages. A separate analysis revealed that the gender and remarriage interaction effect is significant at the .10 level. The Model 1 results also show that men in consensual unions or LAT-relationships tend to be more lonely than men in first marriages. Again, the findings for women are not consistent with those for men: there are no differences in loneliness between women in first marriages and those in consensual unions or LAT-relationships. A separate test revealed a significant effect for the gender and LAT-relationship interaction ($p < .10$), but not for the gender and consensual union interaction. Singlehood is the strongest predictor of loneliness: among both men and women, the unpartnered tend to be more lonely than those in first marriages. A test of the gender*singlehood interaction revealed that singlehood is a better predictor of men's loneliness than of women's ($p < .01$).

The introduction of marital history characteristics in Model 2 results in smaller reductions in the magnitude of the regression coefficients for partnership type among men than among women. Among men, living in a consensual union is no longer a significant predictor of loneliness, but

Table 8.5 Determinants of loneliness (standardized regression coefficients)

	Men (N = 1894)			Women (N = 1983)		
	1	2	3	1	2	3
Type of partnership						
Remarried	.04	.01	−.02	.07 **	.02	−.02
Consensual union	.05 *	.03	−.00 ***	.02 ***	−.00	−.03
LAT-relationship	.07 **	.06 *	.01	.00	−.02	−.04
Single	.31 ***	.30 ***	.19 ***	.23 ***	.11 **	.05
(vs in first marriage)						
Marital history						
Ever divorced		.06 *	.08 *		.08 *	.08 *
Ever widowed		-.00	.02		.13 **	.20 ***
(vs no change)						
Social relationships						
Network size			−.19 ***			−.19 ***
Mean network support			−.11 **			−.10 ***
Mean partner support			−.06 **			−.07 **
Weekly contact children			−.08 **			−.23 ***
No living children			−.01			−.13 ***
Active in voluntary associations			.03			.00
Active in volunteer work			−.01			−.01
Church attendance			−.07 **			−.09 ***
Controls						
Age	.10 ***	.12 ***	.05 *	−.06 *	−.06 *	−.14 ***
Functional capacity	−.11 ***	−.10 ***	−.07 **	−.15 **	−.15 ***	−.14 ***
Eyesight	−.07 **	−.07 **	−.07 **	−.08 **	−.08 **	−.07 **
Hearing	−.02	−.03	−.02	−.10 ***	−.10 **	−.10 ***
Education	−.00	−.00	.03	−.03	−.03	−.02
Income	−.04	−.04	−.03	−.02	−.02	−.00
R^2 (adjusted)	.18 ***	.19 ***	.26 ***	.11 ***	.12 ***	.22 ***
R^2-change	.18 ***	.01 **	.07 ***	.11 ***	.01 *	.10 ***

* $p < .05$; ** $p < .01$; *** $p < .001$.

involvement in a LAT-relationship and singlehood continue to be significant predictors. Among women, the difference in loneliness between women in first and subsequent marriages disappears once marital dissolutions are taken into account, whereas the difference between the first married and those who are single is considerably reduced. It appears then that the type of partnership is more focal to the explanation of differences in loneliness among men, whereas marital history tells us more about differences in loneliness among women. The Model 2 results show furthermore that a previous divorce contributes to higher levels of loneliness independently of the type of partnership. This pattern is observed among both men and women. Given the type of partnership, widowhood does not account for additional differences in loneliness among men. It does among women, however. Women who have lost a spouse by death tend to be more lonely, regardless of their current partner status.

The third step of the analysis examines the extent to which differences in loneliness by type of partnership and marital history are attributable to differences in network characteristics, quality of the partner relationship, relationships with children and community involvement. As the Model 3 results show, once these characteristics are taken into account, the difference in loneliness between men in LAT-relationships and men in first marriages is no longer significant. An additional analysis revealed that of all the characteristics considered, the supportiveness of the partner relationship is the one that accounts for the LAT-relationship effect. The findings suggest that men in LAT-relationships are more lonely than men in first marriages because there are fewer supportive exchanges in their partnerships. The consideration in Model 3 of social relationships leads to a considerable reduction of the magnitude of the coefficient for singlehood. The coefficient remains significant among men but not among women. Additional analyses revealed that two sets of factors account for differences in loneliness between single men and women and those in first marriages: network characteristics and contacts with children. Single men and women tend to have smaller networks and to have lower levels of supportive exchanges with their network members, and for that reason are more vulnerable to loneliness than those in first marriages. Moreover, single parents are less likely to have frequent contacts with their children (to be in touch with one of them at least once a week). Frequent interactions with children help alleviate or prevent feelings of loneliness. This is less strongly so for men than for women ($p < .01$).

Note that, among men, childlessness is unrelated to loneliness. Among women, childlessness is associated with lower levels of loneliness. Childless women tend to be less lonely than those who do not interact with their children frequently. The Model 3 results also show that weekly church attendance helps combat feelings of loneliness, while the active involvement in volunteer work and voluntary associations is unrelated to loneliness. This pattern of results is observed for both men and women. The loneliness-alleviating effect of weekly church attendance is independent of the effects of partnership type and marital history.

The coefficients for divorce remain virtually unchanged after introducing characteristics of social relationships in Model 3. The experience of divorce makes men more and women more prone to loneliness, but this finding cannot be explained in terms of the social relationships in which they are involved. Interestingly, in Model 3 widowhood becomes an even stronger predictor of loneliness among women. Apparently, there is something about widowhood, other than the implications it has for their social relationships, that makes women more prone to loneliness.

Conclusion

'New' partnerships such as consensual unions and LAT-relationships do not surface in civic statistics, which have people's official marital status as their basis. Furthermore the focus on current marital status means no distinctions are made between first and subsequent marriages. Should we consider the absence of information on 'new' partnerships and people's marital pasts an omission? To answer this question, it helps to have an indication, firstly, of prevalence. How many people are we talking about? How much diversity in partnerships is there? Secondly, it helps to have an indication of the implications of partnership diversity.

Findings presented in this chapter show that diversity in partnership histories is not restricted to younger cohorts. Nevertheless, the numbers of older adults with a history of serial partnerships or with experience in intimate relationships other than marriage are quite small. A pattern of divorce and repartnering is characteristic of slightly less than 5 per cent of the sample, whereas slightly less than 3 per cent of the sample were involved in 'new' relationships at the time of the interview. Note that there is overlap between the two categories: approximately 51 per cent of the older adults in consensual unions or LAT-relationships had previously divorced. In assessing the data, it is important to take in mind that there is only a restricted set of eligibles for 'new' partnerships, namely the formerly married and perhaps also the never married (though those who have always been single are unlikely to enter into first partnerships in old age). At the time of the interview, almost two-thirds of the sample were still in their first marriage. Note also that only the form of the relationship, the living arrangement, has been considered here – not the content. We might find greater evidence of individualism in relationships if we examine how marriage partners spend time together and interact with one another. It is also important to consider future trends.

Though relatively few older adults were involved in 'new' partnerships in 1992, their numbers are expected to grow in the future. More and more older adults will have histories involving consensual unions, marital break-ups and non-coresidential partnerships as the cohorts who grew up in the 1960s and 1970s enter the old age population (Cooney and Dunne, 2001; de Jong Gierveld, 2000).

To reach an understanding of the implications of partnership diversity, I examined (a) whether different types of partnerships provide the same kind of protection against loneliness, and (b) whether knowledge about older adults' marital pasts provides a better explanation of loneliness than taking only the current partnership into consideration. The findings indicate that different types of partnerships provide differential protection against loneliness, and that the pattern varies by gender.

Men and women in first marriages tend to be least lonely of all. Among those in first marriages, there are no differences in loneliness by gender. This finding is contrary to what is often suggested, namely that men are more likely to find emotional fulfilment in marriage than are women because wives do more of the relationship work. For first marriages the data do not suggest that men and women derive asymmetric gratifications from being in that relationship. For second or third marriages, the story is different. Whereas the mean level of loneliness of remarried men is similar to that of men in first marriages, remarried women tend to be lonelier than women in first marriages. Remarried men tend to be less lonely than their female counterparts. Findings from a multivariate analysis suggest that the prior experience of divorce or widowhood accounts for the higher level of loneliness in women's second or third relationship. There appears to be a lingering 'shadow of the past' which contributes to feelings of social isolation among remarried women. The idealization of the late first husband (Lopata, 1979) might be one of the reasons why women who remarried after widowhood are relatively lonely. Presumably, the second husband can never meet the qualities of the first.

One of the predictions was that conflicting loyalties to children from the first marriage, ex-in-laws and old friends would contribute to higher levels of loneliness among the remarried. For that reason, indicators for the quality of the relationships with network members and relationships with children had been incorporated in the analysis. These characteristics in and of themselves show clear links with loneliness. However they do not mediate the association between the experience of divorce and widowhood and women's loneliness. An alternative prediction was that remarried men and women would be less lonely than those in first marriages, given the acquisition of new friends and family members that comes with a new marriage. This expansion of the social network prediction was not supported by the data.

Among men, the findings show higher levels of loneliness for those in consensual unions and LAT-relationships compared to those in first marriages. Such differences are not observed among women. The level of loneliness of women in 'new' partnerships is similar to that of women in first marriages. Gender differences in loneliness emerge for those in LAT-relationships, with higher levels of loneliness for men than for women, but not for those in consensual unions. The relatively low level of supportive exchanges in men's 'new' relationships rather than marital history, characteristics of the social network or community involvement account for the elevated loneliness levels among men in these relationships. The findings provide no indication that consensual unions and LAT-relationships form a positive selection of partnerships. On the contrary: men seem to derive lower than average levels of emotional gratification from these relationships, while for women the level of emotional gratification in consensual unions and LAT-relationships seems to be roughly the same as in a first marriage. In other words, there is no support for the idea that only the 'good' consensual unions and LAT-relationships continue to exist, given the absence of legal barriers to leaving the relationship. Neither are there any indications that people in 'new' partnerships have more restricted social networks or are more involved in the community. The absence of ritual and ceremony to publicly mark the start of the relationships had been the basis for this prediction.

Though different types of partner relationships appear to provide differential protection against loneliness, it is important to keep in mind that by far the highest levels of loneliness are observed among the unpartnered. Single men tend to be lonelier than single women, a finding that is consistent with the notion that men's socialization makes it more difficult for them to live outside a partner relationship. Moreover, there are no differences in loneliness between men who have always been single and those previously married. Among single women, differences in marital history are relevant: never married single women are least vulnerable to loneliness. These results confirm a pattern that has been observed before: never-married women tend to fare better in life than their male counterparts. This difference is generally explained in terms of differential selection into marriage. Women tend to marry 'upward', that is, find marriage partners with a social status greater than their own, while men tend to marry 'downward' (Bernard, 1972). Those who remain unmarried tend to be high-resource females and low-resource males.

The findings do not provide a clear answer to the question of which experience makes older adults more vulnerable to loneliness: divorce or widowhood. Divorcees, both men and women, tend to be relatively lonely. However, their relatively high level of loneliness cannot be attributed to differences in the number and quality of network ties, contacts with children or community involvement. It appears then that current feelings of loneliness, both within and outside marriage, continue to be triggered by an emotionally hectic experience from the past. The findings seem to come closest to supporting the notion that divorce, as a deviation from the normal expectable life script, contributes to feelings of marginalization and social exclusion. Widowhood, like divorce, contributes to feelings of loneliness. The way it does, however, seems to differ between men and women. For men, the fact of being single, appears to be loneliness-inducing. For women, the findings provide no explanation for the higher levels of loneliness among the widowed. In other words, differences exist even after taking the type of partnership, network characteristics, contacts with children, and community involvement into account. Perhaps the explanation should be sought in dispositional factors, such as the uncertainty of future prospects, feelings of helplessness, and feelings of abandonment.

Characteristics of older adults' social networks, contacts with children, and community involvement were introduced in the analyses to help gain an understanding of differences in loneliness by partnership type and marital history. However, the majority of the characteristics also independently contributed to the explanation of loneliness. The findings show that older adults with larger and more supportive networks tend to be less lonely. The findings also show that frequent contacts with children help to alleviate or to prevent feelings of loneliness. Childlessness of itself is unrelated to loneliness among men, and – contrary to popular belief – inversely associated with loneliness among women. Apparently, the absence of children does not contribute to loneliness in older adults. Having children but not interacting with them frequently is what makes older adults more prone to loneliness. Finally the findings indicate that whereas voluntary organizations and volunteer work do not appear to be important avenues to social integration, the church is. Older adults who attend church services on a weekly basis are less lonely than those who go to church less frequently or never attend church services. There are several reasons why church attendance might help alleviate loneliness. The first concerns the role of the spiritual leader (minister, priest, imam, rabbi) as a confidant, or as a bridge to a larger social group. Religiosity in and of itself might also help combat feelings of loneliness. A personal relationship with

God can serve as a source of inner peace, confidence and happiness. Thirdly, the church provides a context for socializing with others, not only on days of worship, but also through other activities such as bible study, choir practice, volunteer work, and home visits.

Findings reported in this chapter show that in order to understand the antecedents of loneliness it helps to have details about the type of partnership in which older adults are involved and about their marital pasts. The results also show, however, that the differences in loneliness by marital history are not as pronounced among men as they are among women. Among men, the presence or absence of a partner seems to be more decisive. Among women, additional references to disruption in the marital career provide greater insight. Given these findings, I feel that analyses of gender should be focal in any future study of the implications of diversity in partnership histories for older adults' social integration.

Notes

1   This study is based on data collected in the context of 'Living Arrangements and Social Networks of Older Adults' (NESTOR-LSN), a research programme conducted at the department of Sociology and Social Gerontology of the Vrije Universiteit in Amsterdam and the Netherlands Interdisciplinary Demographic Institute (NIDI) in Den Haag, The program was funded by NESTOR, the Netherlands Program for Research on Ageing, with subsidies from the Ministry of Health, Welfare and Sports and the Ministry of Education, Culture and Sciences.
2   All percentages are based on weighted data. The data were weighted to correct for the overrepresentation of older cohorts, and older males in particular. The data can be considered to be representative for the Dutch population over the age of 55 in 1992.
3   The hypotheses presented in this section are drawn from Dykstra and de Jong Gierveld (2002).

Chapter 9

Social Networks as Mediators Between the Harsh Circumstances of People's Lives, and their Lived Experience of Health and Well-being[1]

Vicky Cattell

This chapter looks at the dynamic relationship between poverty and exclusion, neighbourhood, and health and well-being by considering the role of social networks and social capital in the social processes involved. Based on qualitative research in East London, it argues that social networks are key mediators between the harsh circumstances of people's lives and their lived experience of health and well-being.

Despite a substantial literature on the relationship between deprivation and reduced health chances (Acheson, 1998; Dorling, 1997; Graham, 2000; Townsend and Davidson, 1982) and on the protective influence of social networks on health (Berkman and Breslaw, 1983; Blaxter, 1990; Stansfeld, 1999), the relationship between them remains uncertain. Qualitative studies of poverty have however provided some clues as to the mechanisms involved. These include stress, loss of self-esteem or control, stigma, powerlessness, lack of hope, and fatalism (Cohen et al., 1992; Faith, 1985), some of which have also been linked to negative health outcomes in the health literature (Brown and Harris, 1978; Graham, 1993; North et al., 1993; Wheaton, 1980).

Poverty and Exclusion

Research and policy focus are as much now on poor places as on poor people. The neighbourhood has become a setting for policy approaches aimed at combatting social exclusion (Social Exclusion Unit, 2001) and reducing health inequalities (Department of Health, 2001; Secretary of State for Health, 1998). Discussion over whether health in poor areas can be explained wholly by the socio-economic characteristics of residents, or whether features connected with context can play an independent role (Mcintyre et al., 1993; Sloggett and Joshi, 1994), are paralleled by wider questions in the poverty literature concerning the impact of social exclusion and concentrated poverty on life chances. Social exclusion embraces a view of poverty concerned with multiple aspects of deprivation, with the role of neighbourhood and with process and dynamics over time (Oppenheim, 1998b; Hills, Le Grand and Piachaud, 2002). Concentrated poverty areas are seen not only as places where deprivation is particularly acute, but also as places providing a fertile environment for the mushrooming of social problems. Approaches focus on agency, i.e. on the behaviour and values of the poor (Massey et al., 1994; Murray, 1994), and on structure, particularly exclusion from the 'social, economic, political and cultural systems which determine the social integration of a person in society' (Walker, 1997, p. 8; Wilson, 1987). Both social exclusion and concentrated poverty imply some form of impoverished social networks.

Social Networks and Social Capital

Solid evidence links formal and informal social networks with better health chances (Berkman and Breslaw, 1983; Rogers, 1996; Wolf and Bruhn, 1993). Approaches to explaining these relationships focus on network functions (such as social integration) or benefits associated with network membership. Social ties can provide social support, are a source of sociability, and can confer self-esteem, identity, a sense of belonging and perceptions of control (Brown and Harris 1978; Cohen and Syme 1985; Stansfeld, 1999; Allan, 1996). Social networks can help individuals cope with poverty and adversity, and may generate *social capital* (Wellman and Wortley, 1990), a resource produced when people cooperate. Social capital has been defined by Putnam (1995b, p. 664), one of its major exponents, as 'features of social life – networks, norms [including reciprocity] and trust – that enable participants to act together more effectively'. For Jacobs (1962), an earlier writer on social capital, it refers to networks which provide a basis for trust, co-operation and perceptions of safety. Different forms of social capital have been specified and include obligations and expectations of support, information potential, informal social control (Coleman, 1990), and civic engagement (Putnam, 2000; Putnam et al., 1993).

Despite the concept having undergone vigorous critiques (Blaxter, 2002; Foley and Edwards, 1998; Lynch et al., 2000 ; Portes, 1998; Schuller, Baron and Field, 2000), 'social capital' has generated a great deal of interest and research activity amongst epidemiologists. It is considered to be a key mechanism for example in the relationship between poverty and ill health. First, it is suggested that growing income inequalities exert a negative influence on health through the reduction of social capital in poor areas (Kawachi et al., 1997). It is also argued that inegalitarian societies are less socially cohesive, with high crime rates and populations disconnected from public life (Wilkinson 1996). A difficulty here is that problems concerning place, the scale of analysis and the influence of context are not made explicit. For example, not all deprived neighbourhoods suffer from a lack of social cohesion or a depleted store of social capital (Cattell and Evans, 1999; Silburn et al., 1999). Second, it is suggested that social capital can explain processes by which *relative deprivation* – particularly perceptions of income inequality – impacts on health (Kawachi and Kennedy, 1997; Wilkinson, 1996). Yet strong perceptions of inequality could co-exist with the mutual aid and solidarity – the one a form and the other a source of social capital – evident in some traditional working class communities (see, for example, Frankenberg, 1966). Could different processes be operating here?

An additional problem with work which seeks to link social capital to health is that it is not clear which kinds of networks – strong or weak ties, homogeneous or heterogeneous contacts – are most effective. Durkheim's (1933) distinction between the mechanical solidarity of traditional communities and the organic solidarity of modern times involving cooperation between *unlike* individuals and groups is paralleled by work on social capital which distinguishes between 'thick' and 'thin' forms of trust (see, for example, Newton, 1997). Work in network analysis has shown that strong and weak ties can have different effects and different benefits (Cattell, 1995; Hirsch et al., 1990). Explanations include those which suggest that relationships involving *similar* persons foster understandings and support, whereas those between *dissimilar* persons in loose networks of weak ties provide wider access to diverse resources (Granovetter, 1973; Wellman and Wortley, 1990). If perceptions of inequality are detrimental to health, then perceived homogeneity might be crucial. Merton (1957) suggested that the extent to which individuals see themselves as deprived varies according to the reference group selected for comparison. A critique of traditional working class communities was that their dense supportive networks could also be characterized by exclusion and by suspicion of outsiders (Lockwood, 1966). In today's heterogeneous neighbourhoods we may need to identify conditions which make for more inclusive social networks. Although Marxist sociologists like Westergaard (1975) have argued that the narrow and constraining concerns of neighbourhood are not conducive to the growth of solidarity and universalistic identification, participation in local groups and initiatives could be expected to have some potential for inclusion and solidarity.

The questions to be addressed in this chapter include: do social networks mediate between poverty/exclusion and health; between place and health; and between structures and agency? And do different kinds of networks mediate these factors in different ways? The research sought to identify contextual and other influences on social network characteristics and their inclusivity/ exclusivity; to explore implications of different patterns of social networks and associated forms of social capital for health, well-being and quality of life, and to give particular consideration to variation in the social processes involved. These processes embody four dimensions: psychosocial pathways; norms and values; action and behaviour, and perceptions.

Methodology

A comparative approach based on localities was adopted to explore contextual effects, using intensive qualitative research to explore complexity and process. As Crow (2000) argues, community studies based on qualitative research can illustrate the meaning of macro-level trends for people's lives. The case study areas were located in East London, an area which contains some of the most multiply deprived boroughs and wards in England (Cattell, 1997). Two neighbourhoods were selected: 'Dock Lane' and 'Bridge Street' estates.[2] In each neighbourhood interviews were conducted with 35 to 37 residents and with approximately 15 people whose work took them into the neighbourhood. Selection was via participatory observation, through key contacts, and snowballing. As well as aiming to reflect the demographic make-up of the neighbourhood, efforts were made to include less active, less confident individuals, as well as those who were more participatory. Interviews were informal and conversational. The approach was holistic: interviews explored everyday lives and changing experiences; perceptions of neighbourhood; social networks; reciprocal aid; participation; perceptions of self and political efficacy; attitudes to mixing with others; and perceptions of the wider society and the future. Health was explored from a 'quality of life' and 'well-being' perspective (Bowling 1991), and treated as part of ordinary, everyday life (Cornwell, 1984).

Narratives were used to help explore the relationship between: (i) neighbourhood, social networks and social capital; and (ii) individuals' social networks, social capital and well-being. Utilizing grounded theory methodology

(Strauss and Corbin, 1990), theme analysis was adopted for the neighbourhood data, and typologies constructed from the personal data. I wanted to adopt a means of exploring complexity, accessing inter-relationships and retaining individuals in their time and place whilst facilitating comparison. The typologies were developed in stages, reflecting structural, then cultural elements; analysis progressed to assess their explanatory value and incorporate conceptual links.

The Neighbourhoods

Communities, in the sense of neighbourhoods but also in terms of the social interactions which take place there and residents' perceptions, exist in space, time and social and economic structure. These to some extent shape community life (Bulmer, 1986; Giddens, 1984). The Dock Lane Estate is located in Canning Town, Newham. Housing is mixed: solid postwar terraces, low-rise maisonettes and flats, and less popular towers. Until the mid-1970s, it was a dockside community. Described as 'a whole way of life' by people living and working there, the docks and the dockside factories were the backbone of the area. The once plentiful demand for manual labour has now ceased. Despite similarities in the profile of residents in terms of poverty, deprivation, unemployment, and a high proportion of single parents, Bridge Street, in Waltham Forest, differs from Dock Lane in certain respects. It has a history of sustained community development work and voluntary sector activity, and was undergoing radical redevelopment as a Housing Action Trust (HAT) estate at the time of the research. The (preregenerated) housing included elongated low-rise blocks with endless concrete walkways. Both estates have a history of stigmatization, but on Bridge Street it is a stigma which appears to have been internalized by some residents. The estate's decline and poor reputation were reportedly derived from badly designed and poorly maintained housing, allegedly from an influx of families with problems in the 1980s, and from high crime levels. Each estate had potential for the creation of social capital: Dock Lane was a relatively stable working class community; and Bridge Street had numerous opportunities for involvement in initiatives and organizations.

Neighbourhood Influences on Social Networks and Social Capital

The neighbourhood context, its social and employment history, its services, facilities, housing, opportunities for casual meeting and for participation in associations, as well as each area's reputation, were all found to influence social networks and the social capital generated. Housing design for example could encourage neighbourliness and perceptions of safety, facilitate cooperative child-care practices, or limit opportunities for interaction with neighbours; while housing allocation and relocation polices impacted on population stability and network density. Dwindling resources and facilities like social clubs, local shops and small trades meant that there were now fewer casual meeting places than there once were. Those remaining however continued to have significance for the weak ties necessary for a vibrant community life and which contribute to a sense of well-being: 'If I'm feeling fed up I take myself down to the market, where I see lots of people. You hear some good gossip, you keep in touch with what's going on.' Strangers can be included in this street life if the opportunities to stop and chat are there: 'Even people lining up at the bakers, although they don't know you, will tell you wonderful stories.'

Despite recent economic and demographic change, the Dock Lane estate largely remains a traditional working class neighbourhood, where residents have strong community loyalties, a strong sense of place, and a shared sense of history. One said: 'People round here are proud to be working class, they tell you that Dad was a docker, and Grandfather was a docker.' Work also gave people experience of organizing socially and collectively. As one explained: 'I was 30 years in Knights soap factory, and my husband worked in the docks ...They still have social evenings and outings now, the ex-workers organize them.' Today, despite the closure of the docks, neighbourly support and intergenerational continuity are still strong features of parts of the estate. The traditional norm of reciprocity and the expectations and obligations of mutual aid which it engenders, though certainly not as strong, have to some extent survived changed conditions, particularly in areas where the housing facilitates it. It is however an insular neighbourhood; newcomers can feel excluded.

On Bridge Street, in contrast to Dock Lane, there is little sense of pride in the area, little sense of history. Alienating housing design, anti-social behaviour and high population turnover have made it difficult to develop and sustain local social networks, and undermined any sense of community. Residents were critical of the design of the housing for example, where flats with entrances on the same walkway would lead to upper and lower decks: 'You can't really talk about neighbourliness in the low-rise because its difficult to know who your neighbours are.' In Dock Lane, positive perceptions of fellow residents are a major source of commitment and stability, but in Bridge Street, narratives indicated that rather than neighbourliness and trust there was distrust between residents, family dispersal and strain rather than a local supportive extended family, anomie rather than strong local culture and values, and alienation rather than attachment to the community. A resident said: 'There is no community spirit at all … There's a lot of mistrust, you worry who you talk to.' 'Keeping yourself to yourself' attitudes were prevalent. Residents suggested that a deprived and hostile environment also acted to damage closer relationships, while concerns about the estate's reputation for muggings and drugs discouraged family visits.

Yet there are many very positive aspects to life on the estate. Plentiful opportunities for involvement in projects, self-help groups, tenants' groups as well as courses, toy libraries and so on mean that there is a thriving resilient community which co-exists with the demoralized community. Services and initiatives like educational visiting and a women's project help people not only to cope with problems but also to increase their social ties. Residents' action led to redevelopment as a HAT estate. The social capital produced by self-interested groups can frequently be limited to that group, yet on Bridge Street, bridging ties, seen as essential for generating wider social trust (Putnam, 1995b), were being developed. An active resident reported:

> They [tenants, child care, elderly, Korean, Somali Women, and West Indian groups] used to all keep themselves to themselves, but there's been a lot of groundwork done to bring the groups together. The Summer Festival, for example, had a really good feel about it.

Values could change, as she explained: 'We're all here working in the same community … and that's something a lot of us have learnt, tolerance.' International links with tenants' groups had also been established.

Community has to be actively created on Bridge Street. The majority, however, on both estates, do not join activities and organizations. Constraints include poverty, attendant feelings of defeatism, and the neighbourhood's image. As a Bridge Street woman explained: 'Why join anything, or go on courses? People round here think that no-one on this estate ever gets anywhere, so why bother?'. Putnam (1995b) has suggested that social trust and civic engagement are highly correlated. On Dock Lane, however, resistance to becoming involved comes not from *lack* of trust. The expectation that '*you look after your own*' is both evidence of social capital – of the 'thick trust' kind – and a block to wider social trust.

The Social Network Typologies

Just as it would be an 'ecological fallacy' to assume that we can infer individual-level relationships with health from those observed from aggregate data (Macintyre and Ellaway, 2000), so it would be mistaken to expect social network characteristics which typify a specific spatial context to have generalized local applicability. A deterministic approach would ignore variation in human experience and obscure the role played by human agency in network formation. Network typologies – 'networks of experience' – were developed from residents' narratives. An early emergent pattern related to groups in an individual's network and other key themes. The typologies developed referred initially to the degree of homogeneity or heterogeneity in a network, estimated with reference to the range of 'membership groups' included (Bott, 1957). It has been suggested that values, as well as ways of coping with stress, can be learnt from one's membership groups (Pearlin, 1989). The membership groups identified from residents' accounts included: family, ethnic group, neighbours in the street/block, people in the wider community, school friends, and people connected with present and past work, clubs, churches, voluntary organizations and local initiatives. The typologies also refer to interviewees' positive or negative reference groups – locals, East Enders, social class, ethnicity, rich/poor, and older/younger people – used to explore values, attitudes, and identity. Working closely with individuals' narratives, the typologies were further developed in a way which reflected cultural issues. By developing typologies based on networks and associated norms and values, I was documenting some of the influences of social and economic change and continuity on people's lives. The distinction between the 'parochial' and 'traditional' network type on Dock Lane (see below) for example, captures temporal effects; the apparent paucity of residents on Bridge Street with 'parochial' networks is a reflection of neighbourhood effects.

Residents' networks on each estate corresponded broadly to five models: *socially excluded*; *parochial*; *traditional*; *pluralistic*; and *solidaristic*. Table 9.1 outlines their structural elements; their cultural components are described below. However on Bridge Street there were some residents whose networks were entirely individualistic and innovative. An example is the *relocating* network found amongst some resourceful Bridge Street residents. Pat for example responds to the stigmatized reputation of the estate by disassociating herself from it and becoming involved in local life in an Essex village.

The *traditional* network is that most closely associated with a traditional working class community and culture (Lockwood, 1966; Young and Willmott,

Table 9.1   The East London network typology: structural characteristics

Socially excluded network	A small number of membership groups, limited in size. Examples of residents with these networks include newcomers, unemployed people, women in difficult relationships, isolated older people, single parents without local families (on Bridge Street), carers, a refugee, a woman who immigrated on marriage.
Parochial network	A small number of membership groups, but may be extensive contacts within them. Comprised of a local extended family, plus a smaller number of local friends or neighbours. Dense, homogeneous structure. Examples include single parents, unemployed people.
Traditional network	Made up of family, neighbours, ex workmates, old school, social/sports clubs friends. Tight knit structure. Examples are mainly long term residents, predominantly older people, and a smaller number of younger people who worked locally, involved in unions or clubs.
Pluralistic network	An open network consisting of a relatively large number of membership groups; dissimilar people in terms of age, ethnicity, interests, employment status or occupation, and place of residence. Generally loose knit. Principal examples are people active in voluntary organizations, frequently not born locally.
Solidaristic network	A wide range of membership groups, made up of both similar and dissimilar people; structure both dense and loose; wide range of positive reference groups. Networks share some characteristics of both the traditional and the pluralistic models, strong local ties plus looser contacts.

1957). For the *parochial* network, local ties, particularly family ties, remain strong as they do for the *traditional* group, but its members do not have experience of local work or clubs. In a sense it is *more* parochial than the traditional community, with attitudes tending to be insular. For example: 'I'm not one for friends, my family are my friends' said one resident. The *socially excluded* model incorporates a wide range of people who, temporarily or long-term, have truncated social networks. Both the *pluralistic* and *solidaristic* models reflect wide networks and participation in organizations, but the latter are also integrated into the local community and share some of its traditional attributes. In addition, these residents perceive shared interests with unlike groups. Tolerant attitudes are also more likely to be found here.

Traditional patterns of social networks reflect Dock Lane's traditional characteristics and, along with the *parochial*, are typical of the estate. Reciprocity is a dominant norm and 'looking after your own', a common expectation. Pensioners in the *traditional* group are active in social clubs, their present activity is rooted in their experience of work and youth or sports clubs in the past. *Traditional* network models are found on both estates, but in Bridge Street, which has not been a work-based community and where attachment to place is weakened, they exist in a slightly paler form. On both estates social and economic change, out migration, and residents' perceptions of changing values and behaviours – such as cooperation and collective activity – suggest that residents in the *traditional* category are a diminishing group, more typical of the older generation. On Dock Lane the *parochial* group appears to be taking their place. On Bridge Street, the picture is more fragmented. The *parochial* model of strong, homogeneous, local – especially family – ties is perhaps associated with a traditional community which has lost some of its essential features, but which has nevertheless managed to remain reasonably resilient.

For many residents interviewed on Bridge Street, the locality is much less dominant an aspect of their social networks. Residents involved in tenants' groups and voluntary organizations are an exception; as on Dock Lane their networks can be loosely grouped as *pluralistic* or *solidaristic*. For many of the remainder, social ties are either restricted, or dispersed. A higher proportion of Bridge Street interviewees had networks which currently or in the past corresponded to the *socially excluded* model. Although, as on Dock Lane, personal circumstances were contributory factors, here neighbourhood factors such as a fear of crime and a lack of trust deterred residents from making contacts. A young woman said:

> It would be nice to be able to ask a neighbour in for a cup of tea, or help someone financially ... Or we could babysit for each other. They don't do any of this on this floor ... People don't trust each other.

Networks of Experience and Health and Well-being

A feature of the network typologies was that certain health protecting or damaging attributes and attitudes – such as hope, fatalism, pessimism, self-esteem and perceptions of control – were related to network type. Those with the more restricted networks, for example, were more likely to express feelings associated with negative health outcomes. Here the isolation associated with being a newcomer was easiest to overcome. It was those residents not simply unable temporarily to participate in the life of their communities but socially excluded in a wider or deeper sense who were more at risk. For example, some of the Dock Lane women with *socially excluded* networks linked a violent partner with their isolation, damaged self-esteem, feelings of lack of control and poor physical and mental health. Single parents on Bridge Street were less likely to have family and neighbourly support than their counterparts on Dock Lane; low self-esteem and depression were common.

Additional attributes shared by several of those in the *socially excluded* group included feelings of fatalism and hopelessness. An unemployed Dock Lane man with a number of health problems said: 'What future? There's no future'. His account of his earlier life illustrates the long-term nature of social exclusion as well as his individual trajectory:

> I'm unemployed. I can't read or write. I did labouring years ago. I've been on courses but nothing ever happens, it's always the man next to you what gets the job, the man with qualifications. I never went to school when I was young, I bunked it, my family didn't care. Dad chucked me out when I was 11.

His problems were exacerbated however by his present circumstances. An income and accommodation totally inadequate for the needs of his family were, he reported, causing him and his wife considerable stress.

Fatalism, relating to one's own life and health and the way society works in general, and political cynicism were linked in some cases. Yet health-damaging attributes did not always go hand in hand with either political cynicism or insular attitudes. An unemployed Bridge Street resident in the *excluded* category for example, who took an interest in politics, described his feelings of demoralization. He believed the effects of his situation were in themselves direct obstacles to his becoming involved locally:

> I don't have the power to straighten out my own life so how can I do other things [like joining the Tenants' group]. I feel helpless, ... I want to lead a normal life, and look after my family. But it's not under my control. When you

can't do it the depression and the illness creeps in. I feel tired, very lethargic, dizzy, and I have pains. I hate living on benefits, I try to sign on at a time when no-one will see me.

Social exclusion for this man was a result of his material but also social deprivation – he had few contacts outside his nuclear family. It was exacerbated by living in a tower block with high resident turnover and a neighbourhood depleted of everyday social capital.

In contrast, for those involved in local activities, participation could have health promoting qualities. A Bridge Street resident involved in a local credit union for example reported:

They come in here for a chat, make friends, become more confident and assertive. We had a few people who joined feeling a bit low, when they come in … it picks them up a bit. People are financially happier too.

The more highly active residents in tenants' groups or campaigns tended to feel in control of their lives, their self-esteem was high, and they were more likely to express hope for the future – for themselves, their families and their community. Yet the processes might be more direct. Feeling happy, healthy, hopeful and in control may predispose participation. However there were some residents on both estates who described how becoming involved had changed their lives. Their friendship networks had grown, they were enjoying life, and for many, their sense of well-being also improved. A Dock Lane woman said:

I felt terribly isolated, and had little confidence then … I was on Valium … That part of my health has improved over the last few years, since I've been on my own and involved in the Tenants Association. I feel in control of my life now, I didn't before.

These observations on the relationship between network model and well-being are, perhaps not surprisingly, related to the size of the network, especially at the extremes. But when we look at the benefits bestowed by different networks, and the forms of social capital associated with them, the picture is more complex. Some Dock Lane residents for example had numerically extensive social ties which were very good at providing practical support or conferring identity. However they may be limited in other ways. A further way of understanding the relationships and processes involved indicated by the interview data suggests another link in the chain: the coping resources and mechanisms afforded by, or associated with, different network types.

Coping with Poverty and Life's Difficulties

People with more restricted models – the *socially excluded* or narrower end of the *parochial* group – understandably find it difficult to cope. They lack resources and social capital. Problems may be so overwhelming that they give up trying. For others, life has always been an uphill struggle. Jennifer, a Dock Lane resident in her 40s, expressed it as 'never having had a chance to enjoy life', and added 'Life has always been hard ... I had my family young, so didn't see much of life, I couldn't go out clubbing it and pubbing it'. Jennifer and her husband are unemployed. In order to manage she buys from catalogues, but it is coping at a cost: 'worrying how to cope, who to borrow off now'. In some cases, residents' social contacts may be too low in resources themselves to be able to help. Mulki is a widowed refugee. One of her few contacts on Bridge Street is a fellow countrywoman, but Mulki is reluctant to approach her for help, because she too is widowed, has poor health and six children of her own to bring up.

Frequently, *parochial* networks, through mutual aid and norms of 'bounded reciprocity', can work very effectively. Michelle, for example, a black East Ender, lives with her husband and four children. Her main contacts are her large local extended family. They supply most of each other's needs, be it emotional, financial or help with the children. The coping resources accessed by the *parochial* group are clearly beneficial, but sometimes they are not enough to meet needs, and at times there may be family conflict. Some of the single parents on Dock Lane were unaware of sources of advice on benefit entitlement. Additionally, the tight-knit structure of the networks, illustrated by comments such as 'The kids know my friends, everyone I know they know', means that network members may provide little relief when negative life events strike. Family members may be too involved themselves. As Anne put it: 'I lost my Mum last year ... I can't talk to my two brothers about her, they just break down. I've had a whole year of stress, kidney and stomach trouble'. In contrast, a (*solidaristic*) widow described how her looser contacts helped her overcome bereavement: 'The family were a bit too close, we were all hurt ... Work was my safety valve, a lifeline. They treat you normally, you can have a laugh and a joke with them.'

Those in the *traditional* model cope, like those with *parochial* networks, through mutual aid. This is particularly clear in old age. One older resident offered a nice definition of friendship: 'When I make a bread pudding, I always try to make one for Jim too.' Families were a prime source of support, but people in the *traditional* group were better able to cope successfully partly because their lives reflected a history of coping with poverty cooperatively, but also because they had other membership groups to balance their lives. The contacts they made at work, the social skills learnt, the esteem derived, the support given and received, as well as the experience of organizing collectively, appeared to sustain them across the life course. Mavis, for example, now in her eighties, met most of her friends in the factory. She continues to visit them on the estate, talk over old times in the pensioners' club, and shop for the more infirm. Their experiences and the building-up of resources – social capital – help this group to cope. Benefits included enjoying life. Carol's comments were typical: 'I worked in a factory when I was 15, I loved it, being part of things, and we all stuck up for each other … For all their problems they enjoyed being there.'

The duality of coping was also evident in these narratives. The *traditional* group laid great stress on the norm of coping in adversity, 'getting on with it', taking what life throws at you, being in control, managing on your income and not getting into debt. As a younger woman on Bridge Street said: 'Living here … has not affected my health. You can say yes, it is depressing and get depressed, or you can make the best of it.' An emphasis on coping is reflected in attitudes to both ill health and negative life events; there is a tendency not to seek help from external sources, especially amongst older residents. Not admitting to worrying is seen as a virtue: 'My [bad] health has never prevented me from doing anything … I don't think it's right to waste the doctor's time if you can get the tablets to do it yourself.'

Those in the *pluralistic* group cope actively; they are well informed and are able to access a range of resources. Just as they believe that they can take an active part in improving neighbourhood life, so they recognise that they have a role to play in protecting their health. Members are able to access the 'information potential' form of social capital most effectively: 'I know what I'm entitled to' as one respondent receiving benefits said emphatically. Another resident was able to use her loose ties to find out about health care for her mother. Residents in this group may however miss out on the kind of support associated with dense ties. On Dock Lane for example, a relative newcomer to East London said:

> When I've had a lot of pressure connected with meetings, and the children have been playing up, it's then that I feel isolated. I wish someone would knock on the door and say 'I'll have your kids for an hour'.

She felt strongly that a culture of 'you look after your own' was instrumental in her exclusion from supportive networks.

Residents whose networks correspond to the *solidaristic* model cope interactively. Like the *pluralistic* group, they have the advantages that activity in organizations can bring, but can also access the support of close personal or neighbourhood ties. They are better able to withstand a certain amount of stress associated with events such as break-ins and bereavement, not by 'getting on with it' like '*traditionals*', but because they have both homogeneous and heterogeneous ties. They have built up social capital of both thick and thin trust forms. June, for example, a young mother on benefits in Dock Lane, can ask anyone – neighbours, local friends and family – for help if she is ill, short of money or needs help with the children. She also has contacts made through the tenants' association which keep her well informed. She has gained in other ways from participation: 'It makes you more aware of people's problems, and your own problems do not seem so big ... It gives you a good feeling, a sense of achievement, that you have helped'.

One might suppose that those networks which were most health promoting would maintain a balance between altruism and egoism (Durkheim, 1951). A minority of residents in the *solidaristic* group reported that at times they did too much for others, felt overloaded, and out of control. Where reciprocity was an associational norm however, the balance could be more readily achieved. Participation in self-help groups, such as an association for West African women and their children which encouraged cooperation and mutual support via a wide range of activities, seemed to be particularly beneficial to the quality of life of a number of residents.

Perceptions of Inequality

As well as perceptions of inequality adversely affecting health (Wilkinson, 1996), the reverse also appeared to be happening. Some of the residents active in local initiatives and groups were motivated by their perceptions of inequality and hatred of the poverty they saw around them. For example: 'I've seen such wealth, and such poverty, such inequality. The children round here are so poor ... I can do something to help.' The research indicates that both the nature of the response to perceptions of deprivation and how the structure of inequality is perceived have relevance for the inclusivity of social networks, for the social capital created, and, by extension, for health and well-being.

Those with a narrow range of positive reference groups on the estates tend to see themselves in competition with people who they perceive as different from themselves, but who on many counts are little different. Residents were critical of people getting higher social security benefits than themselves, of the person in the post office queue getting a better pension, of someone with a bigger council house or of someone who managed to get a job. These are poor people too, but they are perceived to be less deserving. Sometimes race is an issue, or age, or being a newcomer. Conversely, those generally tolerant individuals with a broader range of positive reference groups do not see such narrow lines of division. Frequently motivated by political or religious beliefs, they tend to see inequalities between rich and poor and between social classes as the important ones. They are willing to mix with and recognise interests in common with a relatively broad range of groups and are more likely to be active in organizations. On both estates residents with *solidaristic* networks are committed to their community, but for them the community is wider and much more inclusive than it is for other residents. For example 'The more ethnic groups you have in a society, the richer it will be'; and 'Round here it's "You look after your own, don't let others take liberties". Now, I look further afield. I don't judge people.'

Conclusions and Discussion

The social network typologies identified – *socially excluded*; *parochial*; *traditional*; *pluralistic*; and *solidaristic* – reflect spatial and temporal contexts in which social networks are developed and sustained. These 'networks of experience' capture structural constraints and opportunities, but also aspects of human agency, like values and responses, all factors which help shape networks and their inclusivity. Social networks can be seen to perform a dual role in processes involved in health inequalities. They provide a link between macro and micro factors, what Mills (1970) described as the relation of personal troubles of milieu to public issues of social structure, but at the same time they can be part of the process of coping with or resisting structural inequality.

Neighbourhood context emerged as a key influence on the genesis of social networks and social capital; local resources and neighbourhood reputation are both dimensions to consider when exploring area effects. The research provides little evidence however to support notions of a contagion or miasma effect evident in discourses on 'concentrated poverty' in the development of values and behaviour associated with social exclusion (or indeed with social capital). Rather than the concentration of the poor being the problem, it was the stigmatized reputation of an area and its people together with an alienating physical environment which contributed to isolating residents from each other, restricted the flow of information and acted as a block to the development of trust or a local cooperative culture. Local characteristics contributed to differences in patterns of social networks between the neighbourhoods, but there were also commonalities. In exploring diverse influences it would be mistaken to neglect wider contexts. Dominant political ideologies, for example, could be expected to have some influence on norms and attitudes which motivate the active creation of social networks. As suggested elsewhere, normative change in relation to individualism/collectivism as well as decline in local resources can play a role in generational variation in social capital (Cattell and Herring, 2002a, 2002b).

The research confirms the importance of social networks to health and well-being. But it is the link they facilitate between multiple, complex and changing influences on people's lives with *different* benefits or disbenefits which, the research suggests, makes the identification of different network typologies a useful heuristic tool. The distribution of supportive resources, as well as factors associated with health and well-being – perceptions of esteem and control, hope and enjoyment – vary with network characteristics. Different network types, made up of dense or weak, homogeneous or heterogeneous ties, involving 'thick' or 'thin' forms of trust, all contribute to the quality of life. The more varied the range of membership groups, the greater the range of coping resources accessible and the greater the potential benefits for health.

Although the direction of relationships can sometimes be inferred from the data – for example, involvement produces higher perceptions of esteem and control and widens networks, with both promoting active coping – routes are not generally unilinear. Relationships between psychosocial pathways, norms and values, and coping mechanisms and resources appeared essentially dynamic. Can social capital theory illuminate these relationships? A pivotal component for Coleman (1990) is that the norms involved inhere in the structure of social relations. To some extent the research did confirm this embeddedness and the fragility of social capital for individuals. But social capital theory is limited as an explanatory tool for uncovering the connections between wider structures and networks or norms, or for establishing the direction of relationships between norms and networks. The critique of social capital for its circularity (Portes, 1998) is persuasive. What is important perhaps is that these relationships are recognized as sometimes recursive. Hope could be gained through action, for example, but for some active residents hope for a better future was an integral part of their political or religious outlook. Similarly values like tolerance and social consciousness were involved in a dual relationship with the structural characteristics of individuals' social networks. Network types might also be seen as reflecting and being reflected by individualistic, intra-group or collective responses to deprivation and day-to-day problems. The 'networks of experience' approach introduced here informed by notions of the duality of structure/action of structuration theory – structures make social action possible, at the same time, social action creates those structures (Giddens, 1984) – may have potential for further conceptual development of social networks and for their heuristic value in illuminating the social processes involved in health inequalities.

The focus on reciprocity and participation should not detract from underlying poverty issues. Evidence confirms that even if networks can ameliorate the harsher health effects of poverty and deprivation, they are nevertheless no substitute for a more equitable distribution of resources nationally. Social exclusion impeded access to social capital, but there were also more direct pathways evident between exclusion and mechanisms implicated in health effects. Additionally it could be argued that the processes within network typologies described here are simply a reflection of the class structure and that by focusing on an array of coping and other resources, they are encapsulating some of the ways in which class-based health inequalities are created and structured. Middle class people generally have wider, looser and more resourceful social networks; working class people have fewer opportunities to broaden theirs (Pearlin, 1985; Willmott, 1987). Almost all interviewees were from semi-skilled and unskilled backgrounds, yet network models could perhaps be seen to bear some relation to nuances of and changes in the class structure. Of more interest are those aspects of class which embrace human agency – identity, class consciousness and solidaristic action. Perceptions of inequality and deprivation can be both a source of hopelessness and a source of social action, effects to some extent contingent on social consciousness and on ways in which residents perceive the structure of inequality.

Questions remain about the salience of neighbourhood as a source of wider solidarity. Involvement in local activities could help broaden networks and develop tolerance, but participation may equally embody self-interest and bounded solidarity (Cattell and Evans, 1999; Portes, 1998; Stolle and Rochon, 1998). Participation does, in any case, involve only a minority of East London residents. Nevertheless, I propose that the local arena, with certain prerequisites, *can* be a source of wider solidarity. Westergaard (1975) argued that vision was necessary to extend the boundaries of solidarity and that its sources lay in the wider society. There are many constraints on the growth of alternative values and utopian ideas, not least prevailing political ideologies, but their impact is not universal. Individuals with '*solidaristic*' networks for example embraced a vision of a more egalitarian society. Influences were diverse and not confined to local ties and local experience. However an additional factor which characterized their attitudes was tolerance which co-existed with a willingness to cooperate with dissimilar others. If the contribution made by tolerance to solidarity is a significant one, then the saliency of the neighbourhood context, with its potential for supporting integrative social ties, becomes apparent. For Jacobs (1962), it was the loose ties made up of the interactions of a wide range of different people which made a neighbourhood thrive, and its facilities, resources and streets the facilitators of casual interaction. The plentiful meeting places which once dotted the East London landscape have dwindled, but remaining opportunities – like schools and markets – are valued by residents.

The integration and cohesion of diverse neighbourhoods are likely to be key policy concerns for Britain in the twenty-first century. If weak ties are prerequisites for social cohesion (Granovetter, 1973) and inclusion, then appropriate policy interventions can be suggested: first, mixed use developments with plentiful sites for interaction; second, opportunities for structural links between associations of the kind found on Bridge Street; and third, regenerated local employment. If work was a source of thick trust in the homogeneous neighbourhood of the past, could rejuvenated local labour markets in today's heterogeneous neighbourhoods encourage the social exchanges which would help foster tolerance and integration? Similarly could work-based collective activity promote wider solidarity and more inclusive social networks? A likely benefit would be a reduction in inequalities in health both by widening access to productive and empowering social networks and by combating the poverty and social exclusion which disproportionately continue to affect Britain's old industrial and manufacturing areas.

Acknowledgements

I would like to thank Susanne MacGregor for sustained support for the duration of the research, the ESRC for the award which made it possible, and the East London residents who generously shared their experiences with me.

Notes

1   This chapter is based on my Doctoral research (Cattell, 1998), funded by a full-time ESRC award. An earlier and expanded version was published as Cattell, V. (2001), 'Poor People, Poor Places and Poor Health: The Mediating Role of Social Networks and Social Capital', *Social Science and Medicine*, 52 (10), 1501–16.
2   These are pseudonyms.

Chapter 10

Older People in Urban Neighbourhoods: Addressing the Risk of Social Exclusion in Later Life[1]

Thomas Scharf and Allison E. Smith

Introduction

Addressing the causes and consequences of social exclusion represents a key theme in contemporary social policy. This reflects a growing awareness of the social costs that can arise when individuals, families and communities become cut off from wider society. While the concept of social exclusion has appealed to politicians and social scientists alike on the grounds of its breadth and elasticity (Silver, 1994, p. 536), when it comes to the policy-making process there is growing evidence of a narrowing down of the target groups for public intervention. In Britain, the current social exclusion agenda focuses strongly on the needs of children, young adults and those of employment age (for example, Opportunity for All, 2002). Within this context, important questions arise concerning the position of people who have permanently withdrawn from the labour market. In particular, emphasis on the social integration of potentially marginalized groups through paid employment neglects the situation of older people, the majority of whom have retired. The absence of adequate data on the nature of poverty and exclusion experienced by older people (Howarth et al., 1999) merely confirms the marginal position of this group in debates about social exclusion (Scharf et al., 2001).

In this chapter, we seek to develop a broader understanding of ways in which debates about social exclusion might be applied to the situation of older people. This involves the need to reach beyond established discourses on social exclusion that, in Levitas's (1998, p. 27) terms, 'posit paid work as a major factor in social integration'. Our emphasis will be on exploring social inclusion in the context of relationships and resources that exist beyond (paid) employment. A particular focus is upon the situation of older people who live in socially deprived urban neighbourhoods. Such neighbourhoods have been the target of considerable social policy intervention in recent years, as governments seek to reduce the geographic divide between Britain's most deprived areas and the mainstream of society (Social Exclusion Unit, 2001). In this respect, the chapter seeks to examine the degree to which residence in an area of concentrated poverty might compound the impact on older people of other forms of social exclusion.

The chapter is divided into three parts. First, we develop a conceptual understanding of social exclusion in relation to the situation of older people. In emphasizing the multidimensional nature of exclusion, we identify several difficulties associated with application of the concept to the circumstances of older people. Second, we seek to develop a new approach to examining social exclusion of older people. Using data drawn from an empirical study conducted in socially deprived neighbourhoods in three cities, we provide evidence of the multiple risks of exclusion faced by many older people in urban areas of England. Finally, we examine some of the implications of this analysis for an understanding of social networks and for public policy.

Conceptualizing Social Exclusion of Older People

Early debates about social exclusion tended to emphasise the distinction between the *distributional* dimension of poverty and the *relational* focus of social exclusion (see, for example, Room, 1995; Townsend, 1987). However, as Bhalla and Lapeyre (1997, p. 417) note, poverty and exclusion are closely inter-related: 'adequate levels of income are a *necessary* though not *sufficient* means of ensuring access of people to basic human needs'. As a result, attempts to conceive of social exclusion in terms of both its distributional and relational elements are increasingly common (Russell Barter, McCafferty and Woodhouse, 1999, p. 85). Such approaches highlight the multidimensionality of exclusion, suggesting that people can become excluded when particular institutional systems break down (Atkinson and Davoudi, 2000). For example, Berghman (1997, p. 19) disaggregates the idea of exclusion, conceiving social exclusion in terms of the non-realization of citizenship rights within four key societal institutions – the democratic and legal system, the labour market, the welfare system, and the family and community system.

Of growing relevance in discussions of social exclusion are approaches that link exclusion to residence in particular types of neighbourhood (Glennerster et al., 1999; Power, 2002). The importance of the geographical dimension is emphasized by Madanipour et al. (1998, p. 22) who suggest that the different components of social exclusion, as outlined by Berghman and others, can combine to 'create acute forms of exclusion that find a spatial manifestation in particular neighbourhoods'. The environmental dimension of exclusion is particularly important given the way in which neighbourhoods contribute to shaping the identities of those who reside in them. In this respect, Marcuse (1996, pp. 201–2) comments that: 'Neighbourhood has become more than a source of security, the base of a supportive network, as it has long been: it has become a source of identity, a definition of who a person is and where he or she belongs in society'.

Emphasis on the multidimensionality of social exclusion has influenced several attempts to operationalize the concept within research. For example, Burchardt, Le Grand and Piachaud (1999) identify five domains of social exclusion that relate to the individual's ability to participate in what might be perceived as 'normal' social activities: consumption activity (the ability to consume up to a minimum level the goods and services considered normal for society); savings activity (the accumulation of savings, pension entitlements, or property ownership); production activity (engagement in an economically or socially valued activity); political activity (engagement in some collective effort to improve or protect the immediate or wider social or physical environment); and social activity (engagement in significant social interaction with family or friends, and identifying with a cultural group or community).

Gordon et al. (2000) adopt a similar approach when developing a measure of exclusion with four dimensions: impoverishment; non-participation in the labour market; lack of access to basic services; and exclusion from a range of social relations. This latter component is further subdivided into elements such as individuals' non-participation in common social activities, social isolation, a perceived lack of support in times of need, lack of civic engagement and an inability to 'get out and about' (Bradshaw et al., 2000).

There are at least three difficulties arising from current exclusion debates in terms of the situation of older people. These are also reflected in attempts to operationalize the concept in research. The first difficulty concerns the centrality of labour market participation as an indicator of social inclusion (Levitas, 1998). The focus of exclusion debates on work and employment leaves unclear the position of older people who have permanently withdrawn from their occupational roles. For example, in their production domain of exclusion, Burchardt et al. (1999) judge as 'included' and 'engaged in a socially valued activity' those who have reached state retirement age and are retired. This runs counter to research in social gerontology that highlights the exclusionary impact of retirement on many older people (Phillipson, 1998). In terms of the broad spectrum of social roles adopted by older people that reach beyond labour market participation, it is particularly useful to consider their involvement in aspects of community life, their links within and beyond the local community, as well as their informal social relationships. This focus can be conceived of in terms of the degree of access that older people have to different forms of social capital (Smith, Phillipson and Scharf, 2002). Emphasis is placed on involvement in civic activities, the nature of social (support) networks, and the way in which social relationships are characterized by mutuality and reciprocity.

A second difficulty arises from an emphasis in exclusion discourse on the dynamic nature of social exclusion (Byrne, 1999). Household panel studies show how people move in and out of poverty/exclusion as their circumstances change (Burchardt, 2000; Leisering and Walker, 1998). The evidence from such studies leads to the conclusion that, as Perri 6 (1997, p. 3) asserts, 'most people get out of poverty'. This gives rise to the impression that the boundaries of exclusion are essentially fluid rather than rigid. However the situation of older people is likely to be rather different. For those prone to exclusion, the experience of being excluded may be more permanent than would be the case for other groups. Thus while exclusion from political activity or social interaction might represent an episodic characteristic of younger people's lives, older people may face additional difficulties in seeking to escape the enduring impact of such situations. Equally, older people who lack adequate material resources are unlikely to be able to 'get out of poverty' without considerable additional financial support from the state.

A third problem concerns the neighbourhood dimension of exclusion, and its impact on older people's sense of identity (Scharf et al., 2002a). For a variety of reasons, the local residential environment may represent a much more important aspect of exclusion for older people than for other age groups. On the one hand, older people tend to spend more time than younger people in their immediate neighbourhood. On the other, many older people have spent a substantial period of their lives in a particular neighbourhood, deriving a strong sense of emotional investment both in their home and in the surrounding community (Phillipson et al., 2000; Young and Willmott, 1957). Indeed, Rowles (1978, p. 200) suggests that what he refers to as a 'selective intensification of feelings about spaces' might represent 'a universal strategy employed by older people to facilitate maintaining a sense of identity within a changing environment'. This idea is reinforced by Rowles and Ravdal (2002, p. 87) who argue that the 'selective and repeated mental reconstruction and maintenance of these places in consciousness ... provides a sense of reinforcement of the self'.

Discussion of potential environmental impacts on self-identity raises particular concerns in terms of the situation of older people in deprived urban neighbourhoods. In their study of residents living on two estates in East London, Cattell and Evans (1999) comment that older people derived an important part of their identity from their similarity with one another. This desire for similarity is understandable: at one level it is about feeling protected by those with similar attributes; at another, it is about being surrounded by people with a similar history. In most urban areas, however, the desire for 'sameness' may be difficult to realize. This applies in particular to so-called 'zones of transition' which thrive on a rapid turnover of people and buildings. A similar situation may arise for older people living in what Power (2000, p. 12) describes as 'nonviable' estates – those unpopular urban neighbourhoods characterized by low housing demand and subsequent abandonment of housing by all but the very poorest or least mobile residents. Part of the problem here may be that the advantages of the inner city for some (services for minority groups, relatively cheap housing) also translate into disadvantages for others (falling house prices in some cases; destruction of familiar landscapes in others). It is also clear that older people can be highly selective in how they view the consequences of profound urban change, and this translates into often negatively charged perceptions about those around them. A significant result of the rapid change experienced in some urban neighbourhoods would be an undermining of older people's sense of identification with the local community, and the expression of dissatisfaction with the neighbourhood.

Operationalizing Social Exclusion of Older People

Arising from this discussion, there is a need to consider ways in which the idea of social exclusion as a multidimensional concept can be developed to reflect the particular circumstances and needs of older people. To explore more fully the issues raised, we draw upon data from a survey of 600 older people living in nine deprived neighbourhoods in three English cities. Liverpool, Manchester and Newham (London) were ranked as England's most deprived local authorities in the 1998 Index of Local Deprivation (DETR, 1998). To account for the substantial variation that exists within each city in relation to the intensity of deprivation, the research was concentrated on each city's three most deprived electoral wards (Scharf et al., 2002b). While the selected study areas vary in relation to their proximity to the respective city centre, socioeconomic structure and population profile, they share a range of characteristics associated with intense urban deprivation. This includes, for example, above-average rates of unemployment, relatively poor housing conditions, a steady loss of services such as shops and banks, and a high incidence of crime (Power, 2002; Social Exclusion Unit, 1998).

Face-to-face interviews were conducted with 600 people aged 60 and over using a standardized questionnaire. In designing the questionnaire, we were able to draw upon the recently completed survey of *Poverty and Social Exclusion* (Gordon et al., 2000), and upon other major social surveys (such as the *General Household Survey* and the *British Household Panel Survey*). In addition, a number of questions and measures were included that were regarded as especially relevant to the situation of older people.

Conceptually the approach to operationalize social exclusion adopted here displays deliberate overlaps with that of Burchardt et al. (1999) and especially of Gordon et al. (2000). However in its detail we seek to take account of some of the limitations of existing approaches in relation to the particular situation of older people. We conceive of social exclusion as encompassing five distinct dimensions: exclusion from material resources; exclusion from social relations; exclusion from civic activities; exclusion from basic services; and neighbourhood exclusion. For analytic purposes, it is necessary to treat the domains as being independent of one another. However, as outlined previously, we recognise that the domains of exclusion are likely to be interconnected and we explore some of the relationships between them below. As a first step it is necessary to develop appropriate indicators of the different domains and show how in each case these might be summarized in terms of a single measure.

Exclusion from Material Resources

Two indicators of individuals' exclusion from material resources were used in this study. The first is a poverty measure, the second a measure of multiple deprivation. In relation to *poverty*, we followed researchers such as Mack and Lansley (1985) and more recently Gordon et al. (2000) in measuring poverty by identifying those of our respondents who say they lack and are unable to afford what the majority of British people view as basic necessities. Our research draws on the results of a national survey of the adult population that highlighted a range of items and social activities regarded by 50 per cent or more of people as being necessities of daily living (Gordon et al., 2000). In our survey, we presented people with a similar list of 'socially perceived necessities' (Scharf et al., 2002b). From the list of 26 necessities, which encompasses 19 material items and seven common social activities, respondents were asked to identify items that they did not have or activities that they did not do. They were then asked to state whether they lacked the items because they did not want them or could not afford them. Following the approach of the national survey, people lacking two or more of the items because they could not afford them were judged to be in poverty. This technique identified 45 per cent of respondents as poor. Some older people lacked and could not afford a substantial number of necessities, suggesting an intense degree of poverty. For 7 per cent of respondents, this meant going without and not being able to afford 11 or more of the items and activities on the list. Just taking the 19 material items from the list of necessities, and adopting the same threshold of lacking two or more items on the grounds of lack of affordability, identifies 41 per cent of people as living in material poverty (Table 10.1).

The second indicator of exclusion from material resources is a *deprivation* measure. Here we developed the work of Evandrou (2000) whose index of multiple deprivation comprises seven items considered of particular importance to older people (for example, central heating, use of a telephone, access to a car) (see Figure 10.1). This measure categorizes people according to the degree of deprivation faced, ranging from no deprivation (where a person is not disadvantaged on any of the seven characteristics) to high deprivation (disadvantaged on at least five characteristics). Very few respondents (three per cent) in the study reported here were not disadvantaged on any of the

---

A person scores 1 for each of the following characteristics:
  lives in a household without central heating
  lives in a household without a phone
  lives in a household without a car
  lives in local authority or housing association rented accommodation
  lives in a household with more than one person per room
  lives in a household where the head of the household receives income support
  individual has no formal qualifications

No deprivation: score 0, not disadvantaged on any of these characteristics.
Low deprivation: score 1–2, disadvantaged on one or two characteristics only.
Medium deprivation: score 3–4, disadvantaged on three or four characteristics.
High deprivation: score 5 or more, disadvantaged on at least five characteristics.

Figure 10.1   Index of multiple deprivation

Source: adapted from Evandrou (2000).

Table 10.1 Proportion of older people excluded on different domains

Domain of social exclusion	Indicator of exclusion	% of respondents 'socially excluded' on indicator
Exclusion from material resources	In poverty (lacks 2 or more socially perceived necessities on grounds of affordability)	45
	Multiple deprivation (deprived on 3 or more characteristics)	61
Exclusion from social relations	Social isolation (isolated on 2 or more characteristics)	20
	Loneliness (severely or very severely lonely)	16
	Unable to participate in 2 or more common activities	17
Exclusion from civic activities	Non participation in civic activities	47
	Never attends meetings of religious or community organizations	24
Service exclusion	Has cut back on use of at least 3 basic services	14
	Not used 2 or more key services beyond the home	10
Neighbourhood exclusion	Expresses negative views about the neighbourhood	10
	Regards self as being different from local residents	8
	Would feel very unsafe when out alone after dark	44

characteristics of deprivation. Almost two-fifths (37 per cent) experienced low levels of deprivation. By contrast, 60 per cent experienced medium to high levels of deprivation (deprived on at least three characteristics).

The chosen indicator of *exclusion from material resources* combines the two measures outlined above. We count as materially excluded those who are both in material poverty and experiencing medium to high levels of deprivation. This applied to 31 per cent of older people in our study (Table 10.2).

Exclusion from Social Relations

The survey collected a range of data on aspects of older people's participation in informal social relations. Three key indicators were chosen to reflect different forms of exclusion from such relations: social isolation; loneliness; and non-participation in common social activities.

Not all older people maintain or are able to maintain frequent contacts with family, friends and neighbours. The risk of social isolation is thus greater for those who have no children or other relatives, or who have infrequent contacts with family members, friends or neighbours. A social isolation measure, based on the combination of three variables, was generated that sought to take account of these factors (Figure 10.2). According to this measure, 44 per cent of respondents were not isolated on any of the individual items included in the index, and 36 per cent experienced isolation on just one indicator. Put another way, 80 per cent of older people in deprived areas maintained regular contacts with family, friends or neighbours. Respondents isolated on at least two of the three indicators were classed as socially isolated. This applied to one-fifth (20 per cent) of people in our survey.

A person scores 1 for each of the following characteristics:
   has no relatives or children or sees a child or other relative less than once a
   week
   has no friends in neighbourhood or has a chat or does something with a friend
   less than once a week
   has a chat or does something with a neighbour less than once a week

No isolation: score 0, not isolated on any of these characteristics.
Low isolation: score 1, isolated on one characteristic only.
Medium isolation: score 2, isolated on two characteristics.
High isolation: score 3 isolated on all three characteristics.

Figure 10.2   Index of social isolation

Table 10.2 Extent of exclusion on different domains

Domain of social exclusion	Composite indicator of exclusion	% of respondents excluded on domain
Exclusion from material resources	In material poverty and multiply deprived	31
Exclusion from social relations	Socially isolated or (very) severely lonely or unable to participate common social activities	41
Exclusion from civic activities	Non-participation in civic activities and never attends meetings of religious or community organizations	15
Service exclusion	Has cut back on use of basic services or has not used key services beyond the home	24
Neighbourhood exclusion	Expresses negative views about the neighbourhood and feels very unsafe when out alone after dark	21

Loneliness like social exclusion represents a multidimensional phenomenon. Its most salient element has been perceived as a 'deprivation' component that relates to 'the feelings associated with the absence of an intimate attachment, feelings of emptiness or abandonment' (de Jong Gierveld, 1998, p. 74). In this study, loneliness was measured using the De Jong Gierveld Loneliness Scale (de Jong Gierveld and Kamphuis, 1985). This measure is based on the categorization of responses to 11 questions that reflect different aspects of loneliness. Adopting the categories suggested by the scale's authors as our measure of the intensity of loneliness (de Jong Gierveld and van Tilburg, 1999), two-fifths of the sample (40 per cent) were found to be not lonely (lonely on fewer than three of the 11 scale-items). Just over two-fifths (44 per cent) could be described as moderately lonely. Sixteen per cent of respondents experienced either severe or very severe loneliness (that is were lonely on 9 or more scale-items).

Non-participation in common social activities is an indicator derived from the poverty measure outlined above, which includes seven activities that are perceived as social necessities by a majority of the population (Gordon et al., 2000). The indicator encompasses activities such as being able to visit friends or family in hospital, celebrate special occasions such as birthdays, or engage in a hobby or leisure activity. Around two-thirds of respondents (65 per cent) were not excluded from any of these activities on the grounds of lack of affordability, and 18 per cent were excluded from just one activity. However 17 per cent lacked and could not afford to participate in two or more of the common activities.

The summary indicator of exclusion from social relations adopted in this research draws upon the three measures described above. Respondents were judged to be excluded under this domain if they experienced medium or high levels of social isolation, were severely or very severely lonely, or were unable to participate in two or more common activities on the grounds of lack of income. This applied to just over two-fifths (41 per cent) of respondents.

Exclusion from Civic Activities

Participation in civic activities, by engaging with community organizations or becoming involved in the democratic system, represents an important element in debates about social inclusion and exclusion. The emphasis can be conceived in terms of the ability of individuals to realize fully their citizenship rights (Berghman, 1997). We used two measures to assess the degree to which older people were engaged in forms of civic life. First, at a less formal level, respondents were asked whether they attended religious meetings or meetings of community groups. Over two-fifths (42 per cent) attended religious meetings at least on occasion, while one-third (33 per cent) attended meetings of community groups. Almost half of respondents (47 per cent) never attended either type of meeting.

Second, we presented respondents with a list of 11, more formal, civic activities, and asked whether they had undertaken these in the previous three years. The most commonly undertaken activity was voting, with 68 per cent having voted in the previous general election and 66 per cent in the last local election. While just over three-quarters (76 per cent) of older people had undertaken at least one type of civic activity in the stated period, around one quarter (24 per cent) had not participated in any of the listed activities, including voting.

The summary indicator of exclusion from civic activities adopted in this study combines the two elements outlined above. Those who did not participate in meetings of religious or community groups and who were fully disengaged from the democratic process (did not take part in any type of civic activity in the three years leading up to interview) could be termed excluded on this dimension. In this research, the overwhelming majority of respondents (85 per cent) were 'included' on this indicator. However 15 per cent of older people were found to be excluded.

Exclusion from Basic Services

Access to a range of basic services becomes increasingly important in later life, especially for people with mobility problems or poor health. In our research, we sought information about older people's access to and use of a range of services both within and outside the home.

In the home, the overwhelming majority of older people had access to the basic utilities (gas, electricity and water). However, 8 per cent lacked a telephone (five per cent on the grounds of lack of affordability; 3 per cent did not want a telephone). While coverage by basic services was generally good, a significant minority of older people cut back on using these services as a means of making ends meet. Older people were asked whether in the previous five years they had used less water, gas or electricity or had used the telephone less often in order to save money. Around three-quarters (76 per cent) had not cut back on any of the services. Fourteen per cent had used less of three or four of these basic services.

Beyond the home, a different type of indicator of service exclusion was adopted. This was based on the non-usage in the previous year of three key services selected from a longer list of services and amenities. These were a post office, a chemist, and a bus service. While 72 per cent of respondents had used all of these services at least once in the previous year and a further 18 per cent had failed to use just one of the services, 10 per cent had not used two or more of these services in the given time period.

In subsequent analysis, exclusion from basic services is summarized in a single indicator that takes account of respondents' access to services both within and beyond the home. Interestingly, there was relatively little overlap between these separate indicators. Those who cut back on domestic utilities were not the same people as those failing to use essential services beyond the home. Respondents who had used less of three or four services in the home or who had not used two or more services outside the home were judged to be service excluded. This applied to 24 per cent of respondents.

Neighbourhood Exclusion

The neighbourhood dimension of social exclusion seeks to develop an understanding of the distinctive ways in which environmental factors can contribute to exclusion. In this respect, we are interested in examining the degree to which people feel attached to their local area, and in this sense provide an indirect measure of the neighbourhood's impact on respondents' self-identities. Neighbourhood exclusion is reflected in individuals' expression of views about their immediate environment, and about the degree to which they feel safe in the neighbourhood.

In separate questions, respondents were asked whether there was anything that they liked or disliked about their neighbourhood. Just under one-fifth (18 per cent) expressed only dislikes about the neighbourhood. In a separate question, we asked people how satisfied they were with their neighbourhood. One in ten respondents was very dissatisfied with their neighbourhood. Thirteen per cent of respondents strongly disagreed with the statement 'this neighbourhood is a good place to grow old in'. Taking responses to these items together, 10 per cent of the sample expressed negative views about their neighbourhood on at least two of the three questions.

The manner in which forms of spatial segregation impact upon individuals' sense of identity can, in part, be addressed through perceptions of space. In relation to deprived urban neighbourhoods, and particularly the views of older people, an important feature of such perceptions is the degree to which people feel secure when leaving the home. Those who regard their neighbourhood to be unsafe or as a place where they might be vulnerable to crime may be restricted in their ability to participate in a variety of social roles. We asked people: 'How safe would you feel if you had to go out alone after dark?'. Very few respondents (seven per cent) suggested that they would feel very safe in this situation, and 44 per cent reported that they would feel very unsafe. These findings should be interpreted within the context of the heightened incidence of crime experienced by older people in this research (Scharf et al., 2002b).

The composite indicator chosen to represent neighbourhood exclusion focuses on people's perceptions of the area immediately around their home. We judged as excluded on this domain individuals who expressed negative views about the neighbourhood in relation to at least two of the three questions outlined above, and who also reported that they would feel very unsafe in their neighbourhood after dark. It was felt that this group would be most likely to experience difficulty in maintaining a sense of identity within the context of rapidly changing urban neighbourhoods. According to this approach, 21 per cent of respondents were judged excluded on the neighbourhood dimension.

The Experience of Multiple Exclusion

Our research suggests that significant numbers of older people in deprived urban areas appear to be prone to some form of social exclusion. In this study, exclusion from social relations was the most common of the five types of exclusion identified, affecting around two-fifths of older people. A significant minority, amounting to just under one-third, experienced exclusion from material resources. Nearly one quarter were excluded from basic services, and just over a fifth experienced neighbourhood exclusion. By contrast, fewer than one-in-seven older people were excluded from participation in a range of civic activities.

Drawing these findings together, a considerable proportion of older people were found to experience social exclusion in at least one of its different guises. In this respect, the study population divides into three broad categories (Table 10.3). The first group, comprising 30 per cent of respondents, were not excluded on any of the five domains. The second group, representing 31 per cent of the sample, experienced exclusion on a single domain. The final group was numerically the largest. It comprised almost two-fifths of respondents (39 per cent) who were prone to the cumulative impact of multiple forms of exclusion. A small minority (4 per cent) could be regarded as especially vulnerable, in that they were excluded on four or even all five dimensions.

Table 10.3　Older people experiencing multiple forms of exclusion

	Percent	(n)
Not excluded	30	179
Excluded on one domain	31	189
Excluded on two or more domains	39	232
Total	100	600

Who are the socially excluded? The experience of multiple exclusion was as likely to be a characteristic of the lives of older men as of women and did not vary according to individuals' marital status. However social exclusion was linked to age. People aged 75 and over were significantly more likely to be multiply excluded than those aged 60–74 years. While 33 per cent of younger respondents were not excluded on any of the individual domains, this applied to just 23 per cent of the oldest respondents. Forty-three per cent of people aged 75 and over experienced exclusion on two or more domains, compared with 36 per cent of those aged 60 to 74. An even stronger relationship existed between the experience of exclusion and an individual's ethnic background. In this research, people with Indian and Black Caribbean backgrounds were significantly less likely to be socially excluded on any of the domains than those belonging to other groups. The experience of multiple exclusion was most pronounced for Somali and Pakistani older people. Four out of five older Somali respondents (80 per cent) and just over half of Pakistani respondents (52 per cent) experienced exclusion on two or more domains, compared with 24 per cent of Indian, 35 per cent of Black Caribbean and 36 per cent of white respondents.

Some of the complexity of social exclusion and the potential for overlaps between its component domains is illustrated in Table 10.4. Examination of the interplay between different dimensions of exclusion, expressed in terms of statistical significance, reveals a number of interesting features. For example, of older people who were excluded on the material dimension, 58 per cent were also excluded on the domain of social relations, 20 per cent on that of civic activities, and 33 per cent in relation to access to services. These findings underline the important role of poverty and deprivation in limiting older people's ability to participate in key social roles. No clear statistical relationship existed between exclusion from material resources and neighbourhood exclusion. This suggests that those who have difficulty maintaining a sense of identity in deprived neighbourhoods are as likely to be materially disadvantaged as relatively comfortably off. By contrast, in

Table 10.4 The relationship between different dimensions of social exclusion

% of respondents excluded on:

% also excluded on	Material resources	Social relations	Civic activities	Services	Neighbour-hood
Material resources	–	43 **	42 *	43 **	33
Social relations	58 **	–	49	58 **	55 **
Civic activities	20 *	18	–	20	15
Services	33 **	34 **	32	–	24
Neighbourhood	22	28 **	21	21	–

* $p > 0.05$; ** $p > 0.005$

addition to its link with the material domain, exclusion from social relations was closely related to exclusion from basic services and the neighbourhood measure. In this regard, there is evidence of a neighbourhood impact on individuals' ability to engage in social roles. Older people who are (mentally) cut off from their surroundings are more likely to experience limitations in their informal social relationships than those who perceive their neighbourhood more favourably. Exclusion from civic activities and neighbourhood exclusion were most likely to be independent of other forms of exclusion. While the former was related only to exclusion from material resources, the latter was only linked to exclusion from social relations. Such analysis confirms the need to disaggregate the notion of social exclusion in research and raises a number of issues for policy.

Conclusion: Implications for Research and Policy

From the conceptual discussion and the range of data presented, it is possible to make a number of observations about the nature of social exclusion and the way in which it affects older people in deprived areas of England. Most importantly we have been able to demonstrate that older people in deprived areas face multiple risks of exclusion. Using a measure that reflects the multidimensionality of social exclusion in relation to the situation of older people, it was established that seven out of ten respondents could be classed as excluded in relation to at least one aspect of their lives. For almost two-fifths, the experience of exclusion in one area was compounded by vulnerability to additional types of exclusion. The risk of being affected by multiple forms of social exclusion was greatest for those in the oldest age group (75 and over) and for those belonging to some minority ethnic groups. Our research also points to the existence of connections between the different domains of exclusion. In particular, there was a strong relationship between exclusion from social relations and exclusion from material resources, confirming the way in which poverty and deprivation can combine to restrict participation in a range of informal social relationships.

When examining the social roles that older people engage in (beyond the labour market), our research emphasizes the fundamental importance of informal relationships with family, friends and neighbours. While the majority of older people maintain varied and active relationships with members of their social networks, a significant minority appear prone to exclusion from social relationships. One-fifth of older people taking part in this study could be described as being socially isolated, and one in seven were severely lonely. The existence of a link between neighbourhood exclusion and exclusion from social relations suggests that older people's ability to sustain informal social relations is subject to environmental influences. In deprived areas, older people's social networks are vulnerable to the negative influence of perceived risks associated with the local neighbourhood. In particular, concern about becoming a victim of crime limits the involvement of some older people in a range of social relationships.

Our research also raises a number of issues for policy and practice. First, it is important to emphasize the importance of informal social relationships in older people's daily lives, and to develop policies in ways that can facilitate and sustain such relationships. In this respect, it is necessary to consider the physical and psychological barriers that inhibit the maintenance and development of highly valued low-level social interactions in deprived neighbourhoods (such as being able to chat to people in the street, or visit them in their homes). This encompasses a need to design and plan urban areas in ways which are conducive to the development of social relationships. Housing schemes with pleasant and secure public spaces, shopping areas that provide places to sit, and community centres are important in this context. While urban regeneration programmes typically invest large sums in altering the physical environment of deprived areas, resources should also be devoted to measures that foster informal social networks. One way of achieving this goal would be to develop the role of community workers in inner cities. Such workers could assist older people in making contact with others in the neighbourhood and cooperate with existing community organizations to develop opportunities for older people to meet. Measures that succeed in reducing neighbourhood crime are likely to have a positive impact on older people's social integration by removing some of the psychological barriers that prevent people from participating in a range of outdoor activities.

Second, in relation to integration within formal spheres of community life, participation in civic activities can often be of great personal benefit for retired older people. Community engagement not only represents a route by which individuals can remain valued and effective, but also has been shown to rebound on older people's mental and physical health. Most older people in deprived areas displayed a commitment to public involvement to the extent that around two-thirds of respondents in our survey participated in different types of election, and a significant minority engaged in other civic activities. Only 15 per cent of older people were not involved in any type of civic activity. This suggests that that there is likely to be potential for increasing the level of involvement of older people living in deprived urban areas. In this respect, it would be useful to develop further research that examines the reasons why some older people are more likely to participate than others. Material insecurity, low levels of literacy, language barriers, lack of self-confidence, perceived vulnerability to crime, and an absence of opportunities to become involved are likely to prevent some people from engaging with such formal aspects of community life.

Finally, this research highlights the enduring importance to older people in deprived areas of such basic services as local post offices, chemists and public transport. It is important that public policy recognizes the need to maintain access to a good service infrastructure in deprived urban neighbourhoods. Such areas are especially vulnerable to the withdrawal of both public and commercial services. Older people who are already disadvantaged in terms of poverty or ill health are disproportionately affected by the loss of services such as a local post office or shops. As a result, consideration should be given at an early stage to the likely impact on older people of decisions to withdraw services from deprived neighbourhoods.

Note

1   The authors wish to acknowledge the financial support of the Economic and Social Research Council's Growing Older Programme (Grant No. L480254022). We are also grateful to Chris Phillipson and Paul Kingston for their considerable contribution to the research described in this chapter.

Chapter 11

Can Government Influence our Friendships? The Range and Limits of Tools for Trying to Shape Solidarities[1]

Perri 6

Introduction

Governments *unavoidably* have enormous influence over the patterns of social ties in their populations over which they exercise jurisdiction. They do so in their routine operations as well as in specific programmes, whether deliberately or unintentionally. Housing design, slum clearance, and transport policy bring some people together or apart and make it easier or harder for them to reach each other; education famously creates ties between students that can sometimes last for a lifetime; personal social services, health care and training, whether provided individually or in groups, can all have significant impacts upon friendship and acquaintance.

All of this matters, because social networks are significant causal contributors to many outcomes that policy-makers are expected to care about. A vast body of research scattered across every academic discipline that studies human beings has concluded that friends and acquaintances, and the practical resources and the emotional support they offer, measurably increase our chances of thriving (see 6, 2002). This seems to be true in every respect from labour market attainment and upward social mobility to resistance to infectious disease, from postponement of frailty in old age through to avoidance of the pathways into delinquency. The patterns of social ties also make a quantifiable contribution to collective outcomes such as national competitiveness and the chances of community cohesion. These are facts of considerable significance for public policy. The presence of certain configurations of social networks clearly greatly enhances the chances of certain policies being pursued effectively.

If government unavoidably influences social networks which in turn affect crucial outcomes, then how far can public policy feasibly be used *deliberately* to influence those patterns of social ties of friendship and acquaintance?[2]

Another prior question is: What might it mean to intervene 'effectively'? The research on the causal impact of social networks upon all those desirable individual and collective outcomes about which policy-makers rightly care suggests that very different configurations of ties contribute to different goals. For example the configuration of weak ties with little redundancy reaching into diverse cliques that Granovetter (1973, 1995a) found so important for labour market attainment – a finding broadly, but with qualifications, confirmed by the subsequent research (Burt, 1992, 1997, 2001; Granovetter, 1982, 1995b) – do not appear to be particularly beneficial and may actually undermine thriving in later life (Wenger, 1997a, 1997b, 1997c). Again while community activists in disadvantaged estates might serve their communities well by having some weak ties outside that community with which to leverage resources (Douglass, Ard-am and Kim, 2002; Gilchrist, 2000), neighbourhood community development depends heavily on dense patterns of enduring ties of medium strength within those communities (Crow and Allan, 1994); such patterns look very different from those which might most effectively counter unemployment in the very same disadvantaged areas.

This suggests very strongly that all good things do not go together. Policy-makers must at least sometimes strike settlements between incompatible goods and choose policies that might promote certain network forms, realizing that they are thereby foregoing other goods that other network forms might conduce to. (I speak of 'settlements', for 'trade offs' would suggest smooth and continuous curves and the possibility of making finely-grained policy for exactly calibrated incremental shifts, but this is of course not the real world of social policy-making.)

This chapter first sets out a conceptual framework for thinking about the basic varieties of forms of social network available in any society that, at least in principle, policy interventions might seek to promote or undermine, and for thinking about the range of tools of public policy available for seeking to do so. The main body of the argument of the chapter is concerned with a brief review of the literature on several major fields of public policy (taken from a much longer treatment in 6, forthcoming). It provides an analysis of the repertoire of uses of tools that have been described in the literature, an assessment of how direct these tools might be in their effects, and a preliminary assessment of which kinds of solidarity might typically be promoted by their use in programmes that have been studied. Some suggestions are made about what emerges from the literature about the 'effectiveness' of these interventions, at least considered in their own terms in so far as they have been used to influence social structure. These remarks must of course be heavily qualified by the nature of the evidence afforded by the evaluative and public policy literature. This is followed by a short discussion of the implementation challenges inherent in programmes deliberately designed to use public policy to shape social structure.

Conceptual Framework

There are a modest number of distinct forms of personal social networks that can be identified in almost any society. For the present purposes, it will suffice to work with the four basic types shown in Figure 11.1. The figure shows the network 'signatures' which are ideal typical forms of empirically observable networks. These exhibit the work of quite distinct underlying institutional structures which can be regarded as basic social solidarities. This taxonomy is derived from the neo-Durkheimian institutional theory first developed by Douglas (1970, 1982a, 1982b, 1986, 1992) using Durkheim's basic dimensions of social organization in *Suicide* (1951) and in *Moral Education* (1961), and refined by Douglas and Ney (1998), Thompson, Ellis and Wildavsky (1990), Thompson, Grendstad and Selle (1999), Thompson (1996), Schwarz and Thompson (1990), Gross and Rayner (1985), Fardon (1999), Rayner (1988), Mars (1982, 1999), Wildavsky (1998), Schmutzer and Bandler (1980), Coyle and Ellis (1993); Ellis and Thompson (1997); cf. also Fiske, (1991). The Durkheimian explanatory theory on which the classification rests is institutionalist in that it proposes that bringing about change in network forms, at least of a sustainable kind, will over the medium term have to rest on bringing about change at the underlying level of micro-institutions and informal institutions which produce the network 'signatures'.

Each of these forms has certain strengths and certain weaknesses from the point of view of different outcomes that policy-makers care about. Hybrids between two or more of them are also found. However, in any given programme of policy, even attempting to promote hybrids involves making hard choices between them to some degree.

If this account specifies the range of ideal-typical variation in the most elementary forms, then the next question is what tools are available to government so as to influence how networks might change within this bounded range? Drawing on the taxonomies developed by Hood (1983), Salamon with Lund (1989), 6 (1997b), 6 et al. (2002), and Bemelmans-Videc, Rist and Vedung (1998) we can distinguish the categories of tools shown in Table 11.1; the tools are ranked by degree of coercion within each cell. Some tools have

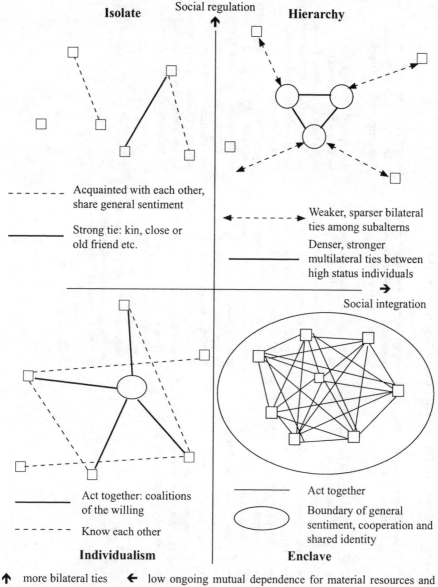

Figure 11.1   Network signatures of the basic institutional forms of social organization

Source: this figure is significantly adapted from Figure 2 in Mars, 1999.

Table 11.1   The tools of government for the shaping of social networks

Generic categories of tool	Types of tools, ranked from strong to weak	Examples of tools used more or less *directly* and *deliberately* to shape social networks	Examples of tools more or less *indirectly* and *unintentionally* shaping social networks
Effectors (for producing changes in culture or behaviour)	• Direct government provision • Government-owned corporations • Regulation, mandation, permission, prohibition • Rights and systems of redress • Contract purchasing • Loan guarantees • Grants-in-aid, matching grants • Tax expenditures • Information delivery: persuasion, propaganda, example, demonstration projects, education, training	• Compulsorily placing people in situations limiting their opportunities to meet and get to know others, or directing them to people like them (e.g., 'total institutions'; 'diversion' programmes for delinquents; or simply separation within schools or workplaces) • Compulsory individualized friendship management e.g., mentoring for unemployed people, counselling e.g., illicit drug use (Nolan, 1998) • Voluntarily offered and entered befriending schemes • Encouragement and persuasion to socialize with particular persons or types of persons, not others e.g., in education • Social skills education	• Restrictions on location of residence and freedom of movement, or on ease of change of residence (e.g., transfer rules in social rented housing sectors) • Cost of transport • Labour management arrangements and nature of job contacts at work, as affected by regulation, taxation, etc (private sector) or direct management (public sector) • Models of housing design, road layout, transport routing, location of collectively consumed services

Table 11.1 cont'd

Generic categories of tool	Types of tools, ranked from strong to weak	Examples of tools used more or less *directly* and *deliberately* to shape social networks	Examples of tools more or less *indirectly* and *unintentionally* shaping social networks
Detectors (for acquiring information)	• Requisition • Inspection • Purchasing, barter • Appeals (including rewards for information)	• Requirements to disclose names of friends and acquaintance when under criminal investigation • Requirements to divulge anonymous or identified information on ties when under counselling e.g., unemployment counselling • Voluntary disclosure e.g., in form to be anonymized in response to government voluntary survey	• Interviews on 'peer group pressure' in education welfare, social work, probation, etc among young people at risk, delinquents, etc • Public health promotion programmes identifying informal networks for health information distribution
Selectors (for managing, selecting, analysing, presenting information)	• Audit • Cost-benefit analysis • Performance indicators and measurement • Cost measurement, resource budgeting • Management review • Scenario-building, risk assessment	• Use of sociometric mapping techniques by employment counsellors	• Mapping techniques used in social services, probation, education welfare on distribution and linkages between young people at risk, delinquents • Network impact auditing on employment services, services for older people, housing programmes etc.

more direct influence than others, although directness is not straightforward to measure. Some tools affect ability to form and sustain ties, while others affect willingness; some combinations may affect both.

Using these tools will often have unintended consequences. Sometimes people respond in the manner hoped for, and sometimes not, and sometimes quite otherwise. Tools must be understood contextually: they do not have predictable effects, irrespective of the prior formation of social networks, institutional context or field of public policy (Peters and van Nispen, 1998). Moreover, their effects must be understood as flowing from the whole set used; analysis of the use of an individual tool is of limited value.

Some Interventions Compared

A review of the literature was undertaken in the fields of housing, education, micro-economic development, services for unemployed people, services for people with mental health difficulties, services for people with learning disabilities, services for older people, interventions targeted to divert young people from delinquency and illicit drug use, community development practice and design strategies for the urban built environment. There is not space here to present an analysis of the literature or even a listing of all the texts examined (see 6, forthcoming). The aim of the review was to identify just how large the repertoire of specific tools by which policy-makers can hope to affect the social networks of citizens actually is, to gather together what is known of their consequences and effectiveness, and to determine just which solidarities these tools are used to promote or reinforce. There is space here only to present a summary of the findings and not the detailed analysis of the literature undertaken.

The Repertoire

Table 11.2 presents a summary of the conclusions on the first question about the extent of the repertoire. Perhaps the most important point to note in considering the table as a whole is the comparative sparseness with which its cells are populated with entries. While some of this sparseness may be due to the incompleteness of the research on which the present review is based, and the limitations of the literature available in English, there are few reasons to believe that a more extensive search would identify many more distinct forms of intervention. Moreover it is clear from the review of the fields considered here that very few of these interventions have been subjected to extensive evaluation, using sociometric analytical methods, for their impact upon social networks either for individual service users or indeed for geographically-bounded communities or communities of interest. Therefore what is known about the efficacy of such interventions remains provisional, based on small initiatives which may not be straightforwardly scalable.

It seems to be the case that in the west today, the informal social ties that are most important for many people are those associated with family or household and those gained through or associated with work. For these are the ties closest to the institutional forces that hold the most powerful accountabilities. By contrast, ties associated with residential neighbourhood or even community of interest are generally of less importance, even for people no longer within the labour market. However most of the really powerful interventions currently available to contemporary welfare states are geared to tackling issues of housing, land use planning, residential management and community development. By contrast, most of the interventions available to deal with family and household are not really designed to influence ties, but practices (e.g. health visiting), or else are blunt instruments for emergencies (e.g. taking children into care). Moreover we lack well-developed strategies to address informal routes into employment and through careers. Similarly our repertoire of interventions around criminal peer association remains inadequate, just as policy-makers' aspirations for network-level interventions in the built environment and in shaping ties between people in adjacent residential zones continue to outrun actual achievements.

It would however be unduly pessimistic to conclude from the sparseness of Table 11.2 and from these limitations that governments can do little that is effective to shape the social networks of their citizens. For the table shows that there is a range of tools, and different combinations can be experimented with. Moreover most of the tools have been developed relatively recently. Many were unknown before the 1960s, and some are very recent indeed. Public services have grown in capabilities to shape the social networks of their target groups or at least their actual clientèles, even if one consequence of this is – and rightly should be – an increase in the level of concern about the potential for intrusion and abuse of such powers.

Interventions and Solidarities

It is important to note that by and large interventions have been much better developed that effectively or deliberately create (or re-enforce)

Table 11.2 Public service strategies by field, as they draw upon or may be used to influence informal social ties

Service field strategy	Housing	Education	Micro-economic development	People who are unemployed	People with mental health difficulties	People with learning disabilities	Older people	Delinquency and illicit drug use	Community development	Built environment
Encourage and enable individual to develop new weak ties				(Some) employment counselling?						
Encourage and enable individual to develop new strong ties, or ties to similarly situated people				Job clubs	Befriending schemes	Befriending schemes	Befriending schemes	Group diversion, intermediate treatment		Communal spaces for residents in defined small areas
Formalize and institutionalize existing ties (to make stronger or denser)			Business borrowers clubs		Drop-in centres	Circles of support			Create local nonprofit organizations	
Use existing ties for new purposes								Peer leaders as health communicators		
Provide defined role-holder as new tie		Mentors		Mentors						
Offer organizational ties in lieu of personal social ties		School referral schemes (esp. Japan)								
Put in situation where new ties to similar others could be formed			Entrepreneurs' networks							

Table 11.2 cont'd

Service field strategy	Housing	Education	Micro-economic development	People who are unemployed	People with mental health difficulties	People with learning disabilities	Older people	Delinquency and illicit drug use	Community development	Built environment
Put in situation where new ties to similar others could be prevented								'Designing out crime'		City-centre pedestrian-ization; zoning for street cafés etc
Put in situation where new ties to dissimilar others could be formed	Mixed tenure scheme	Compre-hensive schooling; bussing								
Put in situation where new ties to dissimilar others could be prevented										
Develop skills in forming and sustaining ties		Life skills training		Life skills training				Life skills training		

enclave structures than either informally hierarchical ones or weakly-tied individualistic ones between people relevantly dissimilar, for the welfare state has long been understood as a set of responses to risk and need. The fiscal imperative to achieve economies of scale, the political imperatives to respond to pre-existing solidarities among client groups and the hierarchical practice of bringing together those of similar status have together meant that those with similar needs, or experiencing similar risk, or presenting similar risks to other citizens, tend to be provided with services that reinforce their social networks with others classified as similar to themselves. So, for example, in the allocation of social rented housing, in creating lunch clubs or job clubs or circles of support, buddying schemes and the like, the priority has been to develop groups on the basis of shared problems and shared identities.

These approaches are reasonably well-understood by social workers, advisors, community development workers, educators and other practitioners for they are taught as part of mainstream professional education and training. This means that the capacities for implementing such approaches are more readily available and better distributed than for other kinds of intervention. Moreover enclave interventions have the appearance of being causally direct, whereas most of the interventions that might support more individualistic styles have the appearance of being causally somewhat oblique and thereby of carrying lower probabilities of success. For example, the creation of physical spaces in pedestrianized city centres or café zones along marinas in which people might or might not mingle is a strategy that is hardly guaranteed to bring about mingling between strangers or the formation of ties of acquaintance between people who consider each other dissimilar by class, ethnicity, interests or lifestyle.

Apart from the creation of formal organizations to shape or even discipline the social networks of their target groups though membership, informal hierarchical interventions are deployed mainly in coercive services, such as the rehabilitation of offenders, 'designing out crime' in the creation of defensible spaces and the blocking of escape routes from high risk areas, and, to a lesser extent, the enforcement of schooling against truants. Most evaluations of the introduction of formal organizations have also neglected to examine closely the social network dimensions of their efficacy. Whatever their efficacy in achieving other goals of community development, such evidence as we have about the effects of introducing voluntary organizations and about the dynamics by which resistance follows upon the introduction of formal organization does not suggest that there are straightforward routes for influencing social ties in the way policy-makers want. Nevertheless, established practices of community development work, built environment design for situational crime prevention and educational welfare work would generally suffice to provide a professional infrastructure that would enable the implementation of more ambitious hierarchical ways of drawing upon and shaping social networks for policy goals. However those ambitions must, the findings suggest, be tempered with realism about the dynamics of resistance and evasion that such assertions of hierarchy can elicit.

It is clear that most of the enclave and the few individualistic interventions are designed to work at the network level of social structure, while some of the hierarchical ones are designed to work at the institutional level to the extent that their architectural and organizational achievements do in fact become entrenched and institutionalized features of the environments in which the targeted groups live and work. However, few operate principally at the institutional level.

Table 11.3 shows the distribution of the initiatives identified by the kinds of solidarity that they might have promoted if they were effective, to the extent that they can work both at the network and the institutional levels of social structure. Those interventions that are marked with an asterisk are ones which the evidence that we currently possess suggests have *not* been effective in promoting the kinds of social network structures that policy-makers have hoped from them – at least in the context of the western world, with its relative aggregate weighting toward greater individualism than either of the strongly socially integrated solidarities. Interventions that seem ineffective in these contexts might be more efficacious when used in social contexts which are initially more communitarian in their institutions. Those beside which a double dagger appears in the matrix are ones where the evidence about their efficacy in changing social networks in Western countries, to the extent that we have been able to interpret it, is equivocal. This may be either because the effects may be modest, because the effects do not last, or because the intervention may provoke significant counter-organization toward other solidarities. Those which appear with a question mark are ones which may or may not in practice conduce to that solidarity.

Of course, it is far from ideal only to consider the efficacy of these interventions singly, although it is understandable that most of the evaluative literature does so. The interventions are often combined, at least to the extent that they are *de facto* administered concurrently upon specific clientèles and upon whole populations, and so there must be interaction effects. We know rather little from empirical research about these interaction effects. Ideally, for policy purposes, we should like to know about the relative weight of at least

Table 11.3   Interventions by solidarities they are designed to promote

Social regulation

↑

Isolate	*Hierarchy*
‡ Segregation of individual offenders within institutions	? Counselling
	? Life skills training
‡ ? School exclusion without re-admission to another school organization	Mentoring
	‡ Funding voluntary
	? Circles of support
	‡ Designing out crime, e.g., closing streets to block criminals' escape routes
	‡ ? City centre pedestrianization; zoning for street cafés and clubs
	School exclusion into specialist units

→ *Social integration*

Individualism	*Enclave*
? Life skills training	Segregated allocation of social rented housing
Entrepreneurs' networks	‡ Buddying schemes
Business borrowers clubs	Befriending schemes
* Comprehensive schooling	‡ Funding voluntary organizations
* Mixed tenure schemes	Drop-in centres
	? Job clubs
	Communal spaces for residents in defined small areas
	‡ ? City centre pedestrianization; zoning for street cafés and clubs
	? Creating local nonprofit organizations

two kinds of interaction effects. First, we should like to know more about the degree to which interventions targeted upon the same or closely overlapping clientèles typically reinforce each other to promote the same solidarity – that is, *positive feedback* effects (on feedback effects in systems theoretic models, see Jervis, 1997). Secondly, we should like to know more about the extent to which the distribution of interventions as a whole, across all the fields of public policy, serves to check these positive feedback tendencies, and to promote a variety or even some kind of balance between the four solidarities – that is, *negative feedback* effects.

The real significance of showing this analysis of effectors by solidarities promoted is that it enables us to provide a richer and much more specific account of the contextual character of the efficacy of the tools of government than conventional approaches have done. What is key for the efficacy of tools is the dovetailing of effectors with appropriate detectors that can enable policy-makers to learn about the balance of forces within the mechanical solidarities in the social structure of the target communities.

The review of the literature does not suggest that the skills and the design capabilities for the selection of detectors, and for the dovetailing of detectors and effectors required, are particularly well developed in any of the fields of public policy under examination. It is perhaps remarkable that it is in services for people who are often most marginal to the larger pattern of social structure, namely those with learning disabilities, where the use of detectors at the individual level of mapping social networks are beginning to be developed (McIntosh and Whittaker, 1998, 2000; Wertheimer, 1995). However in the field of services to older people, there are also important initiatives to provide social workers and those commissioning care with practical tools for network mapping. The work of Wenger and her collaborators has taken on some international importance in this regard (see especially Wenger, 1997b and Wenger and Tucker, 2000). Yet even in these fields, the major innovations have been in the development of detectors that enable the mapping of relational structure more than institutional structure and, in particular, for the measurement of the degree of social integration more than for the degree of social regulation. In this way, even though many of these approaches may not use the concept of 'social capital' or appeal to Putnam's (2000) or Coleman's (1990) theories, they are working within the same broad paradigm that stresses the importance of social integration more than of social regulation. In education, the importance of Coleman's arguments has led to some development of interest in kinship structure in facilitating discipline, and tools for the mapping of this plays some role in education welfare work to prevent or correct truancy. There is also some interest in network mapping of peer groups, but this tends to be of a more research and academic nature than a practical one for school-based pastoral work. Moreover the focus of mainstream education on the administration of curriculum means that the institutional support for these capabilities is relatively limited.

However what is most important for the present argument is that even the network mapping tools offered to practitioners in some of these fields are still not adequately grounded in and integrated with tools for the measurement of the dynamics. Social structure is still seen insufficiently in process terms. This is another disappointing example of the ways in which practice has lagged behind theory, for anthropologists had developed ways of showing the processual and dynamic character of the institutions underlying social structure some forty years ago; within the Durkheimian tradition, this was shown powerfully in the work of Turner (1995).

Directness and Obliqueness

The distinction between direct and oblique strategies is not, as has been noted already, an absolute one. At best it can only constitute a spectrum or a dimension along which strategies and interventions can be roughly but hardly exactly arranged. At the most direct end of the spectrum lie straightforward prohibitions of association between individuals – for example, between delinquent schoolchildren in the context of a school or between prisoners found to have conspired together. Indeed it is hardly a coincidence that the clearest examples of the most direct interventions are to be found in the most coercive institutions, and that their aims are typically to enforce for punitive purposes more or less isolate forms of organization. Also relatively direct are those interventions that effectively force people together, and again these are easiest to administer in the context of coercion. The duty on parents to ensure that their children attend school gives an opportunity to public authorities to require certain associations which will typically take a limited number of forms. The duty on unemployed claimants of benefits to accept certain kinds of work, authorized training or other preparation for work also directly influences the pattern of social ties. Slightly less direct but still toward the more direct end of the spectrum are those interventions in which the service user's participation is voluntary, but where public bodies put pressures of incentive or sanction around compliance. These include encouragement for people in certain categories to use drop-in centres, befriending schemes and the like, or the provision of a mentor or a 'buddy'. Next we can identify those schemes in which involvement is purely voluntary, such as networks of entrepreneurs in local micro-economic development initiatives. In all of these direct initiatives, some use is made of the 'artificial friend' – individuals whose time is provided by the service to act as a surrogate friend or acquaintance in order to sustain informal as well as role-based relationships with the intended beneficiary.

Moderately oblique are life skills or friendship skills training in which capabilities for forming and sustaining ties are explicitly provided but actual ties are not. More oblique interventions are those which create spaces in which people who are institutionally classified as different from one another are brought together in the hope that they will form some social ties, without skills or ties being explicitly provided. Comprehensive schools are supposed to mix children from different social classes (although they do not necessarily do so in practice). So too people from different tenures are placed together in deliberately mixed tenure schemes with the (as it turns out, vain) hope that they will develop informal social ties. The most oblique or least direct initiatives are those which create opportunities for forming or sustaining ties or which block off only a few opportunities, such as city centre pedestrianization or closing streets to minimize criminals' escape routes.

Table 11.4 reorganizes the findings to show both this (admittedly crude) relative ranking of directness alongside the findings of the review of the literature about their efficacy. The table reveals one important point, even if that point is not altogether surprising. Essentially the better chances of efficacy seem to be found to be associated with those interventions located roughly in the middle of the table. This may be regarded as unsurprising to the extent that the very indirect interventions are probably *too* indirectly causally related to the outcomes of social network change, while the most direct are most likely to run into resistance for their instrumental treatment of people's friendships, save in those special contexts of authorized coercion in which that resistance can be overridden.

The table also makes it clear that there are sharp limits to the acceptability of interventions which are both explicit and coercive in character; in general those limits are just the limits of appropriate coercion in a liberal democratic society.

Implementation Challenges and Capabilities

There are many questions about public authorities' abilities to implement strategies using these interventions acceptably and effectively. Still more importantly, there are major questions about whether public authorities possess sufficient understanding of the institutional dynamics by which the four different kinds of solidarities identified in this paper interact with one another, let alone of the ways in which they might think about the relative weight and balance of the solidarities that they might seek to promote or protect. Yet without that understanding, it is almost impossible to design strategies and interventions that will be legitimate yet not vulnerable to a variety of unintended consequences.

Table 11.4   Directness and obliqueness of interventions

Degree of directness or indirectness	Type of intervention	Examples	What is known about efficacy and conditions for efficacy
Most direct (negative) ←	Prohibitions of association between individuals	Between delinquent schoolchildren in the context of a school or between prisoners found to have conspired together	Can be effective, but most likely in coercive institutions
Most direct (positive) ←	Force people together	Compulsory schooling Duties on unemployed benefit claimants to take part in prescribed activities	Can be effective, but most likely in coercive institutions
	Service user's participation is voluntary, but where public bodies put pressures of incentive or sanction around compliance	Encouragement for certain people to use drop-in centres, befriending schemes etc; provision of a mentor or a 'buddy'	Limited efficacy; depends on characteristics of service user; most effective in sustaining enclave forms
Provide an 'artificial friend'; purpose of intervention explicitly about social networks ←	Service user's involvement is purely voluntary	Networks of entrepreneurs	Can be effective

Table 11.4 cont'd

Degree of directness or indirectness	Type of intervention	Examples	What is known about efficacy and conditions for efficacy
→ *Provide conditions under which social ties might be formed*	Capabilities for forming and sustaining ties are explicitly provided	Life skills; friendship skills training	Can be effective; depends on characteristics of service users
→ *Social network purpose of intervention is either implicit or may even be incidental to another purpose*	Create spaces in which people who are institutionally classified as different from one another are brought together	Comprehensive schooling; Deliberately mixed tenure housing schemes	Not very effective, especially ineffective in overcoming enclave in favour of e.g., more individualism
→ *Least direct*	Create opportunities for forming or sustaining ties or else that block off only a few opportunities	City centre pedestrianization; 'designing out crime'	Only effective in limited negative goals

Some of the implementation problems are essentially simple in character – not necessarily simple to solve, but at least straightforward to understand. For example, many of these interventions require professionals to have very specific skills which are scarce and expensive to provide through training. Moreover while some new skills may have been developed in recent years, it is also possible that some of the skills required to address the social network dimensions of the kinds of problems which concern public services have actually been lost. For example the discipline of probation work has changed hugely since the early 1980s. During the postwar decades in the UK and many other countries, probation was taught and indeed generally conceived as within the general orbit of social work. Much of the daily effort of probation officers was focused on social work practices of rehabilitation, advice, support, including assisting ex-offenders to find work sometimes through the use of informal networks and the development of new kinds of informal networks beyond their criminal associates. Indeed in the early years of the profession, a common slogan was 'advise, assist and *befriend*'. Since the 1980s, however, the profession has been completely repositioned. Today probation work is firmly part of law enforcement. The daily work of probation officers is concerned with surveillance, the administration of tagging and the conduct of corrective programmes. Most rehabilitation work undertaken now is designed on a cognitive-behavioural basis, working with psychological models of individual change (Raynor and Vanstone, 2002).

Social work too has changed hugely since the 1980s. Although the techniques of group work and of community-based 'patch' work are still taught to social work students, much of the daily work of social workers is now devoted to such matters as the purchasing of material forms of care services for frail elderly people or people with disabilities. Similarly social workers involved in family interventions are now more likely to be case managers, coordinating interventions of a therapeutic nature with the availability of benefits advice and educational support. There remains more scope for social network based approaches in certain areas of work with children, but even here the political pressures to focus on interventions to curb or prevent sexual abuse, violence or neglect typically take priority over more developmental work.

Community policing has always been a minority sport within that profession. The rising fear of crime, taken together with the technologies that have enabled more data-intensive 'intelligence-led' policing, have resulted in community policing now being conducted mainly through inter-agency and interprofessional structures such as Crime and Disorder Reduction Partnerships. Few police officers would see these areas of work as ones that offer major opportunities for promotion. Although in such inter-agency structures there is some scope for work that is sensitive to the social network dynamics that play a part in the genesis of criminality, even here much more attention is given to detection and individual-level corrective interventions. Similarly the increasing pressure on teachers to focus their efforts on the administration of a centrally specified curriculum and on discipline has left rather less time for the kinds of 'pastoral' work that might have provided the basis for educational interventions of a network-sensitive character.

The point here is certainly not to look back wistfully to a lost golden age of post-war public services as if they were peculiarly equipped to address the social network level dynamics of the problems for which taxpayers were willing to support them. Clearly that would seriously misrepresent the history of the post-war welfare state, which was widely criticized from both left and right for its 'one-size-fits-all', paternalistic, insensitive and often very limited approach to service delivery and intervention. Indeed, many of the intellectual developments in understanding social network dynamics post-date by a decade or more the decline of post-war models of probation, social work, policing and education. However in any assessment of the implementation capabilities for new approaches that give greater weight to the social network structures and processes, it is important to recognize that the weaknesses in the contemporary skill base do reflect quite conscious decisions made in the last quarter of the twentieth century. These reflect a move toward more cognitive-behavioural approaches, to more material care and to more content-rich rather than process-rich approaches in education.

Nevertheless, there are also some more encouraging trends in the development of new skills. One example is the recent renaissance of community development work, moved from its post-war organizational base in social services into economic development and regeneration functions and into 'neighbourhood renewal' partnerships (Social Exclusion Unit, 1999). It remains the case that much of this work is concerned with the development of formal community-based non-profit organizations rather than the cultivation and development of informal ties. Moreover there are powerful criticisms to be made of the ways in which some of this work may actually have contributed to the stigmatization of poor communities, reinforcing their enclaving for the wider society (Taylor, 2002). The plethora of such initiatives may have exhausted the capacity of the relatively few individualist brokers who can exercise leadership in disadvantaged areas (Forrest and Kearns, 1999). Nevertheless the growing recognition of the importance of networks of informal ties between small businesses for successful entrepreneurship has induced a commitment to the development of skills in understanding and developing such ties.

In many fields of local governance too there has developed great interest and some investment in skills in practices of conflict management, mediation and resolution, which are based at least in part on the recognition of the importance of informal social ties between people with conflicting interests. Community visioning and planning exercises, multiple stakeholder conferences held to conciliate in disputes over the siting of controversial facilities, and the use of local citizens' juries before which a wide range of interests are brought as ways of conducting deliberation, have all proliferated in many countries during the 1990s. The use of internet-based conferencing and consultation has also grown, becoming important foci of debate about the changing nature of democratic governance (Lowndes et al., 1998; Stewart, 1995; Stewart, Kendall and Coote, 1994). It is possible – but it would be unwise to make any stronger claim – that the institutionalization in at least some public authorities of the skills for conducting such exercises may bring about a practice that could have some impact on the wider citizenry. It may bring people together who might then sustain at least acquaintanceship in ways that might conduce to the achievement of goals other than the immediate goals of consultation, conciliation, development of consensus or civic pride. However it is important to be cautious, for the history of experiments in inducing public participation in state-led exercises of this kind is not entirely happy. Typically after an initial surge of interest only the already well-connected and active remain involved. Moreover there is a real danger that initiatives may be undertaken more to be seen to be consulting than genuinely to elicit participation; initiatives of which this true will hardly elicit much social connectedness either (Blaug, 2002).

Meeting many of the implementation challenges will require quite new ways of working for professionals; they require attention to be shifted from the kinds of material, environmental, cognitive-behavioural and other non-social or at least non-structural factors that form their normal daily concerns. Since no one has suggested that these other issues should be neglected in favour of focusing on social network issues, adequate attention to the development of these interventions will require additional resources if they are not to represent still more unwelcome trade-offs of priorities and resources. These are nevertheless only (!) questions of the adequacy of resources. Other challenges are interorganizational in nature. For example any intervention which seeks even to achieve fairly straightforward goals about social ties, such as combating isolation for older people or developing weak ties to increase labour force participation, requires coordination between many different agencies. One may be optimistic (6 et al., 2002) or pessimistic (Challis et al., 1988) about the capabilities of agencies making local policy decisions and providing public services for this coordination. However, at the very least, some very specific and perhaps elaborate institutional arrangements are required for this to be achieved sustainably.

In this particular field, a major practical and moral problem for implementation must be the collection of data with which to monitor what is achieved by way of impact upon friendship and acquaintance. The practical problems of designing instruments by which to measure patterns in social relations and social structure are not insuperable and there is a huge body of social network research methodology on which to draw. However using data of this kind as the basis for assessing performance of interventions is extremely problematic. Not only are there many influences upon friendship and acquaintance that lie far beyond the influence of public service interventions, there are also many difficulties in identifying lines of causation. This would create major problems of fairness in the use of social network data for measuring performance (Bennett, 2002). More fundamental is the problem of trying to work out what the behavioural consequences would be. All use of trend data as indicators for performance management and audit creates incentives for organizations to behave strategically (Carter, Klein and Day, 1993) and very often it is almost impossible to predict in advance just how behaviour might actually change.

Other implementation challenges, however, may be still more fundamental in character. It is a long-established saw in the academic lore of implementation studies that a policy cannot be expected to be implemented successfully if it is based upon a suspect hypothesis about the relationship between cause and effect (Bardach, 1977; Pressman and Wildavsky, 1973). It is far from clear that the body of understanding that we possess about how and how far policy action and service interventions can shape social networks meets the conventional political scientist's test. It is scattered across a plethora of different professional disciplines, weakly integrated and poorly grounded in sociological and anthropological theory.

Moreover the same corpus of work descending from Pressman and Wildavsky and from Bardach's writings in the 1970s on policy implementation also bequeaths us the maxims that the less direct the causal links between intervention and outcome, and the greater the number of intervening variables, the more complex the relationships of cooperation and dependency involved (for example in inter-professional coordination). So too, the greater the plurality of values between settlements which must be struck, the lower the probability of successful implementation (Hill and Hupe, 2002). Applying these tests to what we know about the relationships might well lead one to doubt that much can be achieved.

But before concluding that policy action to shape social networks is one of those things that can only be done when it is not intended, that is as an incidental by-product of pursuing other goals (Lindblom and Cohen, 1979), it is worth reflecting that even if the conditions for successful implementation are not met, the public administration research does not suggest that literally nothing can or will be done. Implementation is not something that either happens successfully (in the sense of replicating in administrative reality the hopes of the policy formulators) or else does not happen at all. In the absence of the conditions for success, what can be done, as Lindblom (1959; 1979) argued many years ago, is likely to be a deal of muddling through, of patchy and incremental change, of experimentation from which learning will be fragmentary and only spasmodically diffused, all characterized by far weaker efficacy than one might like. But that may still be worth doing if the results are better (considered against some prevailing settlement between the multiple values and goals that plural societies must bring to political judgment about the impact of policy upon social relations and institutions) than those that can be expected from allowing the activities of civil government to have the vast impacts that they will have in any case upon these things.

Conclusion

The range of capabilities that have been developed by which public authorities can deliberately influence social network forms reflect the much greater priority attached to this in social policy than economic policy, at least until relatively recently. For even micro-economic regeneration programmes have tended to be dominated by physical infrastructure programmes rather than programmes to cultivate the social structures that might sustain economic vibrancy. Moreover within social policy the majority of interventions have been developed in order to influence the social networks of the poor and disadvantaged. For those who insist that social policy interventions should always be targeted on the basis of need, and for whom the needs of the poor and disadvantaged extend to what are seen as deficits in their patterns of friendship and acquaintance, this will seem to stand in need of no further justification. For those who recognize that the relative closure of the social networks of the better-off is itself a constitutive element of structural advantage, the present distribution of capabilities raises policy issues of equity in relation to goals as well as of effectiveness in their achievement.

Even within the range of tools available to governments to influence the network situations of the poor and disadvantaged, it is clear that most of the effort has gone into developing interventions at the level of the individual client's personal network, rather than, say, the geographical community. Moreover, even at this level, a surprisingly high proportion of the effort goes into the deployment of more or less direct interventions, including the provision of 'artificial friends'.

Yet the analysis offered in this chapter does not suggest that such direct interventions explicitly concerned with social networks are particularly effective, save in very limited contexts. They may be all that can be done in particular settings, and these settings may indeed be the ones that, for example, some unemployed people or some people with mental health problems actually live in. Even so it would be dangerously complacent to assume that these interventions will be effective for all those experiencing such difficulties.

Moreover the community development literature as well as some mental health studies suggest that in addition to promoting whatever solidarity is intended by policy-makers, these interventions typically elicit negative feedback in the form of the counter-development of other solidarities. In response to the development of formal organization some people will peel off into more enclaved groups, some will prefer to plough their own furrows and some will retreat into passivity and civic privatism. The well-known existence of cycles in community action (Hirschman, 1982) provides good evidence of the risks. Indeed the syndrome is a more general one, as neo-Durkheimian institutional theory predicts (Thompson, 1992). The enclave responses of many of the service user movements in public services have arisen partly in response to the hierarchical forms of service provision – asylums, paternalistic housing management, clinically dominated health care provision, legalistic disregard of victims' interests in the criminal justice system, and so on. The frustrations that the 'lowerarchy' can come to feel in such hierarchical systems have also contributed to this. Probably, if we had better longitudinal data and evaluation studies on the social network consequences of each of the interventions reviewed above we should see the same dynamics at work.

The priority then must be to design a whole mix of different interventions which reflect understandings of how various policies can affect social networks. Social science can contribute something to the more intelligent design of policy and interventions here, although empirical evaluative research on the effects of public policy interventions upon the social networks of citizens is in its infancy. However, perhaps the key contribution of social scientists will be to point out that all good things do not go together, that we have to care about the complete variety of institutional forms of social solidarity, that the network forms we promote are rooted in institutions and not the other way around, and that political judgment in this field must consist in the astute cultivation of forms of settlement between all four of the basic solidarities.

Notes

1   This chapter is taken from parts of several chapters of 6 (forthcoming). I am grateful to Chris Phillipson and Graham Allan for encouraging me to write this chapter, and for their comments and suggestions.

2   Ideally, the question ought not to be asked quite so baldly. A critical prior question is whether government *should* be in the business of trying to influence their citizens' friendships and acquaintance. There is no space here to deal with this question of legitimacy, and so I must ask the reader to assume for the sake of present argument that a set of goals and a set of side-constraints can be specified for which and under which it might be legitimate for public authorities to use at least their existing services and capacities to try to influence those patterns of ties.

Chapter 12

Community Issues and Social Networks[1]

Marilyn Taylor

The past decade has seen a revival of ideas about community, mutual aid and social capital in public policy and academic debate. These ideas are seen as particularly strong weapons in the fight against the fragmentation, uncertainty and potential unsustainability of contemporary life, where traditional institutions are felt to be breaking down and where too strong a dependence, first on the state and then the market, is seen to have eroded the sense of collective responsibility on which social cohesion, good governance and economic prosperity depends. While these are ideas which are promoted throughout society, they are seen as particularly potent weapons in the battle against social exclusion, especially in the most disadvantaged neighbourhoods, which have become cut off from economic prosperity, from political life and, in the eyes of some, from the moral consensus on which society depends.

For policy-makers, as I have argued elsewhere (Taylor, 2002, 2003), the values of moral cohesion, responsibility, reciprocity, consensus, trust and safety that are implicit within the concepts of community and social capital have the potential to address a number of overlapping concerns in the twenty-first century: a rapidly increasing demand for welfare, partly due to increased life expectancy; a perceived moral crisis; a breakdown of democracy and political legitimacy as voting figures in the UK and elsewhere plunge; increasing concern about sustainability and the legacy we are leaving for future generations.

Community is not a new idea. The 'lost community' mantra has been recited at frequent intervals over the centuries, along with the belief that 'we are being cast adrift in a world in which the previous rules of social interaction and social integration no longer apply' (Forrest and Kearns, 2001, p. 2126). Nor is it as straightforwardly positive as it sounds. Both community and social capital are contested concepts, with a 'dark' as well as a 'good' side and both are full of tensions and contradictions. There are particular issues to be addressed when applying such concepts to neighbourhoods and population groups that are defined by their exclusion and dislocation from mainstream society. Harking back to a mythical and romantic idea of community can be a particularly savage irony when applied to places and groups whose networks and traditional institutions have been destroyed by economic change, whose members are isolated by poverty and who are further excluded by the operation of market choices, insensitive allocations policies and media stereotyping: 'Poverty is isolating. You do not want anyone to know what you are feeling, what you need because of the indignity of the situation, so you put on a brave face and do not let anyone into your private life' (UK Coalition Against Poverty, 1998, p. 4). In this chapter, after briefly revisiting some of the flaws in the communitarian heaven, especially as applied to excluded communities, I shall consider the ways in which ideas of community, social capital and networks can realistically be used to redress the imbalance of power which is at the heart of social exclusion.

The Importance of Community

The story of human evolution is commonly characterized as the survival of the fittest. But a closer reading suggests that it is mutuality and reciprocity that are at its core:

> When struggle is replaced by co-operation, that substitution results in the development of intellectual and moral faculties which secure to the species the best conditions for survival ... The fittest are not the physically strongest, nor the cunningest, but those who learn to combine so as to mutually support each other, strong and weak alike, for the welfare of the community (Charles Darwin, cited in Kropotkin, 1904, p. 2).

Forrest and Kearns (2001) describe 'residentially based networks' as 'the basic building blocks of social cohesion, through which we learn tolerance, cooperation and acquire a sense of social order and belonging'. But the importance of networks goes much wider. Danny Burns and his colleagues (Burns, Williams and Windebank, forthcoming) describe how even economists, usually stereotyped as promoting competition and individualism, use models based on trust and reciprocity to explain human behaviour – in the development, for example, of game theory and the example of the prisoner's dilemma (Axelrod, 1984). Networks and social capital have been linked with economic prosperity, lower crime, higher educational attainment, health and quality of life (Performance and Innovation Unit, 2002). Thus, countries with high level of social connectiveness suffer less economic damage in times of recession than others and are also able to respond more effectively to economic opportunities as they arise (Chaney, 2000).

Particular links have been made with health. Gilchrist (2001), summarizing some of the growing body of research on social capital and health reports how relationships and regular interaction with others appear to create some kind of protection against disease and mental distress. Individuals with robust and diverse networks, she reports, lead healthier and happier lives than those who are more isolated or whose networks are comparatively homogenous (Argyle, 1989; 1996; Yen and Syme, 1999). Burns, Williams and Windebank (forthcoming) suggest that social capital provides a physiological triggering mechanism, stimulating people's immune systems to fight disease and buffer stress.

Community and a range of ideas associated with it – social capital, networks, partnership – are words which are suffused by positive assumptions – of consensus, trust, accessibility and engagement. Community can be exclusive, defined as much by who is outside as who is in; the moral certainties generated by community can be oppressive instead of secure; and too much trust can lead to corruption and abuse. The 'old boy network' has plenty of social capital as does the Mafia, but these do not benefit the community at large. Social capital can support unhealthy lifestyles (smoking and excessive alcohol use, for example) (see Morrow in this volume). It also underpins 'deviant' moralities – Hoggett (1997) cites gang law and drugs cartels as examples – the influence of criminal minorities is a pervasive feature of the exclusion and fear that many people experience in excluded communities.

Ideas of community also contain within them contradictions that are missing from much of the community and social capital discourse: the tensions between diversity and cohesion that government is currently struggling with, tensions between the particular interests that prompt people to join together and the common good, tensions between the individual and the collective and, as we have already seen, between inclusion and exclusion. All these tensions are reproduced within neighbourhoods, networks and population groups, the more so, the more value is attached to belonging.

Community and Social Exclusion

Implicit in much of the rhetoric of community and social capital is an assumption that what really separates the successful from the unsuccessful neighbourhood is the degree to which there is social cohesion and a sense of community (Forrest and Kearns, 2001). Rebuilding the networks that have been damaged by welfare dependency and economic change would seem to make a lot of sense. But as I have argued elsewhere (Taylor, 2003), there are particular anomalies in prescribing 'community' to the poor. The first of these is that, for the most excluded, poverty and the struggle for survival leaves little room for developing social networks, participating in collective activities or discharging their communitarian responsibilities. Despite considerable interest in new forms of mutual and community exchange as a resource for excluded communities, Williams and Windebank (2000) suggest that poor communities engage in less of this activity than the relatively affluent. Another recent study (Prime, Zimmeck, and Zurawan, 2002) found that people from the higher socioeconomic groups were twice as likely to engage in formal volunteering activity as those in the lowest. The correlation was slightly weaker when it came to informal activity, but still present.

A second anomaly in prescribing community to those excluded by the market and economic restructuring is that this restructuring has itself undermined the foundations on which communities are built as industries have withdrawn or relocated and the institutions built around them have suffered. Gilchrist (2003) argues that, while evidence of an apparent decline in social capital in industrialized countries is often blamed on various cultural factors, it can equally be attributed to the negative impact of social and economic policies which erode collective solidarity. A third anomaly is the way in which exclusion itself breeds exclusion. The stereotypes that are imposed on excluded communities by the media, professionals and most other outsiders are often displaced onto newcomers or people whose faces do not fit, as the rise of the British National Party in some northern cities illustrates.

In 1972, Suttles argued that two of the most important considerations when choosing a neighbourhood to live in were status and safety. He argued that there were two main ways in which people could satisfy these requirements: one was to buy into an area where the character of fellow residents is assured by the costs of living there; the other was to cultivate one's neighbours. People in the most excluded areas do not have the former choice and the reputation that is attached to many neighbourhoods makes it feel unsafe to cultivate the neighbours. Too often, therefore, community becomes the site of fear and dislocation rather than the safe haven painted by much of the community rhetoric, let alone the breeding ground that Forrest and Kearns suggested for habits of tolerance and cooperation.

Unpacking Community

Atkinson (2000) reminds us that excluded spaces are not homogeneous. Community has not always been lost. Some neighbourhoods may indeed be fragmented, with highly transient populations; some have been abandoned. But others may have relatively stable populations with strong and long-term networks and it is unwise to assume that people who live in excluded areas have fewer local ties than those who live elsewhere. Indeed, self-help and mutual support can be powerful tools for survival in a hostile environment. However, they are not enough. More and more people are suggesting that the supposed tight-knit communities of the past, with a clear moral order, are not what is needed in society today. Successful communities are characterized as much by weak as strong ties, both within the neighbourhood and across their boundaries. People need many overlapping networks which give them choices within and beyond their locality.

This has been captured in the distinction that is increasingly being made between different types of social capital (Performance and Innovation Unit, 2002):

- bonding social capital: strong relationships and networks within communities (social glue);
- bridging social capital: weaker relationships and networks across social groups and communities (social oil);
- networks and connections between communities and institutions (linking social capital).

As Forrest and Kearns (2001) argue, bonding social capital may help people in excluded communities to cope, but it will not help them to overcome their problems. Likewise, Gilchrist (2003) argues that networks which are closed and homogeneous do little to challenge existing power structures or 'received wisdom'. In his study of social movements, Tarrow (1994, p. 60) argued that 'the ties of homogenous groups are inimical to broader mobilization. Weak ties among social networks that were not unified were much stronger than the strongest ties of workbench or family'. What excluded communities often lack are the weaker ties and overlapping networks which are integral to most of our lives today – bridging and linking social capital – that expose us to different points of view and expand our opportunities.

The different forms of social capital may play different roles for different population groups. Perri 6 (1997) has suggested that bonding social capital may be more important for young people as they define their identity and for older people who are less mobile and need care. Forrest and Kearns (1999) report that entrepreneurs from minority ethnic communities in one city they studied tapped into wider social networks across the city and were less likely to want to leave the neighbourhood they lived in than were others, because they had access to these wider networks. Different types of social capital may also be required for different purposes. Key early texts on 'weak ties' focused on employment opportunities, for example (see Granovetter, 1973), while work outside the social capital tradition has distinguished between the roles played by kin, friends and neighbours (see, for example, the work of Philip Abrams summarized in Bulmer, 1986) and what can be expected of each. While we need to know much more about the significance of community networks and different types of social capital across different generations, cultures and gender and what purposes they serve, community policies need to pay more attention to the importance of developing ties beyond the neighbourhood or community of interest.

Reconnecting the Rich

Ironically, the lack of bridging social capital may not only be a characteristic of the disadvantaged. It could be argued that it is a characteristic too of the very rich, as they lock themselves away in 'gated communities'. The answer to exclusion might be not so much to focus attention on the need for community among the poor, but to reconnect the rich.

In the nineteenth century, Benjamin Disraeli alerted society to the danger of the emerging gulf between rich and poor in his references to 'two nations'. The language of social exclusion is rooted in the republican tradition of solidarity in France. It focuses our attention on the relationship between the excluded and the wider society, and the processes through which exclusion occurs. We therefore need to understand community in relation both to the public sphere and in the context of the power relations that define and structure the way community is defined.

It is possible to argue that if networks and social capital are to empower the excluded they need to operate within a concept of the public sphere which can encourage debate between different conceptions of the public good and promote solidarity. However, Bauman (1999) deplores the loss in today's society of the *agora*, a space which is the province of neither the public nor the private, but is 'the place where private problems meet in a meaningful way', where private troubles can be reforged into public issues and which can thus provide collective levers for the alleviation of private misery and uncertainty. The advance of the market has commodified the public arena and eroded public space in ways which sever social ties, threaten the security from which trust is derived and reduce the likelihood of the chance encounters on which familiarity and networks are built. In excluded communities, Forrest and Kearns (1999) argue, the erosion and stigmatization of public services has had a negative effect, meaning that there is less public presence than there used to be, and adding to the sense of insecurity. Community is invoked to rebuild some sense of commonality, but is prey, as we have seen, to fragmentation and particularism. It may be that new and different kinds of public space are being created, through the internet, through forms of deliberative democracy, through the media, and through new issue-based social movements. If this is the case, there may be gains as well as losses. But it remains to be seen how far these different spaces will foster the kinds of solidarity and social capital that can address exclusion.

The promotion of networks and community has been separated from ideas of the public sphere. It has also been divorced from understandings of power. Networks and social capital can, as we shall see later in this chapter, give people access to power. But they are also structured by existing power relationships. Social capital is as unevenly distributed as any other form of capital and can be used to prop up power elites – Bourdieu's analysis (1986) implies that social capital is likely to reproduce socioeconomic class distinctions and inequalities. The strong normative element to later conceptualizations of social capital has been heavily criticized (Foley and Edwards, 1999). The communitarian agenda sought to promote community as a way of creating a shared morality to areas which had become divorced from the wider society. But the assumption was that this would be the existing moral order and existing hegemonies. Power privileges certain ways of knowing and understanding over others. To include the excluded, it is necessary to challenge those ways of knowing and understanding and allow different narratives to come to the fore. 'The very constitution of the public sphere', argues Flyvbjerg (1998, p. 206, citing Hirschman) derives 'not solely from rational discourse and consensus but "from a field of conflict, contested meanings and exclusion"'.

The Role of Networks in Addressing Social Exclusion

So far in this chapter, I have been critical of the language of community and social capital in addressing exclusion. I have suggested that these are concepts which mask a wealth of contradictions, especially when applied to excluded communities. I have suggested also that policies to promote community neglect both power issues and the erosion of the public sphere within society. But it does not follow that we should abandon these ideas. The increasing prevalence of this discourse is a considerable advance on previous preoccupations with the relative benefits of state and market. Its use brings into focus a huge territory of relationships which have been ignored for too long in political and economic debate. However, the foregoing discussion suggests that it needs to be used in a way which engages with concepts of power and the public.

Even at a very basic level, networks empower. People who have been excluded and isolated are easily stripped of any sense of power and agency. They internalize their experiences and blame themselves for their exclusion. Networks can create new spaces where they can share this experience and reforge private troubles into public issues, as Bauman (1999) suggests. Society's dominant cultural narratives tend to exclude or stereotype the least powerful in society, but when people meet in networks and share their stories, they can create a new, shared narrative. Instead of blaming themselves or accepting the labels of personal inadequacy that are typically imposed by the outside world, they can begin to frame what Woliver (1996) calls 'narratives of resistance'.

The challenge for change agents, therefore, is to 'activate the web of networks submerged in everyday life', along with the alternative 'frameworks of sense' that they generate (Melucci, 1988, p. 248). This is often done through encouraging small-scale activities and giving people opportunities to engage at many different levels. Informal networks are easiest to access; they feel more natural to people. They allow people to opt in and out, and this can be particularly important for people in stressful situations.

Effective informal networks can be encouraged simply through providing spaces and opportunities to meet casually. Short-term activities, such as social and arts events, community festivals or more formal urban design and 'planning for real' exercises act as recruiting mechanisms for both informal networks and more formal organizations – a kind of social glue. Networks can also be encouraged by making the spaces that already exist safer and more attractive. Gilchrist (2003) defines the task of the community worker as the stewardship of social capital, constantly monitoring the holes and breaches in the web of local networks, moving to plug gaps and mend severed ties. She acknowledges, however, that this it is difficult and sometimes risky work, often requiring considerable ingenuity to find a connection or to step into unfamiliar cultural or organizational territory.

Change and inclusion will require not only bonding social capital but bridging and linking social capital. Firstly, bridging social capital – a wide range of overlapping activities and networks – will provide opportunities for people with different identities, allegiances and interests to work together without losing those identities and interests. Informal contacts and networks need thus to be a crucial element of government's community cohesion agenda. It will be particularly important to build informal links between neighbourhoods and communities of interest both to increase understanding across these divides and to ensure that the most excluded within neighbourhoods both benefit from and contribute to area-based initiatives. Isolated and fragmented communities are easily 'outflanked' (Clegg, 1989) and their divisions can be exploited by those who resist the empowerment and inclusion agenda.

Secondly, linking social capital needs to be built between communities and the institutions that affect their lives. Gilchrist (2001) argues that networking across these boundaries contributes to empowerment by reconfiguring power relations and mobilizing a 'critical mass of strategic allies'. At the very least, the development of trusting networks across these boundaries allows power to become more transparent and creates more pathways through which power can be accessed. More radically, Carley and Smith (2001) argue that, in the face of dynamic, complex and interconnected problems, 'action' networks that span sectors and localities are capable of rapid learning, tap a wide range of knowledge and can thus generate power. Both bridging and linking social capital require change agents who can act as 'connectors', 'catalysts' (Gilchrist, 2000) or 'social relays' (Ohlemacher, 1992) and make the connections between different communities – people who encourage people to share ideas and resources across real or perceived boundaries, to coordinate their activities and to identify and exploit opportunities for change.

Change requires formal as well as informal ties. But in his analysis of social movements, Tarrow (1994) counsels against relying solely on networks as a way forward. The power of unincorporated organizations, he argues, is limited. If communities are to become active agents, they need to channel the energy that can be generated through the myriad potential networks within them and take more formal action. If networks are to be the foundation for longer-term engagement, they need to be embedded in sustainable organizations and institutions. Formal activities allow people to take more sustained action and to achieve longer-term goals.

Nonetheless, informal links within and across communities and organizations will still be important:

Informal interaction associated with meetings, training and other joint events will encourage the development of mutual understanding and respect, making it easier to explore and resolve conflicts, to reach consensus and compromise where necessary and to clarify aims and objectives as these ... change over time (Gilchrist, 2003).

Finding ways of making face-to-face contact on neutral territory can increase mutual understanding, help defuse potential tensions and provide the 'social oil' (Performance and Innovation Unit, 2002) to make formal cooperation work more effectively. Informal links also ensure that communication is not pushed solely through the bottlenecks of formal meetings and partnerships. They help to ensure that these more formal structures are embedded in and accountable to the communities they serve.

Maximising Network Opportunities

Developing policies that can maximize the opportunities created by networks requires from policy makers and those who implement their policies a much more acute understanding of the conditions which encourage their development than has been evident in the policy debate so far. Firstly, it requires a much more rigorous assessment of the capacity of loose informal networks to move into the spaces implied by the current emphasis on community and an understanding of their limits as well as their potential. Mulgan and Landry (1995) argue that to see mutual help as a general solution to the problems caused by dependence on large corporate and government systems is to ignore its ephemeral nature and the limitations of time and resource that characterize involvement in such activity. We need to know much more about how networks operate within communities and how they link into more formal activities, if their contribution is to be maximized.

Second, policies that seek to build on community networks need to understand the different driving forces that underpin informal networks and formal systems. Hoch and Hemmens (1987) argue against the assumption of a 'seamless web' between mutuality and formal systems, suggesting, for example, that attempts to co-opt informal care can endanger its social integrity. They claim that professionals fail to recognise the different logics of formal and informal systems, the first instrumental, the second expressive. While informal care depends on reciprocity and the character of personal relationships, for example, professional systems are expected to be detached (Burns and Taylor, 1998).

Thirdly, despite their centrality in government rhetoric, 'community' and social capital are only one narrative in current policy. There are other strong narratives and theories of change, some of which are compatible with community, some less so. The latter have the potential to damage social capital and to limit the potential of networks. Earlier in this chapter reference was made to the impact of wider economic trends on communities – the closure of a major employer can undo years of renewal initiatives in a stroke. But there are other contradictions. The more networks are expected to take on societal responsibilities, for example, the more they will attract scrutiny. Instead of being based on trust, they become subject to regulation and lose their distinctive character:

> Thus, a woman may decide to look after some of her friends' children as a way of making a little money. For her friends, this frees them to work or get involved in other activities. But she runs the risk of being regarded as in breach of regulation – even if she does it for nothing. A group may decide to set up a [local exchange trading system]. But they may find that a benefits officer regards them as being unavailable for work, that business complains of unfair (untaxed) competition or that the Inland Revenue are watching their development closely, because the system sees what they are doing as untaxed exchange (Burns and Taylor, 1998, p. 25).

These arguments suggest that if government and other players wish to promote 'community' in the sense of supportive networks, which give people a sense of identity and foster reciprocity, policy makers need to find ways of creating an environment in which community networks can flourish and provide a foundation for more formal engagement without becoming formalized themselves. This requires a delicate balancing act and is most likely to be articulated through an arm's length or indirect approach, which supports community development and intermediary organizations, which can develop a more flexible approach than is possible with government (Burns and Taylor, 1998).

Promoting informal networks as the basis for tackling exclusion also requires new approaches to risk which allow flexibility to govern the interface between the informal and the formal. There is a tension at the heart of this government's policies, which undermines its intention to promote community and social capital. Its commitment to decentralize services and devolve responsibilities sits uncomfortably with its tendency to maintain control at the centre through standardized performance management and audit systems. The focus on the measurable and short-term gains that pervades government policy erodes the time and development needed to create social capital and gives little value to the more intangible aspects of community building that are needed if the hard outputs are to be achieved. As I have argued elsewhere, the rules and regulations attached to partnerships seem expressly designed to replace trust rather than to foster it (Taylor, 2003).

It is not only the state which seeks to formalize informality. The market has turned many services that have traditionally been exchanged without cost into commodities with a price attached. The best example of this is in developing countries, where herbs which have been used for centuries as traditional medicines are now bought up by companies or where the purchase of water rights places traditional springs out of bounds to indigenous communities. This either strips networks of the currencies and knowledge that make them work or turns their members into criminals.

Another tension within current policy is the tension between leadership and participation. The very centrality of partnership in policy can destroy its potential, with the pace and complexity of partnership working divorcing people from their communities, eroding their networks and overcrowding the agendas of allies within government. It is all too easy to criticize the 'usual suspects', many of whom put an immense amount of effort into their communities and find themselves in the unenviable position of being pig in the middle between partners who question their representativeness and communities who are frustrated at the lack of progress. But it is equally true that community leaders can lose touch with the people whose interests they are expected to reflect or represent. As a respondent in my own research suggested:

> One of the most difficult things about doing an enabling job is to get other people to learn how to enable. Once you've empowered somebody, to get them to empower other people is quite difficult. Power sticks to people and then the whole system gets clogged up.

Policy and practice needs to ensure that expectations of community leaders and representatives are realistic, that support is provided to make sure that leaders remain embedded in and accountable to their communities, and that a foundation of more widespread community engagement is built at an early stage as the basis for engagement in policy initiatives and partnerships. In order to ensure this, we need to know far more than we do about what makes for effective leadership. Most of the research on community involvement has focused on the interface between communities and institutional partners.

Relatively little addresses community leadership and the sources of power and accountability that back this up or how partnership affects the networks of those involved (but see Purdue et al., 2000).

A final tension that needs to be addressed if policies are to promote renewal and partnership is the competitive nature of special funding initiatives. In the past, this competition has had the perverse effect of asking communities or sub-communities to parade their disadvantage in an inverse form of 'place marketing', competing with other to show how disadvantaged they are and feeding the stereotypes they experience at the same time as they seek to escape from them. More recent policies have placed less emphasis on competition between localities, and tackled this by spreading programmes like the Neighbourhood Renewal Fund more widely. Some form of selection is inevitable, but poses two difficult challenges for those who seek to build networks that bind rather than divide. One is that only slightly less disadvantaged neighbourhoods outside the boundaries of those neighbourhoods which are selected for new initiatives become resentful; another is that, within such initiatives, groups may still find themselves competing for money in ways that divide and fragment.

Conclusions

Danny Burns and I have argued elsewhere (Burns and Taylor, 1998) that, while the activities of community networks may seem small-scale, taken as a whole they combine to provide a huge web of social and economic activities which can be said to form the bedrock of our society. Networks are the foundation on which more formal activities both within communities and in partnership with them must be built if they are to be sustainable. In fact, the evidence is that many excluded communities have plenty of social capital. But it may not be the kind of social capital that they need if they are to reconnect to the mainstream. This chapter follows others in distinguishing between the strong ties of close and closed communities and the weaker ties which fuel the networks of the twenty-first century. Inherent in the notion of exclusion is the loss of ties between excluded communities and the wider society of which they are a part.

The task of the change agent is therefore to reconnect at all levels, embedding formal partnerships in informal ties and using formal partnerships to strengthen and make sustainable informal links. Policy needs also to promote weak ties and bridging social capital rather than harking back to the traditional, imagined ways of life that are not 'the way we live now'. It needs to encourage informal networking across communities in ways which respect diversity as well as promoting common interests and to encourage informal linking social capital across institutional boundaries alongside more formal partnership working. But networks can be an elusive and frustrating resource to work with and too heavy a touch risks distorting or incorporating them. Nowhere is this more so than in the most excluded communities, where networks are easily damaged and may operate, in an increasingly regulated and commodified society, on the edges of legality.

This means that building networks and social capital will require a better understanding of the ties that do exist within and across excluded communities, rather than either overromantic or apocalyptic assumptions. It will require a long-term investment in the skills that foster dialogue and build bridges – skills which are needed both in excluded communities and among those who work with them. It will require policies which focus attention not only within excluded communities but on the links between them and the wider society of which they are a part. And it will require an awareness of the ambiguities and challenges within current policy, which can destroy the integrity of informal networks at the same time as seeking to promote them.

Finally, this chapter has argued that, if there is a decline in community, this is not something that is confined to the most marginalized and excluded communities. The exclusion of significant parts of the population from the benefits of economic and social change is the responsibility of the whole of society and not just those who are at the sharp end of change or who work in the increasingly threadbare public services which act as a safety net for them. As commitment to the public sphere and public service declines, it is perhaps not surprising if people withdraw and become 'apathetic', focusing on their own struggle for survival. In these circumstances the social capital that is supposed to draw people out of poverty is likely to be as unfairly distributed in society as any other capital. The welcome focus on the needs of the most disadvantaged communities needs to be matched by reconnecting the rich, by rebuilding and revaluing the public sphere and by acknowledging the need to confront issues of power within communities and across their boundaries.

Note

1   This chapter draws on M. Taylor (2003), *Public Policy in the Community*, London: Palgrave.

Chapter 13

Public Policy and Social Networks: Just How 'Socially Aware' is the Policy-making Process?

Vicki Nash

As the foregoing chapters have made clear, social networks can have a significant impact on the achievement or non-achievement of key public policy goals such as social integration, or the reduction of unemployment and poverty. It should also be obvious that the process operates in both directions, and that public policy decisions can play a significant role in shaping personal social networks. Whilst this may seem like a straightforward enough claim, it is not clear that policy-makers take enough account of these effects and mechanisms. The government's Strategy Unit may have produced a report on policy options for building social capital, but there is, as yet, very little evidence of a more consistent approach to thinking about the social network effects of policy (Strategy Unit, 2002). This chapter asks why this should be the case and how closer integration between research into social networks and public policy could be achieved. It is suggested that despite the current focus on neighbourhoods and communities, British policy-making fails to consistently take account of social as well as economic considerations, and in particular, it fails to take sufficient account of the effect of policy on social networks.

A Promising Start – Where Policy is Already 'Socially Aware'

Given the plethora of high-quality research being undertaken in the field of social network theory, it could be hoped that much of this will find its way into the policy process to inform decision-making. Most of the political debates about the value of social science research funding have focused precisely on the usefulness of resultant findings (King, 1998). The ESRC is itself explicitly committed to this ideal, stating on its website: 'We are committed to communicating ... research as widely as possible, ensuring it has the maximum possible influence on policy-makers, in government, business and on the general public' (ESRC, 2002). Several mechanisms are in place to help support this aim, including the running of monthly media campaigns and the existence of a public affairs and parliamentary relations programme. However, it is not clear that even this is sufficient to ensure easy filtering of social research findings into the policy process. Whether we look at the rhetoric of policy announcements, at the structure of policy evaluation processes or simply decisions themselves, there is a distinct lack of clarity and focus on social as opposed to economic factors.

It is first important to clarify what we mean when we ask whether the UK policy-making process is sufficiently sensitive to concerns about social relationships. Most obviously, nearly all governments are concerned with matters such as crime or social care, and these are clearly 'social' as well as economic issues. Secondly, it could simply be argued that the ideological distinction between Right and Left has traditionally been marked by a respective focus, on the one hand, on matters of the free market and individual liberty, and on the other, social equality and solidarity. On this view, willingness to consider social factors when making policy would simply be reflective of a government's ideological position.

This is not quite the point however. Labour governments may have traditionally been more concerned with matters of social equality and solidarity, but as they have been pursued, these ideals are primarily economic ideals, a fact which perhaps owes much to the legacy of Karl Marx. The Left has been no more concerned with the general quality and character of social relationships in day-to-day life than have parties to the Right. It is rather that in the UK, parties on both sides of the spectrum have, at least in recent years, appeared far more at ease discussing economic benefits and processes rather than social benefits and processes. Where parties such as 'New Labour' have expressed a commitment to supporting community, or more recently, social cohesion, there has been a distinct lack of clarity as to what sort of social relations are sought. In some cases this lack of clarity may even have resulted in policies misguidedly seeking to support certain sorts of social relationship not actually beneficial for the individuals concerned (see, for example, Taylor, 2002; and in this volume). Except for the rhetoric of community (and perhaps also that of parenting, caring and the family), the terminology of economics springs far more easily to politicians' lips than the language of sociology.

The complaint then is that British governments this century have not shown great receptivity to the findings of social research which offer information about the effect of policy on social relationships and vice versa.

It would obviously be unfair to claim that British public policy displays no understanding of social factors and their implications for policy-making, and there are signs that matters are improving. Some policy fields have proved more receptive than others. Little attention, for example, has been devoted to the social factors underlying crime such as peer-group effects and socialization. The move towards comprehensive education, on the other hand, was at least in part underpinned by British sociological research into the implications of the grammar school system. More recently, several policy reports and initiatives, especially those in regeneration, show an admirable awareness of the inter-relation between policy, policy goals and key social factors such as social networks, social capital and peer-group effects. Whilst much more integration between policy and research is still needed, it is worth discussing some of these areas in order to illustrate the (limited) extent to which such an understanding is starting to translate into political action.

Social Exclusion and Neighbourhood Renewal

The establishment of the Social Exclusion Unit in 1997 marked a political determination on behalf of the newly elected Labour government to understand and address the social and geographic determinants of poverty. The Unit, quickly established a range of policy action teams (PATs) to investigate and report on particular aspects of social exclusion with a view to constructing an overall strategy. These PATs brought together experienced civil servants with academics and practitioners in the field. The resulting reports, based heavily on case studies and examples, were largely successful in presenting a fairly subtle account of the various social, economic and environmental factors which compound to exacerbate the many facets of social exclusion. PAT 9 on community self-help displayed particularly detailed understanding of the importance of local social relationships for quality of life, and began by stating that 'networks which link local residents to each other are essential to the effective functioning of communities and thus of society at large' (Social Exclusion Unit, 1999, p. 1). The report goes on to list the various goods which such networks help to provide, although it also lauds the benefits of 'strong communities' which from a more academic perspective, is not a particularly coherent (or attractive) ideal. Several of the other reports, such as those on anti-social behaviour and education, also noted the role that personal social networks can play in reducing or increasing exclusion.

Similarly, the later development of the National Strategy for Neighbourhood Renewal could itself be seen as a positive move. By explicitly focusing on the amelioration of neighbourhood welfare rather than just individual hardship, policy-makers were driven to consider the nature and effects of relationships between residents living in deprived areas. The resultant initiatives supporting capacity-building and a participative approach to regeneration could be argued to reflect a genuinely well-meaning attempt to improve the quality and use of these ties (Cabinet Office, 2001). It is worth noting that this is not necessarily a new approach; more than any other policy area perhaps, regeneration policy has, spasmodically, adopted a sociologically-informed approach. The 1970s Community Development Project, for example, was similarly concerned with supporting local social networks and empowering residents by developing skills and confidence (see Lees and Smith, 1975; Loney, 1983).

Housing

Given the current emphasis placed on the principle of tenure mix it might be thought that housing policy at least has been designed with a view to engineering the development of certain sorts of social networks, in particular, helping people on lower incomes develop social ties with members of more affluent groups. There are encouraging signs from some of the PAT reports that policy-makers were at least aware of the possible benefits of social networks arising between different income groups even if no explicit references are made to Granovetter-style research in the 'unpopular housing' report (Social Exclusion Unit, 1999b). The Housing Green Paper also refers to the importance of supporting 'sustainable communities' via a 'better mix of housing types' (DETR, 2000a), and this principle is now enshrined in policy and planning guidance notes (DETR, 2000b). Despite these references, it is not clear that there has been any serious attempt to determine what might qualify as 'balanced and sustainable communities' and the main driver for mixed tenure housing seems to be a concern that, unlike sink estates, neighbourhoods should prove economically sustainable.

Transport and Public Space

Recent developments in transport policy are amongst the most encouraging from the perspective of initiatives which might be driven by a concern to improve the quality of local social relationships. The piloting of continental-style Home Zones and the more recent expansion of the scheme are driven by a twofold determination to improve road safety in residential areas and to encourage interaction amongst residents and their children. Initial evaluations suggest that this is proving successful (Biddulph, 2001). The current policy focus on the public realm is also encouraging – a reassurance that after years of cutting maintenance budgets there is some awareness of the role that public space plays in stimulating social interaction. The Home Zone initiative is so far the most positive move, with little extra funding having been released by central government for improving the quality of the public realm despite a recent cross-cutting spending review in this area. There are, however, signs that local government may act to improve matters, being encouraged to do so by the introduction of new responsibilities and indicators (Local Government Act, 2000).

Why is this not Good Enough?

It could be argued that there is one very good reason why governments tend not to concern themselves with the conjunction between policy and social relationships, namely that our relationships with others are private matters, beyond the legitimate reach of the state. Liberal political theory has traditionally drawn a sharp distinction between the public and private realm on the basis that interference with individual liberty can only be justified when others' liberty is threatened (Mill, 1859; Rawls, 1971, 1996). In the public eye, deliberate intervention by policy-makers to support certain sorts of social ties or norms thus runs the risk of being seen simply as rather sinister 'social engineering'.

Perri 6 (2002, and this volume) has previously discussed these normative reasons why politics should not be concerned with the 'governance of friends and acquaintances'. There he quite successfully counters these arguments by highlighting one crucial point: if government cannot help but affect our social relationships why should it not ensure that *at least it does no harm*. Normative arguments for non-intervention seem to be rather less weighty when some effect on social networks and relationships is inevitable. To use the examples which Marilyn Taylor has previously raised (Taylor, 2002), if policy is to have the effect of encouraging certain sorts of social ties to develop in deprived areas, then should we not at least ensure that those relationships do not work to the detriment of the area's fortunes?

The first reason, then, why more integration between policy and social research might be needed is because there are plenty of examples where the achievement of a policy goal is actually undermined by an initiative designed to help deliver that goal. Such perverse effects can be observed to occur as a result of policies shaping people's social relationships. It is, for example, widely recognized that, especially for the young, prison can serve as an effective way of building criminal networks and skills and exposing vulnerable individuals to negative peer-group effects. Previous housing policy similarly worked to reinforce the effects of poverty by ensuring that low-income families in social housing were in the past exposed only to other low-income families on mono-tenure estates. A more detailed understanding of social networks and other social research could have helped to identify initiatives with such potentially perverse effects.

The second reason why it matters is because there are certain policy goals which cannot be fully attained unless some attention is paid to underlying social relationships. Equality of opportunity is one such goal. Any government that aspires to promote equality of opportunity may devote significant efforts to ensuring that the standards of state-provided education are raised and that overt discrimination of various forms is stamped out. But so long as social networks prove effective means of gaining information and opportunities, true equality of opportunity will be foiled by any system that sees certain income or social groups dominating good schools or universities. As Perri 6 (2001) has noted, middle class families can become very effective at 'hoarding privilege' in this way, but unfortunately it is difficult to identify any measures which might counter this phenomenon that would not also be seen as quite repressive. Other policy goals may even more naturally require such attention to social networks for their fulfillment, with care for the elderly and eradication of child poverty being two of the most obvious candidates.

In other cases, particular policy goals may not so obviously demand attention to underlying social relationships and networks, but they may nonetheless benefit from such a focus. The rather loose concept of social capital has at least proved an effective means of communicating this message to the policy community. Academically, Putnam's work may raise as many questions as it answers, but politically, it is no great surprise that he has advised both Bill Clinton and Gordon Brown. Putnam's most recent attempt to collate and present some of the research relating to the impact of 'social capital' on key policy issues such as crime, health, education and economic prosperity is arguably most valuable for its communication of the message that social as well as economic infrastructure affects a nation's welfare (Putnam, 2001). This is a message which the UK government has started to react to, with the Strategy Unit reporting on possible policy options that could build social capital and the Office for National Statistics researching ways of measuring it (Strategy Unit, 2002; ONS, 2001). Health officials can pride themselves on being rather ahead of the game, with the Health Development Agency (previously the Health Education Authority) commissioning a programme of research into the effects of social support and social capital on health in 1996 (see, for example, Cooper et al., 1999).

The third and final reason why government should take more account of social relationships and their implications for policy is because at the end of the day our quality of life can be significantly affected by the pattern and character of social relationships we find ourselves immersed in. This means that how we relate to others can itself become a political issue when those relationships break down. Figures from the most recent British crime survey depict the strange situation of a populace becoming ever more afraid of crime, believing it to be rising dramatically, even as most categories of offence show a gradual reduction in reported incidences (Home Office, 2002). This has now become an important political issue, with the Policing White Paper proposing new ways of raising the numbers of policemen out on the streets and creating opportunities for members of the public to patrol their own neighbourhoods as Community Support Officers (Home Office, 2001a).

An even more authoritative political response was demanded when apparently race-related rioting broke out in three northern English towns in the summer of 2001. The stark vision of what looked like complete community breakdown resulted in the immediate commissioning of inquiry reports and the eventual establishment of the Community Cohesion Unit (Home Office, 2001b, 2001c). Whilst the factors that sparked these riots are undoubtedly complex, it seems clear that entrenched problems such as poverty and racism played a significant role. What was rather more shocking though, was the extent to which different ethnic groups were portrayed as living 'lives in parallel' that never crossed, and the role that policy decisions had potentially played in this (Home Office, 2001b). It is worth noting that this should not have come as a surprise; sociological studies carried out in Birmingham in the 1960s had warned what might happen in that city if housing and other policies were not changed (Rex and Moore, 1967). Twenty years later, after no such change, severe rioting broke out, and yet, as Marshall (1990) points out, still sociological research is not seen as relevant to real social and economic problems. The challenge now faced by the Community Cohesion Unit is not simply to ensure that other communities never face the misery and violence that community breakdown can bring, but to determine exactly what is meant by cohesion and how that might be achieved, which must involve working closely with academics engaged in relevant social research.

In all the cases laid out above, the argument is that there are very good policy reasons why government should embrace a more subtle understanding of the interaction between policy and social relations. Government cannot avoid having an effect on how we relate to others, nor can it ignore the impact that social factors exert on desired policy outcomes or individual welfare. It is not that government must do all it can to promote certain sorts of social networks or relationships, only that there are good policy reasons for governments to avoid inhibiting the development of potentially valuable networks or causing harm to those that already exist. In order to do this, we clearly need to know as much as possible about the sorts of relationships and networks which are valuable to individuals in particular situations. But we also need to know more about the ways that policy impacts on such factors, and in many cases this may be a highly uncertain process. Social investment is rather more difficult than economic investment in that you cannot simply pour new social ties or norms such as trust into a community in the same way that you can invest money. The role of government has to be as facilitator not manager, but even this requires a very sensitive understanding of social dynamics.

What are the Barriers to a More Sociologically-informed Approach?

The research reported in the first section of this book makes it clear that there is a great deal that policy-makers could learn from current sociological research into social networks. Frustrating though it might seem, the prospects of this research being absorbed are rather poor. Even if normative objections to 'social engineering' can be overcome, there just does not seem to be the same hunger in UK government for social research as there is for economic or scientific research. The value of social science research may well have been accepted by the policy community, but all too often 'social science' simply means economics. Policy-makers have economic advisers, not social advisers, and governments are judged on how they run the economy and public services rather than on their impact on civil society. It could even be argued that UK governments have been uncomfortable thinking about the interaction between policy and social factors such as networks, relationships and norms.

The days when social research by figures such as Michael Young and the Institute of Community Studies was lapped up by policy makers now seem a long time gone. It is not clear why such a change of heart occurred. Has sociology lost its communicative power as the discipline has become more academically respectable? Does economics offer policy-makers a simpler range of choices and a clearer set of excuses? There are several reasons why sociological research loses out in the policy-making process and if closer integration between policy and research is to be achieved, it is worth considering how each of these might be addressed.

Do They Even Speak the Right Language?

The economic effects of a policy can be communicated to policy-makers or the public with relative ease, using the language of jobs lost or gained, changes in inflation or net value in pounds and pence. Even if this message is inevitably a simplified version, it is a message that is easily understood. The metrics that are used – jobs, money, points on the inflation rate – are all quantifiable measures that people can, without specialist training, appreciate and interpret for themselves. It is not clear that there are any such commonly-understood metrics which would effectively describe the social effects of a policy decision. We might say that a particular policy destroyed trust between residents of a certain area, or that it failed to help elderly single people build personal support networks, but as these examples should show, the effects are not immediately quantifiable, and even if under certain methodologies they are, they are not quantifiable in a way easily understood by the layman.

As well as the lack of any common metrics by which social effects and changes can be communicated, another problem concerns the language itself. Both economics and sociology are potentially as jargon-laden as each other, but at least the basic vocabulary of economics falls within most people's lexicons. It is not obvious that the same is true of sociology. In the context of the research discussed in this book, even the basic premise of a social network or of different types of social tie might have to be explained before it would be clearly understood by someone not trained in sociology. As for discussion about nodes, structural holes and sociometric analysis, this is unlikely to become mainstream in the foreseeable future.

There is one further reason why the language of much social research is not well-suited to the demands of the policy process. That is the use of different terms in different disciplines which either do not precisely equate or which fail to correspond precisely to issues which are current policy concerns. In social psychology, for example, social identity theorists examine the extent to which 'self-esteem' is supported by a basic psychological process of categorizing and comparing oneself to others (Tyler et al., 1997). Sociologists of class structure and stratification have studied how 'self-direction' at work affects individual welfare such as health outcomes (Kohn and Schooler, 1983; Kohn and Slomczycinski, 1990), whilst other sociologists address similar issues under the title of 'self-efficacy' (Gekas, 1989). In all three cases, policy-makers might be interested in research which shows how class, social group or employment position impact on an individual's sense of self-respect and consequent well-being, but the use of different terms means that the implications of different research projects from different disciplines are much harder to collate. Other terms are interpreted in different ways by different researchers. The concept of social capital is one which has been interpreted in subtly different ways by theorists within a discipline, such that the concept introduced by Bourdieu does not quite equate with that introduced by Coleman, which again, is used slightly differently to Putnam's own interpretation (Bourdieu, 1988, 1991; Coleman, 1990; Putnam, 1993; see Baron, Field and Schuller, 2001 for a discussion). All of these subtle differences of terminology, meaning or focus make it much harder for the findings of sociology and other fields of social research to be filtered through into the policy-making process.

How Certain are We?

A second reason why it is difficult to integrate the findings of social research into policy-making is that on many occasions such research will not offer the certainty or predictability of an economic approach. Modern mainstream economics, grounded on assumptions of methodological individualism and increasingly sophisticated core principles, is well-placed to provide axioms and models which deliver precise predictions. It is hard to imagine social research ever producing similarly efficient macro-level models.

Whilst it should be relatively easy to argue that this need not matter, there are bigger concerns. First, it is clear that we still do not know nearly enough to understand, for example, all the effects a particular policy will exert on the social networks of different sections of the population. Secondly, from what we do know, it is clear that the social network effects of a particular policy may help some groups and hinder others. It is therefore very hard for social research in this area at least to offer policy-makers anything like the certainty they might need in designing new initiatives. It is worth briefly examining each of these problems in turn.

Social network theory has undoubtedly come a long way since its early sociometric origins (Scott, 1991). The research discussed in this book shows just how subtle and detailed an account can now be offered of the inter-relation between social networks and various external forces. But this is not yet enough. Consider, for example, all that would need to be known in order to fully understand the likely social impact of a policy that reduces the maintenance of public spaces such as parks or streets. Not only would we need to know which groups currently use those spaces, we would need to know what they do there – do mothers make contact watching their children in the sandpit or do children make friends playing football in the street? We would also need to know what type of interaction might start to occur if the maintenance is reduced – will dealers start selling drugs in a now unlit park, or will children be enrolled in football clubs and leisure centres if their street becomes unsafe? Far-sighted planners such as Jane Jacobs may well have understood broad social principles well enough to predict some of the consequences of such policy decisions (Jacobs, 1962), but can researchers yet offer anything more? More crucially, should we expect them to? It is not clear that social research should have to offer the degree of predictability that economics purports to provide, but if it can't offer this, how are its findings to be politically useful?

Quite apart from the 'usefulness' of less nomothetic research, rather crucially such research exposes decision-makers to risk. Those who are supposedly accountable for new initiatives or decisions could well shy away from research that cannot provide a clear and persuasive case for acting one way rather than another. It is easy, and often appropriate, for decision-makers to seek refuge in the 'evidence' that justifies their position; social research, even when heavily quantitative, may not offer any such sanctuary.

The second sense in which social research such as social network theory cannot offer policy-makers certainty consists in the likelihood that any one policy may be good for some people's social networks but bad for others. Perri 6 in his chapter raises the possibility of tragic outcomes for policy interventions, whereby no matter which option is adopted, one group will suffer – the idea that 'all good things do not go together'. There is no need to say much more on this topic, except to note that this is an eternal policy problem. Most public policy decisions involve trade-offs, either between different policy goals (such as equity and efficiency) or between the welfare of different groups. That social research such as that presented in this volume highlights occasions on which trade-offs will occur is a strength not a weakness, and in many cases may provide the more subtle account of potential winners and losers than economic analysis alone. Quite how these considerations will be built into traditional methods of cost-benefit analysis is another, more challenging question.

What Do We Want to Achieve?

The final reason why it might be hard for governments to take on board the findings of social research such as social network theory is that it remains rather unclear what they should promote. Is there a particular pattern of 'healthy' social relations which public policy should support or are individual needs and networks so complex that no single overall 'pattern' can be recommended?

In the case of particular social groups where there is a history of research consensus, it is definitely possible to generalize and claim that certain types of social network with certain sorts of norms are more helpful than others. We can broadly say, for example, that elderly people are likely to benefit from close supportive social ties to family and friends that will help to provide physical and emotional help. Those who are looking for jobs would, on the other hand, benefit from a broader circle of contacts who might provide new information about employment opportunities. Unfortunately, even this gets complicated. Somebody who is unemployed is not just in need of a job, but may also be a teenager undergoing a difficult emotional transition which requires support from family and friends. We cannot even say for any one individual that a particular set of social ties is ideal. If this is true, how can we possibly hope to arrive at such an ideal for the UK as a whole?

Arguably such a universal ideal is not necessary. There are however two types of scenario in which some model of beneficial social networks would be helpful, namely those where policy is designed to help a particular group of people, and those where policy will shape interaction in particular localities. In the first scenario, it may be possible to recommend one type of social network over another; in the second case this is not possible, but nonetheless some sort of guidance is needed, if policy-makers are to become at least network-aware in their thinking.

Some policies are targeted at individuals who, by definition, share a common status or identity. Thus for example, unemployment policy, such as the New Deal, is directed at those without jobs. In this policy context it would appear to make sense for initiatives to be designed in such a way as to at least not harm the sorts of social network associated with success in finding a job, and possibly even to support them. Other policies which affect the same individuals may seek to support different types of social network. Thus the Connexions service aims to provide young people with the support and advice they will need to get through the transition from childhood to maturity and independence. It is not evident that there is any conflict between these two aims, and as such a particular policy may seek to promote certain types of ties for a particular group. In other words, a blueprint is possible.

The second scenario in which a limited normative account of social relationships is needed concerns policies which will have an impact on interaction in a particular area. Although many people now find some of their closest or most meaningful ties outside their neighbourhood or even their town, the quality and character of local social relationships can impact dramatically on residents' quality of life, partly as a result of the networks that are supported. Policy decisions across a wide variety of issues will inevitably have some effect on the character of local social relations, whether this be by affecting who lives next to whom, who can travel easily where or what spaces are made available for people to interact in. As has been argued elsewhere in this book, given that policy must inevitably have such effect, it makes sense to ensure that at least the effect is a benign one. Unfortunately it is not immediately clear what sorts of social relationships policy-makers should be concerned to protect or promote. Individuals living in the area will have such different needs and experiences, it is hard to imagine how we could generalize enough to offer a preferred 'model' of local social relations. Yet without such a blueprint, how can we help policy-makers to minimize network harm?

The current government talks in terms of supporting 'community' and 'strengthening communities'. Whilst this might have rhetorical appeal, evoking nostalgic memories of supportive close-knit working class towns, this interpretation of 'community' has some very negative connotations, as Taylor (2002) has pointed out. As such, 'strong communities' are not an appropriate policy goal. There is an alternative. Whether or not we use the term community, it is possible to describe a less exclusionary vision of local social relations which policy should support. At minimum, most people want not to fear their neighbours. Beyond that, individuals may need very different things from the people they live near. Some may desire complete anonymity, others support and friendship, others still just the name of a good plumber or school. Here the safest principle to adopt could simply be to hedge bets and opt for courses of action likely to support a wide range of social ties. A recent IPPR publication argued that on this basis, policy-makers have a duty to ensure that overall they support such a diversity of social ties (Nash, 2003). This means supporting the provision of many opportunities for interaction (especially between different social groups), and ensuring that neighbourhoods and public spaces feel reassuring enough that people will want to use them. It may also mean avoiding obvious damage to existing ties between groups, as might be caused by the removal of transport links.

Such an account of the sorts of social relations which national and local government could support is unavoidably vague. There is room for social research to inform and develop this model, especially where a predominance of certain groups makes particular sorts of ties more valuable. It would be perfectly legitimate, for example, for research on social exclusion and social networks, such as that presented in this volume, to inform the current debate on capacity-building and neighbourhood renewal by providing a more detailed picture of the sorts of social relations that would most help residents living in deprived areas and how those might be supported. Indeed, the political value of the research presented in this book comes precisely in its capacity to inform policy-making in each of the two scenarios presented here. The aim should be, first, to ensure that policies targeted at particular groups do not damage the network needs of that group, and second, to help inform our understanding of the relationship between policy decisions and network outcomes within the context of particular localities.

Steps to a More Integrated Approach

It is clear from the research presented in this book that the quality of political decision-making could be improved by further integration of policy and research in this field. This chapter has argued that some of the reasons why policy has been slow to pick up on the findings of social research such as social network theory is because there are institutional barriers as well as normative concerns. Both Perri 6 and Marilyn Taylor have highlighted the normative issues, and in both cases, the conclusion seemed to be that in so far as policy cannot avoid having an impact on the quality and character of people's social relationships, it should at least endeavour to ensure that a rule of harm minimization is observed. The institutional barriers are rather more difficult to overcome. They concern the way that policy decisions are made and the language or concepts that are used, and in particular the hegemony of economics as the social science of choice. It will be hard for social research to surmount these barriers, but it is certainly not impossible, and there are changes that could be made on both sides.

Closer Links between Academic Research and the Policy Agenda

As this book demonstrates, social research can deepen our understanding of the conditions which make the achievement of policy goals more or less likely. Areas of policy which focus on the needs of particular social groups such as the unemployed, the elderly or the young can most obviously benefit from academic research and evaluation which identify the network challenges facing these groups. Both academics and government could do more to ensure closer links between policy and research in some of these key areas. On the government's part, it must be recognized that much academic research is grant-driven, and as such there is immense need for more research programmes similar to the Social Networks and Social Exclusion programme. On the academic side, it is essential that researchers undertaking research in this field begin with a clear awareness of the policy relevance of their work; that efforts are made to ensure that the methodology used will enable any policy implications to be fully and clearly drawn out; and that dissemination strategies display an awareness of different audiences. There could also be value for academic researchers to make links with relevant NGOs or think-tanks, but managing this process so that it does not jeopardize the independence of research is clearly important. More boldly, sociologists need to look at the quality of their own social networks when it comes to disseminating their findings effectively amongst those in positions of political power.

Simplification and Harmonization of Terminology

Academic research will never be jargon-free as specialist language is frequently needed to ensure conceptual clarity. However it is essential that research findings be communicated in a way that makes them accessible to a variety of audiences including the policy audience, and this may mean translating even seemingly simple terms (such as 'weak or strong ties') for a lay audience. More thought should also be given to how research findings are indexed or linked. For example, key words associated with particular books or articles should be designed to ensure that a non-specialist policy-maker could find research relevant to their field. Department or personal websites should also be designed with this point in mind, and where abstracts are available online, some consideration should be given as to whether they are accessible to different audiences. The production of regular policy briefs by a department is also likely to be helpful.

Case Studies that Highlight the Economic Effects of the 'Social' and the Social Effects of the Economic

Given the dominance of economics in the formulation of policy and of the Treasury in the funding of initiatives, it would be valuable for disciplines such as social network theory to be able to point to the economic implications of their research. The inter-connection between social and economic aspects of a particular policy problem would be much clearer if case studies were carried out which examined or modelled their interplay. Thus, for example, it is perfectly possible to estimate the economic cost of services provided by informal carers of elderly people. In similar vein, it would be valuable if more attempts were made to understand the social impact of economic decisions such as those to close down a particular bus route, or indeed, the real economic impact which takes into account costs associated with the social impact. Traditional cost-benefit models may become more flexible with regard to factoring in more complex social costs and benefits as models incorporating principles of sustainable development are mainstreamed throughout government.

More Multidisciplinary Research

Policy problems rarely fall within the aegis of a single discipline. There is thus a need for more coordinated research into policy-relevant issues to take place across disciplines. The research that has been undertaken around issues of social exclusion, whether through universities, research programmes or policy action teams exemplifies what can be accomplished when research teams from a variety of academic backgrounds focus attention on a common policy problem.

More Willingness to Embrace both Economic and Sociological Evidence

There is ultimately a burden of responsibility which must rest on individual policy-makers. As has been pointed out, there are good reasons why economic language and modelling might dominate the policy-making process. The language and concepts are familiar and the theories and principles provide a possibility of more certainty and precision than most social research could hope to offer. This certainty and precision in turn offer easy justification for decisions, and hence a greater sense of accountability. This may be true, but unless the social consequences of policy decisions are also taken fully into account, it cannot be said that decisions have been made in the light of the full knowledge available. As such, the more difficult, more slippery concepts such as social networks and norms should be embraced and considered in all relevant circumstances.

Conclusion

This chapter has argued that research such as that presented in this volume has a vital role to play in informing the policy-making process. There may be a tendency in that process to favour economic over social research and implications, but unless more attempts are made to integrate policy and research in this area, there is a real danger that policy goals will never be properly fulfilled and that policy initiatives will have perverse effects. Changes are needed in the ways that research is undertaken and disseminated. However some of the biggest barriers remain at the institutional level. Until these barriers are removed, social researchers will have to work hard to ensure that their findings are incorporated into the policy-making process and research programmes such as this will play an ever more vital role.

Bibliography

Abbott, P. and Wallace, C. (1992), *The Family and the New Right*, London: Pluto Press.

Acheson, D. (1998), *Independent Inquiry into Inequalities in Health*, London: HMSO.

Adams, R.G. (1986), 'Secondary friendship networks and psychological well-being among elderly women', *Activities, Adaptation and Aging*, **8**, pp. 59–72.

Adams, R.G. (1987), 'Patterns of network change: A longitudinal study of friendships of elderly women', *The Gerontologist*, **27**, pp. 222–27.

Adams, R. and Allan, G. (eds) (1998), *Placing Friendship in Context*, Cambridge: Cambridge University Press.

Albrow, G. (1996), *The Global Age: State and Society Beyond Modernity*, Cambridge: Polity Press.

Albrow, M., Eade, J., Fennell, G. and O'Byrne, D. (1994), *Local/Global Relations in a London Borough: Shifting Boundaries and Localities*, London: Roehampton Institute.

Allan, G. (1979), *A Sociology of Friendship and Kinship*, London: Allen & Unwin.

Allan, G. (1989), *Friendship: Developing a Sociological Perspective*, Hemel Hempstead: Harvester Wheatsheaf.

Allan, G. (1996), *Kinship and Friendship in Modern Britain*, Oxford: Oxford University Press.

Allan, G. and Crow, G. (2001), *Families, Households and Society*, Basingstoke: Palgrave.

Allan, G., Hawker, S. and Crow, G. (2001), 'Family diversity and change in Britain and Western Europe', *Journal of Family Issues*, **22**, pp. 819–37.

Allatt, P. and Yeandle, S. (1992), *Youth Unemployment and the Family: Voices of Disordered Times*, London: Routledge.

Antonucci, T.C. (1985), 'Personal characteristics, social support, and social behaviour', in R. Binstock and E. Shanas (eds), *Handbook of Aging and the Social Sciences*, New York: Van Nostrand Reinhold and Company.

Antonucci, T.C. (1994), 'A life-span view of women's social relations', in B.F. Turner, and L. Troll (eds), *Women Growing Older: Psychological Perspectives*, London: Sage.

Antonnuci, T.C. (2001), 'Social relations: An examination of social networks, social support, and sense of control', in J.E. Birren and K. Warner Schaie (eds), *Handbook of Psychology of Aging*, Orlando: Academic Press.

Antonucci, T.C and Akiyama, H. (1987a), 'Social networks in adult life: A preliminary examination of the convoy model', *Journal of Gerontology*, **4**, pp. 519–27.

Antonucci, T.C and Akiyama, H. (1987b), 'An examination of sex differences in social support among older men and women', *Sex Roles*, **17**, pp. 737–49.

Antonucci, T.C. and Akiyama, H. (1995), 'Convoys of social relations: Family and friendship within a life span context', in R. Blieszner and V. Hilkevitch Bedford (eds), *Handbook of Aging and the Family*, Westport, Conn.: Greenward Press.

Arber, S. and Attias-Donfut, C. (2000), *The Myth of Generational Conflict*, London: Routledge.

Argyle, M. (1989), *The Psychology of Happiness*, London: Routledge.

Argyle, M. (1996), 'The effects of relationships on well-being', in Baker, N. (ed.), *Building a Relational Society: New Priorities for Public Policy*, Aldershot: Arena.

Atkinson, R. (2000), 'Narratives of policy: The construction of urban problems and urban policy in the official discourse of British government 1968–98', *Critical Social Policy*, **20**, pp. 211–32.

Atkinson, R. and Davoudi, S. (2000), 'The concept of social exclusion in the European Union: Context, development and possibilities', *Journal of Common Market Studies*, **38**, 3: pp. 427–48.

Axelrod, R. (1984), *The Evolution of Co-operation*, New York: Basic Books.

Balfour, J.L. and Kaplan, G.A. (2002), 'Neighborhood environment and loss of physical function in older adults: Evidence from the Alameda County study', *American Journal of Epidemiology*, **155**, pp. 507–15.

Ballard, R. (ed.) (1994), *Desh Pardesh: The South Asian Presence in Britain*, London: Hurst.

Bardach, E. (1977), *The Implementation Game: What Happens After A Bill Becomes Law?*, Cambridge, Mass.: Massachusetts Institute of Technology Press.

Barnes, B. (1995), *The Elements of Social Theory*, London: UCL Press.

Barnes, J.A. (1954), 'Class and committees in a Norwegian island parish', *Human Relations*, **7**, pp. 39–58.

Baron, S., Field, J. and Schuller, T. (eds) (2000), *Social Capital: Critical Perspectives*, Oxford: Oxford University Press.

Baron, S., Riddell, S. and Wilkinson, H. (1998), 'The best burgers? The person with learning difficulties as worker', in T. Shakespeare (ed.), *The Disability Reader: Social Science Perspectives*, London: Cassell.

Batalova, J.A. and Cohen, P.N. (2002), 'Premarital cohabitation and housework: Couples in cross-national perspective', *Journal of Marriage and Family*, **64**, pp. 743–55.

Bauman, Z. (1988), *Freedom*, Milton Keynes: Open University Press.

Bauman, Z. (1999), *In Search of Politics*, Cambridge: Polity Press.

Bauman, Z. (2000), *Liquid Modernity*, Cambridge: Polity Press.

Beck, U. and Beck-Gernsheim, E. (1996), 'Individualization and "precarious freedoms": Perspectives and controversies of a subject-oriented sociology', in P. Heelas, S. Lash and P. Morris (eds), *Detraditionalization: Critical Reflections on Authority and Identity*, Oxford: Blackwell.

Beck, U. and Beck-Gernsheim, E. (2001), *Individualization*, London: Sage.

Bell, S. and Coleman, S. (eds) (1999), *The Anthropology of Friendship*, Oxford: Berg.

Bellah, R., Madsen, R., Sullivan, W., Swindler, A. and Tipton, S. (1985), *Habits of the Heart: Individualism and Commitment in American Life*, Berkeley: University of California Press.

Bemelmans-Videc, M-L., Rist, R.C., Vedung, E. (eds) (1998), *Carrots, Sticks and Sermons: Policy Instruments and Their Evaluation*, New Brunswick, NJ: Transaction Books.

Bengston, V.L. and Achenbaum, W.A. (eds) (1993), *The Changing Contract Across Generations*, New York: Aldine De Gruyter.

Bennett, J. (2002), 'Monitoring local authorities' impact on social relations', paper presented at the Institute for Public Policy Research seminar, *Valuing community: assessment the impact of policy on local social relations*, London: 2 June 2002.

Berger, B. and Berger, P. (1983), *The War Over the Family*, Garden City, NJ: Doubleday.

Berghman, J. (1997), 'The resurgence of poverty and the struggle against exclusion: A new challenge for social security?', *International Social Security Review*, **50**, pp. 3–23.

Berkman, L.F. (1985), 'The relationship of social networks and social supports to morbidity and mortality', in S. Cohen, and S. Syme (eds), *Social Support and Health*, Orlando: Academic Press.

Berkman, L.F. (1986), 'Social networks, support, and health: Taking the next step forward', *American Journal of Epidemiology*, **123**, pp. 559–562.

Berkman, L. and Breslaw, L. (1983), *Health and Ways of Living: The Alameda County Study*, Oxford: Oxford University Press.

Berkman, L. and Glass, T. (2000), 'Social integration, social networks, social supports and health', in L. Berkman and I. Kawachi (eds), *Social Epidemiology*, New York: Oxford Press.

Berkman, L. and Syme, S. (1979), 'Social networks, host resistance, and mortality: A nine year follow-up study of Alameda County residents', *American Journal of Epidemiology*, **109**, pp. 186–204.

Bernard, J. (1972), *The Future of Marriage*, New York: Bantam Books.

Berndt, T.J. (1996), 'Exploring the effects of friendship quality on social development', in E. Bukowski, A. Newcomb and W. Hartup (eds), *The Company They Keep: Friendship in Childhood and Adolescence*, Cambridge: Cambridge University Press.

Bhalla, A. and Lapeyre, F. (1997), 'Social exclusion: Towards an analytical and operational framework', *Development and Change*, **28**, pp. 413–33.

Biddulph, M. (2001), *Home Zones: A Planning and Design Handbook*, Oxford: Policy Press.

Black, P., Crossley, N., Fagan, C., Savage, M. and Turney, L. (eds) (2002), 'Globalisation and social capital', Sociological Research Online 7, www.socresonline.org.uk/socres/7/3.

Blaug, R. (2002), 'Engineering democracy', *Political Studies*, **50**, pp. 102–16.

Blaxter, M. (1990), *Health and Lifestyles*, London: Tavistock.

Blaxter, M. and Poland, F. (2000), 'Moving beyond the survey in exploring social capital', in C. Swann and A. Morgan (eds), *Social Capital for Health: Insights from Qualitative Research*, London: Health Development Agency.

Blazer, D. (1982), 'Social support and mortality in an elderly community population', *American Journal of Epidemiology*, **116**, pp. 684–94.

Blumstein, P. and Schwartz, P. (1983), *American Couples: Money, Work, Sex*, New York: William Morrow and Company, Inc.

Boissevain, J. (1979), 'Network analysis: A reappraisal', *Current Anthropology*, **20**, pp. 392–94.

Bonvalet, C., Gotman, A. and Grafmeyer, Y. (eds) (1999), *La Famille et Ses Proches: L'amenagement des territoire*, INED Cahier No. 143, Paris: Presse Universitaire.

Bosworth, H. B. and Schaie, K. W. (1997), 'The relationship of social environment, social networks and health outcomes in the Seattle longitudinal study: Two analytical approaches', *Journal of Gerontology: Psychological Science and Social Science*, **52**, pp. 197–205.

Bott, E. (1957), *Family and Social Network*, London: Tavistock.

Bourdieu, P. (1988), *Homo Academicus*, Cambridge: Polity Press.

Bourdieu, P. (1991), *Language and Symbolic Power*, Cambridge: Polity Press.

Bourdieu, P. (1984), *Distinction: A Social Critique of The Judgment of Taste*, London: Routledge and Kegan Paul.

Bourdieu, P. (1986), 'The forms of capital', in Richardson, J.G. (ed.), *Handbook of Theory and Research for the Sociology of Education*, New York: Greenwood Press, pp. 241–58.

Bourdieu, P. and Wacquant, L. (1992), *An Invitation to Reflexive Sociology*, Chicago: Chicago University Press.

Bowling, A. (1991), *Measuring Health: A Review of Quality of Life Measurement Scales*, Milton Keynes: Open University Press.

Bowling, A. (1994), 'Social networks and social support among older people and implications for emotional well-being and psychiatric well-being', *International Review of Psychiatry*, **6**, pp. 41–58.

Bowling, A. and Grundy, E. (1998), 'The association between social networks and mortality in later life', *Reviews in Clinical Gerontology*, **8**, pp. 353–61.

Bozon, M. (1991), 'Women and the age gap between spouses: An accepted domination?', *Population*, **3**, pp. 113–48.

Bradshaw, J., Williams, J., Levitas, R., Pantazis, C., Patsios, D., Townsend, P., Gordon, D. and Middleton, S. (2000), 'The relationship between poverty and social exclusion in Britain', Paper presented to 26th General Conference of International Association for Research in Income and Wealth, Cracow, 27 August to 2 September, 2000.

Bridge, G. (1995), 'Gentrification, class and community: A social network approach', in A. Rogers and A. Vertovec (eds), *The Urban Context*, Oxford: Berg.

Broese van Groenou, M. (1991), *Gescheiden Netwerken: De Relaties met Vrienden en Verwanten na Echtscheiding* [*Separate Networks: The Relationships with Friends and Kin after Divorce*], unpublished dissertation, University of Utrecht.

Broese van Groenou, M., van Tilburg, T. G., Leeuw, E. de, and Liefbroer, A.C. (1985), 'Appendix: Data collection', in C. Knipscheer, J. de Jong Gierveld, T.G. van Tilburg and P.A. Dykstra (eds), *Living Arrangements and Social Networks of Older Adults*, Amsterdam: VU University Press, pp. 185–97.

Brown, G.W., and Harris, T. (1978), *Social Origins of Depression*, London: Tavistock.

Buchmann, M. (1989), *The Script of Life in Modern Society: Entry into Adulthood in a Changing World*, Chicago: University of Chicago Press.

Bulmer, M. (1986), *Neighbours: The Work of Philip Abrams*, Cambridge University Press.

Bulmer, M. (1987), *The Social Basis of Community Care*, London: Allen & Unwin.

Burchardt, T. (2000), 'Social exclusion: Concepts and evidence', in D. Gordon and P. Townsend (eds), *Breadline Europe: The Measurement of Poverty*, Bristol: Policy Press.

Burchardt, T., Le Grand, J. and Piachaud, D. (1999), 'Social exclusion in Britain 1991–1995', *Social Policy and Administration*, **33**, pp. 227–44.

Burgess, R.J. and Huston, T.L. (eds) (1979), *Social Exchange In Developing Relationships*, New York: Academic Press.

Burns, D., Williams, C. and Windebank, J. (forthcoming) *Mutual Aid and Self-help*, London: Palgrave.

Burns, D. and Taylor, M. (1998), *Mutual Aid and Self-help: Coping Strategies For Excluded Communities*, Bristol: Policy Press.

Burt, R.S. (1992), *Structural Holes: The Social Structure of Competition*, Chicago: University of Chicago Press.

Burt, R.S. (1997), 'The contingent value of social capital', *Administrative Science Quarterly*, **42**, pp. 339–65.

Burt, R.S. (2001), 'Structural holes versus network closure as social capital', in N. Lin, K. Cook and R.S. Burt (eds), *Social Capital: Theory and Research*, New York: Aldine de Gruyter.

Byrne, D. (1999), *Social Exclusion*, Buckingham: Open University Press.

Cabinet Office (2001), *The National Strategy for Neighbourhood Renewal*, London: Cabinet Office.

Campbell, C., Wood, R. and Kelly, M. (1999), *Social Capital and Health*, London: Health Education Authority.

Caplan, G. (1974), *Support Systems and Community Mental Health: Lectures on Concept Development*, New York: Behavioral Publications.

Carley, M. and Smith, H. (2001), 'Civil society and new social movements', in M. Carley, P. Jenkins and H. Smith (eds), *Urban Development and Civil Society: The Role of Communities in Sustainable Cities*, London: Earthscan.

Carstensen, L. (1992), 'Social and emotional patterns in adulthood: Support for socioemotional selectivity theory', *Psychology And Aging*, **7**, pp. 331–38.

Carter, N., Klein, R. and Day, P. (1993), *How Organisations Measure Success: The Use of Performance Indicators in Government*, Routledge: London.

Cassel, J. (1976), 'The contribution of the social environment to host resistance', *Americal Journal of Epidemiology*, **104**, pp. 107–23.

Castells, M. (1996), *The Rise of the Network Society*, Oxford: Blackwell.

Cattell, R. (1966), 'The meaning and strategic use of factor analysis', in R. Cattell (ed.), *Handbook of Multivariate Experimental Psychology* Chicago: Rand McNally.

Cattell, V. (1995), *Community, Equality and Health; Positive Communities for Positive Health and Well Being?*, London: Middlesex University, School of Sociology and Social Policy Occasional Paper.

Cattell, V. (1997), *London's Other River: People, Employment and Poverty in the Lea Valley*, London: Middlesex University, Social Policy Research Centre.

Cattell, V. (1998), 'Poverty, community and health: social networks as mediators between poverty and well being', unpublished PhD thesis, University of Middlesex.

Cattell, V. and Evans, M. (1999), *Neighbourhood Images in East London: Social Capital and Social Networks on Two East London Estates*, York: Joseph Rowntree Foundation/York Publishing Services.

Cattell, V. and Herring, R. (2002a), 'Social capital, generations and health in East London', in C. Swann and A. Morgan, A. (eds), *Social Capital for Health: Insights from Qualitative Research*, London: Health Development Agency.

Cattell, V. and Herring, R. (2002b), 'Social capital and well-being: Generations in an East London neighbourhood', *Journal of Mental Health Promotion*, **1**, pp. 8–19.

Ceria, C., Masaki, K., Rodriguez, B., Chen, R., Yano, K. and Curb, J. (2001), 'The relationship of psychosocial factors to total mortality among older Japanese-American men: The Honolulu Heart Program', *Journal of American Geriatrics Society*, **49**, pp. 725–31.

Challis, L., Fuller, S., Henwood, M., Klein, R., Plowden, W., Webb, A., Whittingham, P. and Wistow, G. (1988), *Joint Approaches to Social Policy: Rationality and Practice*, Cambridge: Cambridge University Press.

Chaney, P. (2000) 'Social capital and community development', *Scottish Journal of Community Work and Development*, **6**, pp. 51–8.

Chappell, N. (1991), 'The role of family and friends in quality of life' in J. Birren, J. Lubben, J. Rowe and D. Deutchman (eds), *The Concept and Measurement of Quality of Life in the Frail Elderly*, New York: Academic Press.

Chappell, N. and Badger, M. (1989), 'Social isolation and well-being', *Journal of Gerontology: Social Sciences*, **44**, S169–76.

Charlton, J. (1998), *Nothing About Us Without Us: Disability, Oppression and Empowerment*, Berkeley: University of California Press.

Cheal, D. (2002), *Sociology of Family Life*, Basingstoke: Palgrave.

Cherlin, A. (1980), 'Changing family and household: Contemporary lessons from historical research', *Annual Review of Sociology*, **9**, pp. 51–66.

Chipperfield, J.G. and Havens, B. (2001), 'Gender differences in the relationship between marital status transitions and life satisfaction in later life', *Journal of Gerontology: Psychological Sciences*, **56B**, pp. 176–86.

Chodorow, N. (1978), *The Reproduction of Mothering: Psychoanalysis and the Sociology of Gender*, Berkeley: University of California Press.

Chou, K. and Chi, I. (1999), 'Determinants of life satisfaction in Hong Kong Chinese elderly: A longitudinal study', *Aging and Mental Health*, **3**, pp. 328–35.

Clarkberg, M., Stoltzenberg, R. and Waite, L. (1995), 'Attitudes, values and entrance into cohabitational versus marital unions', *Social Forces*, **77**, pp. 945–68.

Clegg, S. (1989), *Frameworks of Power*, London: Sage.

Cobb, S. (1976), 'Social support as a moderator of life stress', *Psychosomatic Medicine*, **38**, pp. 300–14.

Cochran, M., Larner, M., Riley, D., Gunnarsson, L. and Henderson, C. (1990), *Extending Families: The Social Networks of Parents and Their Children*, Cambridge; Cambridge University Press.

Cohen, R., Coxall, J., Graig, G. and Sadiq-Sangster, A. (1992), *Hardship Britain: Being Poor in the 1990s*, London: Child Poverty Action Group.

Cohen, S. (2001), 'Social relationships and susceptibility to the common cold', in C. Ryff and B. Singer (eds), *Emotion, Social Relationships and Health*, New York: Oxford, pp. 221–32.

Cohen, S., Doyle, W.J., Skoner, D.P., Rabin, B.S. and Gwaltney, J.M. (1997), 'Social ties and susceptibility to the common cold', *Journal of the American Medical Association*, **277**, pp. 1940–44.

Cohen, S. and Syme, S. (1985), *Social Support and Health*, Orlando, Fla: Academic Press.

Cohn, S., Underwood, L. and Gottlieb, B.H. (2000), *Social Support Measurement and Intervention*, New York: Oxford University Press.

Coleman, J.S. (1988), 'Social capital and the creation of human capital', *American Journal of Sociology*, **94**, pp. 95–120.

Coleman, J.S. (1990), *Foundations of Social Theory*, Harvard: Harvard University Press.

Cooney, T. and Dunne, K. (2001), 'Intimate relationships in later life: Current realities, future prospects', *Journal of Family Issues*, **22**, pp. 838–58.

Cooper, H., Arber, S., Fee, L. and Ginn, J. (1999), *The Influence of Social Support and Social Capital on Health*, London: Health Education Authority.

Cornwell, J. (1984), *Hard Earned Lives: Accounts of Health and Illness from East London*, London: Tavistock.

Coyle, D.J. and Ellis, R.J. (eds) (1993), *Politics, Policy and Culture*, Boulder, Co.: Westview.

Crohan, S. and Antonucci, T. (1989), 'Friends as a source of social support in old age', in R. Adams and R. Blieszner (eds), *Older Adult Friendship: Structure and Process*, Beverly Hills: Sage.

Cronbach, L. (1951), 'Coefficient alpha and the internal structure of tests', *Psychometrika*, **16**, pp. 297–334.

Crow, G. (1999), 'Sociology and the discovery of society's hidden dimensions', *Self, Agency and Society*, **2**, pp. 1–22.

Crow, G. (2000), 'Developing sociological arguments through community studies', *Social Research Methodology*, **3**, pp. 173–87.

Crow, G. (2002), *Social Solidarities: Theories, Identities and Social Change*, Buckingham: Open University Press.

Crow, G. and Allan, G. (1994), *Community Life: An Introduction to Local Social Relations*, Hemel Hempstead: Harvester Wheatsheaf.

Cutrona, C. and Russell, D. (1986), 'Social support and adaptation to stress by the elderly', *Psychology of Aging*, **1**, pp. 47–54.

Dalley, G. (1988), *Ideologies of Caring: Rethinking Community and Collectivism*, Basingstoke: Macmillan.

Dannefer, D. (1996), 'The social organization of diversity and the normative organization of age', *The Gerontologist*, **36**, pp. 174–7.

Davies, J. (ed.) (1993), *The Family: Is It Just Another Lifestyle Choice?*, London: Institute of Economic Affairs.

Davis, K. and Todd, M. (1985), 'Assessing friendship: prototypes, paradigm cases and relationship description', in S. Duck and D. Perlman (eds), *Understanding Personal Relationships*, London: Sage.

de Jong Gierveld, J. (1969), *De Ongehuwden [The Unmarried]*, Alphen a/d Rijn: Samson.

de Jong Gierveld, J. (1998), 'A review of loneliness: Concepts and definitions, determinants and consequences', *Reviews in Clinical Gerontology*, **8**, pp. 73–80.

de Jong Gierveld, J. (2000), *Tussen Solitude en Solidariteit: Nieuwe Levensstrategieën van Senioren [Between solitude and solidarity: New life strategies for seniors]*, Mededelingen van de Afdeling Letterkunde, Nieuwe Reeks, Deel 62, no. 8, Amsterdam: Koninklijke Nederlandse Akademie van Wetenschappen.

de Jong Gierveld, J. and Dykstra, P. (1994), 'Life transitions and the network of personal relationships: Theoretical and methodological issues', in D. Perlman and W.H. Jones (eds), *Advances in Personal Relationships*, Vol. 4, London: Jessica Kingsley.

de Jong Gierveld, J. and Kamphuis, F. (1985), 'The development of a Rasch-type loneliness scale', *Applied Psychological Measurement*, **9**, pp. 289–99.

de Jong Gierveld, J. and van Tilburg, T. (1999), *Manual of the Loneliness Scale 1999*, Amsterdam: Department of Social Research Methodology, Free University of Amsterdam (updated version 18.01.02).

DeVellis, R. (1991), *Scale Development: Theory and Applications*, Newbury Park: Sage.

Degenne, A. and Forsé, M. (1999), *Introducing Social Networks*, London: Sage.

Dennis, N. and Erdos, G. (1992), *Families Without Fatherhood*, London: Institute of Economic Affairs.

Department of Health (2001), *Tackling Health Inequalities: Consultation on a Plan for Delivery*, London: Department of Health.

DETR (1998), *Updating and Revising the Index of Local Deprivation*, London: Department of the Environment, Transport and the Regions.

DETR (2000a), *Housing Green Paper*, London: Department of the Environment, Transport and the Regions.

DETR (2000b), *Policy and Planning Guidance 3 on Housing* to be found at: http://www.planning.odpm.gov.uk/ppg3/index.htm.

Dicks, B., Waddington, D. and Critcher, C. (1998), 'Redundant men and overburdened women: Local service providers and the construction of gender in ex-mining communities', in J. Popay, J. Hearn and J. Edwards (eds), *Men, Gender Divisions and Welfare*, London: Routledge.

Dorfman, R., Lubben, J., Mayer-Oakes, A., Atchison, K., Schweitzer, S., Dejong, J. and Matthais, R. (1995), 'Screening for depression among a well elderly population', *Social Work*, **40**, pp. 295–304.

Dorling, D. (1997), *Death in Britain: How Local Mortality Rates have Changed 1950s to 1990s*, York: Joseph Rowntree Foundation.

Douglas, D. (1985), *Creative Interviewing*, London: Sage.

Douglas, M. (1970), *Natural Symbols: Explorations in Cosmology*, London: Routledge.

Douglas, M. (ed.) (1982a), *Essays in the Sociology of Perception*, London: Routledge & Kegan Paul.

Douglas, M. (1982b), 'Cultural bias', in M. Douglas (ed.), *In the Active Voice*, London: Routledge & Kegan Paul.

Douglas, M. (1986), *How Institutions Think*, London: Routledge & Kegan Paul.

Douglas, M. (1992), *Risk and Blame: Essays in Cultural Theory*, London: Routledge.

Douglas, M. and Ney, S. (1998), *Missing Persons: A Critique of Personhood in the Social Sciences*, Berkeley, Cal.: University of California Press.

Douglas, M., Ard-am, O. and Kim, I. (2002), 'Urban poverty and the environment: social capital and state-community synergy in Seoul and Bangkok', in P. Evans (ed.), *Liveable Cities? Urban Struggles for Livelihood and Sustainability*, Berkeley: University of California Press.

Duncan, S. and Edwards, R. (1999), *Lone Mothers, Paid Work and Gendered Moral Rationalities*, Basingstoke: Macmillan.

Durkheim, E. (1933), *Division of Labour in Society*, New York: Free Press.

Durkheim, E. (1951), *Suicide: A Study in Sociology*, London: Routledge.

Durkheim, E. (1961), *Moral Education*, New York: Free Press.

Dykstra, P.A. (1993), 'The differential availability of relationships and the provision and effectiveness of support to older adults', *Journal of Social and Personal Relationships*, **10**, pp. 355–70.

Dykstra, P.A. (1995), 'Loneliness among the never and formerly married: The importance of supportive friendships and a desire for independence', *Journals of Gerontology, Social Sciences*, **50b**, S321–9.

Dykstra, P.A., and de Jong Gierveld, J. (2002), 'Gender differences in Dutch older adult loneliness' (under review).

Ell, K. (1984), 'Social networks, social support, and health status: A review', *Social Service Review*, **58**, pp. 133–49.

Ellis, R. and Thompson, M. (eds) (1997), *Culture Matters: Essays in Honour of Aaron Wildavsky*, Boulder: Westview.

Erwin, P. (1998), *Friendship in Childhood and Adolescence*, London: Routledge.

ESRC (2002), to be found at:
http://www.esrc.ac.uk/esrccontent/aboutesrc/public_awareness.asp.

Essex, M. and Nam, S. (1987), 'Marital status and loneliness among older women: The differential importance of close family and friends', *Journal of Marriage and the Family*, **49**, pp. 93–106.

Etzioni, A. (1993a), *The Parenting Deficit*, London: Demos.

Etzioni, A. (1993b), *The Spirit of Community: Rights, Responsibilities and the Communitarian Agenda*, London: HarperCollins.

Etzioni, A. (1996), *The New Golden Rule: Community and Morality in a Democratic Society*, New York: Basic Books.

Evandrou, M. (2000), 'Social inequalities in later life: The socio-economic position of older people from ethnic minority groups in Britain', *Population Trends*, Autumn, pp. 11–18.

Faith in the City: The Report of the Archbishop of Canterbury's Commission on Urban Priority Areas (1985), London: Church House.

Fardon, R. (1999), *Mary Douglas: An Intellectual Biography*, London: Routledge.

Fast, J., Derksen, L., Keating, N. and Otfinowski, P. (forthcoming), 'Characteristics of informal care networks of frail seniors', *Canadian Journal of Aging*.

Featherstone, M. (1991), *Consumer Culture and Postmodernism*, London: Sage.

Felton, B. and Berry, C. (1992), 'Do the sources of the urban elderly's social support determine its psychological consequences?', *Psychology and Aging*, **7**, pp. 89–97.

Finkelstein, J. (1989), *Dining Out: A Sociology of Modern Manners*, Cambridge: Polity.

Fischer, C.S. (1982), *To Dwell Among Friends*, Chicago: University of Chicago Press.

Fiske, A. (1991), *Structures of Social Life*, New York: Free Press.

Flyvbjerg, B. (1998), 'Empowering civil society', in M. Douglass and J. Friedmann (eds), *Cities for Citizens: Planning and the Rise of Civil Society in a Global Age*, Chichester: Wiley & Sons.

Foley, M.W. and Edwards, B. (1998), 'Beyond Tocqueville, civil society and social capital in comparative perspective', *American Behavioral Scientist*, **42**, 5–20.

Forrest, R. and Kearns, A. (1999), *Joined-up Places? Social Cohesion and Neighbourhood Regeneration*, York: Joseph Rowntree Foundation.

Forrest, R. and Kearns, A. (2001), 'Social cohesion, social capital and the neighbourhood', *Urban Studies*, **38**, pp. 2125–43.

Foster, J. (1999), *Docklands: Cultures in Conflict, Worlds in Collision*, London: UCL Press.

Francis, D. (1984), *Will You Still Need Me, Will You Still Feed Me, When I'm 84?*, Bloomington: Indiana University Press.

Francis, D. (1991), 'Friends from the work place', in B. Hess and E. Markson (eds), *Growing Old in America*, 4th edn, New Brunswick, NJ: Transaction Publishers.

Frankenberg, R. (1966), *Communities in Britain: Social Life in Town and Country*, Harmondsworth: Penguin.

Fukuyama, F. (1995), *Trust: The Social Virtues and the Creation of Prosperity*, New York: Free Press.

Gans, H. (1962), *The Urban Villagers*, New York: Free Press.

Gardner, K. (2002), *Age, Narrative and Migration*, Oxford: Berg Publishers.

Gekas, V. (1989), 'The social psychology of self-efficacy', *Annual Review of Sociology*, **15**, pp. 291–316.

George, L. (1996), 'Missing links: The case for a social psychology of the life course', *The Gerontologist*, **36**, pp. 48–255.

Giddens, A. (1984), *The Constitution of Society*, Cambridge: Polity Press.

Giddens, A. (1991), *Modernity and Self Identity*, Cambridge: Polity Press.

Gilchrist, A. (2000), 'The well-connected community: Networking to the edge of chaos', *Community Development Journal*, **35**, pp. 264–75.

Gilchrist, A. (2001) *Strength through Diversity: Networking for Community Development*, PhD thesis, University of Bristol.

Gilchrist, A. (2003) 'Networking for health and social capital', in M. Grey, A, Harrison, J. Orme, J. Powell and P. Taylor (eds), *Public Health for the 21st Century: New Perspectives on Policy, Participation and Practice*, Buckingham: Open University Press.

Gillies, V., Ribbens McCarthy, J. and Holland, J. (2001), *Pulling Together, Pulling Apart: The Family Lives of Young People*, London: Joseph Rowntree Foundation/ Family Policy Studies Centre.

Gilligan, C. (1982), *In a Different Voice*, Cambridge, Massachusetts: Harvard University Press.

Gironda, M and Lubben, J. (2003), 'Preventing loneliness and isolation in older adulthood', in T. Gullotta and M. Bloom (eds), *Encyclopedia of Primary Prevention and Health Promotion*, New York: Kluwer Academic/Plenum Publishers.

Gironda, M., Lubben, J. and Atchison, K. (1999), 'Social support networks of elders without children', *Journal of Gerontological Social Work*, **27**, pp. 63–84.

Glass, T., Mendes de Leon, C., Seeman, T. and Berkman, L. (1997), 'Beyond single indicators of social networks: A LISREL analysis of social ties among the elderly', *Social Science and Medicine*, **44**, pp.1503–7.

Glennerster, H., Lupton, R., Noden, P. and Power, A. (1999), *Poverty, Social Exclusion and Neighbourhood: Studying the Area Bases*, London: CASE paper 22, Centre for Analysis of Social Exclusion, London School of Economics.

Glick, P.C. and Norton, A.I. (1977), 'Marrying, divorcing, and living together in the US today', *Population Bulletin*, **32**, 5.

Gordon, D., Adelman, L., Ashworth, K., Bradshaw, J., Levitas, R., Middleton, R., Pantazis, C., Patsios, D., Payne, S., Townsend, P. and Williams, J. (2000), *Poverty and Social Exclusion in Britain*, York: Joseph Rowntree Foundation.

Gove, W.R. and Shin, H.-C. (1989), 'The psychological well-being of divorced and widowed men and women: An empirical analysis', *Journal of Family Issues*, **11**, pp. 4–35.

Gove, W., Style, C. and Hughes, M. (1990), 'The effect of marriage on the well-being of older adults: A theoretical analysis', *Journal of Family Issues*, **11**, pp. 4–35.

Graham, H. (1993), *Hardship and Health in Women's Lives*, Hemel Hempsead: Harvester Wheatsheaf.

Graham, H. (ed.) (2000), *Understanding Health Inequalities*, Buckingham: Open University Press.

Granovetter, M. (1973), 'The strength of weak ties', *American Journal of Sociology*, **78**, pp. 1360–80.

Granovetter, M. (1982), 'The strength of weak ties: A network theory revisited', in P. Marsden and N. Lin (eds), *Social Structure And Network Analysis*, Beverly Hills: Sage.

Granovetter, M. (1995a), *Getting A Job: A Study of Contacts and Careers*, 2nd edn, Chicago: University of Chicago Press.

Granovetter, M. (1995b), 'Afterword 1994: Reconsiderations and a new agenda', in M. Granovetter (ed.) (1995a), *Getting A Job: A Study of Contacts and Careers*, 2nd edn, Chicago: University of Chicago Press.

Grieco, M. (1987), *Keeping It in the Family: Social Networks and Employment Changes*, London: Tavistock.

Griffiths, V. (1995), *Adolescent Girls and their Friends: Feminist Ethnography*, Aldershot: Avebury.

Gross, J. and Rayner, S. (1985), *Measuring Culture: A Paradigm for the Analysis of Social Organisation*, New York: Columbia University Press.

Guadagnoli, E. and Velicer, W. (1988), 'Relation of sample size to the stability of component patterns', *Psychological Bulletin*, **103**, pp. 265–75.

Gubrium, J.F. (1974), 'Marital desolation and the evaluation of everyday life in old age', *Journal of Marriage and the Family*, **36**, pp. 107–13.

Hagestad, G. and Neugarten, B. (1985), 'Age and the life course', in R. Binstock and E. Shana (eds), *Handbook of Aging and the Social Sciences* (Vol. 2), New York: Van Nostrand Reinhold.

Hall, P. (1999), 'Social capital in Britain', *British Journal of Political Science*, **29**, pp. 417–61.

Hareven, T.K. (1977), 'Historical time and family time', *Daedalus*, **106**, pp. 57–70.

Hareven, T.K. (1986), 'Historical changes in the social construction of the life course', *Human Development*, **29**, pp. 171–80.

Hareven, T.K. (2000), *Families, History and Social Change: Life-Course and Cross-cultural Perspectives*, Boulder: Westview.

Harris, C.C. (1987), *Redundancy and Recession in South Wales*, Oxford: Basil Blackwell.

Harvey, M., McMeekin, A., Randles, S., Southerton, D., Tether, B. and Warde, A. (2001), 'Between demand and consumption: A framework for research', *CRIC Discussion Paper No. 40*, The University of Manchester and UMIST.

Heer, W. de (1992), *International Survey on Non-response*, Netherlands Central Bureau of Statistics.

Heitzmann, C.A. and Kaplan, R.M. (1988), 'Assessment of methods for measuring social support', *Health Psychology*, **7**, pp. 75–109.

Held, T. (1986), 'Institutionalization and deinstitutionalization of the life course', *Human Development*, **29**, pp. 157–62.

Hey, V. (1997), *The Company She Keeps: An Ethnography of Girls' Friendships*, Buckingham: Open University Press.

Hill, M. and Hupe, P. (2002), *Implementing Public Policy*, London: Sage.

Hills, J., Le Grand, J. and Piachaud, D. (eds) (2002), *Understanding Social Exclusion*, Oxford: Oxford University Press.

Hirsch, B.J. (1981), 'Social networks and the coping process: creating personal communities', in B. Gottlieb (ed.), *Social Networks and Social Support*, Beverly Hills: Sage.

Hirsch, B., Engel-Levy, A., Du Bois, D. and Hardesty, P. (1990), 'The role of social environments in social support', in B. Sarason, I. Sarason and G. Pierce (eds), *Social Support: An Interactional View*, New York: Wiley.

Hirschman, A.O. (1982), *Shifting Involvements: Private Interest and Public Action*, Oxford: Blackwell.

Ho, C. (1991), *Salt-water Trinnies: Afro-Trinidadian Immigrant Networks and Non-assimilation in Los Angeles*, New York: AMS Press.

Hoch, C. and Hemmens, G. (1987), 'Lining formal and informal help: conflict along the continuum of care', *Social Service Review*, September, pp. 432–46.

Hochschild, A. (2001), 'Global care chains and emotional surplus value', in W. Hutton and A. Giddens (eds), *On The Edge: Living with Global Capitalism*, London: Vintage.

Hoggett, P. (ed.), *Contested Communities: Experience, Struggles and Policies*, Bristol: The Policy Press.

Home Office (2001a), *Policing a New Century*, London: Home Office.

Home Office (2001b), *A Report of the Independent Review Team* (chaired by Ted Cantle), London: Home Office.

Home Office (2001c), *Building Cohesive Communities: A Report of the Ministerial Group on Public Order and Community Cohesion*, London: Home Office.

Home Office (2002), *Crime in England*, London: Home Office.

Hood, C.C. (1983), *The Tools of Government*, Basingstoke: Macmillan.

Hooyman, N.R. and Kiyak, H.A. (1999), *Social Gerontology: A Multidisciplinary Perspective*, Needham Heights, Mass.: Allyn and Bacon, Inc.

House, J. (2001), 'Social isolation kills, but how and why?', *Psychosomatic Medicine*, **63**, pp. 273–4.

House, J. and Kahn, R. (1985), 'Measures and concepts of social support', in S. Cohen and L. Syme (eds), *Social Support and Health*, New York: Academic Press.

House, J., Landis, K. and Umberson, D. (1988), 'Social relationships and health', *Science*, **241**, pp. 540–45.

Howarth, C., Kenway, P., Palmer, G. and Miorelli, R. (1999), *Monitoring Poverty and Social Exclusion 1999*, York: Joseph Rowntree Foundation.

Hurlbert, J. and Acock, A. (1990), 'The effects of marital status on the form and composition of social networks', *Social Science Quarterly*, **71**, pp. 163–74.

Hurwicz, M.L. and Berkanovic, E. (1993), 'The stress process of rheumatoid arthritis', *Journal of Rheumatology*, **20**, pp. 1836–44.

Hutson, S. and Clapham, D. (eds) (1999), *Homelessness: Public Policies and Private Troubles*, London: Continuum.

Jacobs, J. (1962), *The Death and Life of Great American Cities*, London: Jonathan Cape.

James, A. (1993), *Childhood Identities: Self and Social Relationships in the Experience of the Child*, Edinburgh: Edinburgh University Press.

James, A. and Prout, A. (1997), *Constructing and Reconstructing Childhood*, 2nd edn, London: Falmer Press.

Jamieson, L. (1998), *Intimacy: Personal Relationships In Modern Societies*, Cambridge: Polity Press.

Jervis, R. (1997), *System Effects: Complexity in Political and Social Life*, Princeton: Princeton University Press.

Jung, J. (1990), 'The role of reciprocity in social support', *Basic and Applied Social Psychology*, **11**, pp. 243–53.

Kahn, R. and Antonucci, T. (1980), 'Convoys over the life course: Attachment, roles and social support', in P. Baltes and O. Brim, *Life Span Development and Behaviour*, Vol. 3, New York: Academic Press.

Kaiser, H.F. (1960), 'The application of electronic computers to factor analysis', *Educational and Psychological Measurement*, **20**, pp. 141–51.

Kaplan, G.A., Seeman, T.E., Cohen, R.D., Knudsen, L.P., and Guralnik, J. (1987), 'Mortality among the elderly in the Alameda County study: Behavioral and demographic risk factors', *American Journal of Public Health*, **77**, pp. 307–12.

Karney, B. and Bradbury, T. (1995) 'The longitudinal course of marriage quality and stability: A review of theory, method and research', *Psychological Bulletin*, **118**, pp. 3–34.

Kawachi, I., and Kennedy, B. (1997), 'Socioeconomic determinants of health. Health and social cohesion: Why care about income inequality?', *British Medical Journal*, **314**, pp. 1037–40.

Kawachi, I., Kennedy, B.P., Lochner, K. and Prothrow-Smith, D. (1997), 'Social capital, income inequality, and mortality', *American of Journal of Public Health*, **87**, pp. 1491–8.

Keating, N., Fast. J., Forbes, D. and Wenger, C. (2002), *Informal Care Networks of Canadian Seniors with Long-Term Health Problems*, Final Report submitted to the National Health Research and Development Programe, Canada.

Keating, N., Otfinowski, P., Wenger, C., Fast, J., Derksen, L. (2003), 'Understanding the caring capacity of informal networks of frail seniors: A case for care networks', *Ageing in Society*, **23**, pp. 115–27.

Keilman, N. (1988), 'Dynamic household models', in N. Keilman, A. Kujisten, and A. Vossen (eds), *Modelling Household Formation and Dissolution*, Oxford: Clarendon Press.

Keith, P.M., Hill, K., Goudy, W.J., and Power, E.A. (1984), 'Confidants and well-being: A note on male friendship in old age', *The Gerontologist*, **24**, pp. 318–20.

Kelsey, K., Earp, J.L. and Kirkley, B.G. (1997), 'Is social support beneficial for dietary change? A review of the literature', *Family and Community Health*, **20**, pp. 70–82.

Kendig, H. (ed.) (1986), *Ageing and Families*, Sydney: Allen & Unwin.

King, D. (1998), 'The politics of social research: Institutionalizing public funding regimes in the United States and Britain', *British Journal of Political Science*, **28**, pp. 415–44.

Knipscheer, K., de Jong Gierveld, J., van Tilburg, T. and Dykstra, P. (eds) (1995), *Living Arrangements and Social Networks of Older Adults*, Amsterdam: VU University Press.

Knoke, D. and Kuklinski, J. (1991), 'Network analysis: Basic concepts', in G. Thompson, J. Frances, R. Levaèiæ and J. Mitchell. (eds), *Markets, Hierarchies and Networks: The Coordination of Social Life*, London: Sage.

Kohli, M. (1986), 'The world we forgot: A historical review of the life course', in V. Marshall (ed.), *Later Life: The Social Psychology of Aging*, Beverly Hills: Sage, pp. 271–303.

Kohli, M. and Rein, M. (1991), 'The changing balance of work and retirement', in M. Kohli, M. Rein, A.-M. Guillemard and H. van Gunsteren (eds), *Time for Retirement: Comparative Studies of Early Exit from the Labor Force*, New York: Cambridge University Press.

Kohn, M. and Schooler, C. (1983), *Work and Personality: An Inquiry into the Impact of Social Stratification*, New Jersey: Norwood.

Kohn, M. and Slomczynski, K. (1990), *Social Structure and Self-Direction: A Comparative Analysis of the United States and Poland*, Oxford: Blackwell.

Krause, N., Herzog, A. and Baker, E. (1992), 'Providing support to others and well-being in late life', *Journal of Gerontology: Psychological Sciences*, **47**, pp. 300–11.

Krause, N. and Jay, G. (1991), 'Stress, social support, and negative interaction in later life', *Research On Aging*, **13**, pp. 333–63.

Kropotkin, P. (1904), *Mutual Aid: A Factor of Evolution*, London: Heinemann.

Kuijsten, A. (1999), 'Households, families and kin networks', in L. van Wissen, and P. Dykstra (eds), *Population Issues: An Interdisciplinary Focus*, New York: Plenum Press.

Lamont, M. (1992), *Money, Morals and Manners: The Culture of the French and American Upper-Middle Class*, London: Chicago Press.

Lang, F. and Cartensen, L. (1994), 'Close emotional relationships in later life: Further support for proactive aging in the social domain', *Psychology and Aging*, **9**, pp. 315–24.

Larson, R., Mannell, R. and Zuzanek, J. (1986), 'Daily well-being of older adults with friends and family', *Psychology and Aging*, **1**, pp. 117–26.

Lees, R. and Smith, G. (1975), *Action Research in Community Development*, London: Routledge & Kegan Paul.

Leisering, L. and Walker, R. (eds) (1998), *The Dynamics of Modern Society*, Bristol: Policy Press.

Lesthaeghe, R. and Moors, G. (2002), 'Life course transitions and value orientations: Selection and adaptation', in R. Lesthaeghe (ed.), *Meaning and Choice: Value Orientations and Life Course Decisions*, The Hague/Brussels: NIDI CBGS Publications.

Lesthaeghe, R. and Surkyn, J. (1988), 'Cultural dynamics and economic theories of fertility change', *Population and Development Review*, **14**, pp. 1–45.

Levin, C. (2000), 'Social function', in R.L. Kane and R.A. Kane (eds), *Assessing Older Persons: Measures, Meaning, and Practical Applications*, Oxford: Oxford University Press.

Levitas, R. (1998), *The Inclusive Society? Social Exclusion and New Labour*, Basingstoke: Macmillan.

Leyton, E. (ed.) (1974), *The Compact: Selected Dimensions of Friendship*, Newfoundland: Institute of Social and Economic Research, Memorial University of Newfoundland.

Liefbroer, A. and Dykstra, P. (2000), *Levenslopen in Verandering: Een Studie naar Ontwikkelingen in de Levenslopen van Nederlanders Geboren tussen 1900 en 1970* [*Changing Lives: A Study on Developments in the Life Courses of the Dutch 1900–1970 Birth Cohorts*], WRR Voorstudies en achtergronden V 107, Den Haag: Sdu Uitgevers.

Lin, N., Ye, X. and Ensel, W. (1999), 'Social support and depressed mood: A structural analysis', *Journal of Health and Social Behavior*, **40**, pp. 344–59.

Lindblom, C.E. (1959), 'The science of muddling through', *Public Administration Review*, **19**, pp. 78–88.

Lindblom, C.E. (1979), 'Still muddling, not yet through', *Public Administration Review*, **39**, November/December, pp. 517–26.

Lindblom, C.E. and Cohen, D. (1979), *Useful Knowledge: Social Science and Social Problem Solving*, New Haven, Conn.: Yale University Press.

Litwak, E. (1960), 'Occupational mobility and extended family cohesion', *American Sociological Review*, **25**, pp. 9–21.

Litwak, E. (1985), *Helping the Elderly: The Complementary Roles of Informal Networks and Formal Systems*, New York: The Guilford Press.

Lockwood, D. (1966), 'Sources of variation in working class images of society', *Sociological Review*, **14**, pp. 249–67.

Loney, M. (1983), *Community Against Government: The British Community Development Project 1968–78 – A Study of Government Incompetence*, London: Heinemann.

Lopata, H.Z. (1979), *Women as Widows: Support Systems*, New York: Elsevier.

Lowenthal, M.F. and Haven, C. (1968), 'Interaction and adaptation: Intimacy as a critical variable', *American Sociological Review*, **33**, pp. 20–30.

Lowndes, V., Stoker, G., Pratchett, L., Leach, S. and Wingfield, M. (1998), *Enhancing Public Participation in Local Government*, London: Department of the Environment, Transport and the Regions.

Lubben, J. (1988), 'Assessing social networks among elderly populations', *Family Community Health*, **11**, pp. 42–52.

Lubben, J. and Gironda, M. (1997), 'Assessing social support networks among older people in the United States', in H. Litwin (ed.), *The Social Networks of Older People*, Westport, Conn.: Greenwood.

Lubben, J. and Gironda, M. (2000), 'Social support networks' in D. Osterweil, K. Brummel-Smith and J. Beck (eds), *Comprehensive Geriatric Assessment*, New York: McGraw Hill Publisher.

Lubben, J. and Gironda, M. (2003), 'Centrality of social ties to the health and well-being of older adults', in B. Berkman and L. Harootyan (eds), *Social Work And Health Care in an Aging World: Education, Policy, Practice, and Research*, New York: Springer Publishing Co.

Lubben, J., Gironda, M. and Lee, A. (2002), 'Refinements to the Lubben Social Network Scale: The LSNS-R', *The Behavioral Measurement Letter*, **7**, pp. 2–11.

Lubben, J., Weiler, P. and Chi, I. (1989), 'Health practices of the elderly poor', *American Journal of Public Health*, **79**, pp. 371–4.

Luggen, A. and Rini, A. (1995), 'Assessment of social networks and isolation in community-based elderly men and women', *Geriatric Nursing*, **16**, pp. 179–81.

Lynch, J., Due, P., Muntaner, C., and Davey Smith, G. (2000), 'Social capital: Is it a good investment strategy for public health?', *Journal of Epidemiology and Community Health*, **54**, pp. 404–8.

Macfarlane, A. (1970), *The Family Life of Ralph Josselin, A Seventeenth Century Clergyman*, Cambridge: Cambridge University Press.

Macintyre, S., and Ellaway, A. (2000), 'Ecological approaches: Rediscovering the role of the physical and social environment', in L. Berkman and I. Kawachi (eds), *Social Epidemiology*, Oxford: Oxford University Press.

Macintyre, S., McIver, S. and Sooman, A. (1993), 'Area class and health: Should we be focussing on people or places?', *Journal of Social Policy*, **22**, pp. 213–34.

Mack, M. and Lansley, S. (1985), *Poor Britain*, London: George Allen & Unwin.

Madanipour, A., Cars, G. and Allen, J. (eds) (1998), *Social Exclusion in European Cities: Processes, Experiences and Responses*, London: Jessica Kingsley.

Manting, D. (1994), *Dynamics in Marriage and Cohabitation: An Inter-temporal, Life Course Analysis of First Union Formation and Dissolution*, Amsterdam: Thesis Publishers.

Marcuse, P. (1996), 'Space and race in the post-Fordist city', in E. Mingione (ed.), *Urban Poverty and the Underclass: A Reader*, Oxford: Blackwell.

Marlow, A. and Pitts, J. (eds) (1998), *Planning Safer Communities*, Lyme Regis: Russell House Publishing.

Mars, G. (1982), *Cheats at Work: An Anthropology of Workplace Crime*, 3rd edn, Aldershot: Ashgate.

Mars, G. (1999), 'Criminal social organisation, cultures and vulnerability: An approach from cultural theory', in D. Canter and L. Alison (eds), *The Social Psychology of Crime: Criminal Groups, Teams and Networks*, Aldershot: Ashgate.

Marshall, G. (1990), *In Praise of Sociology*, London: Unwin Hyman.

Martire, L.M., Schulz, R., Mittelmark, M.B. and Newsom, J.T. (1999), 'Stability and change in older adults' social contact and social support: The cardiovascular health study', *Journal of Gerontology: Series B: Psychological and Social Sciences*, **54B**, S302–11.

Mason, J. (1999), 'Living away from relatives: Kinship and geographical reasoning', in S. McRae (ed.), *Changing Britain: Families and Households in the 1990s*, Oxford: Oxford University Press.

Massey, D., Gros, A. and Kumiko, S. (1994), 'Migration and the concentration of poverty', *American Sociological Review*, **59**, pp. 1153–89.

Mayer, A.C. (1966), 'The significance of quasi-groups in the study of complex societies', in M. Banton (ed.), *The Social Anthropology of Complex Societies*, London: Tavistock.

McCallister, L. and Fischer, C. (1978), 'A procedure for surveying personal networks', *Sociological Methods and Research*, **7**, pp. 131–47.

McDowell, I. and Newell, C. (1987), *Measuring Health: A Guide to Rating Scales and Questionnaires*, New York: Oxford University Press.

McIntosh, B. and Whittaker, A. (eds) (1998), *Days of Change: A Practical Guide to Developing Better Day Opportunities with People with Learning Difficulties*, London: King's Fund.

McIntosh, B. and Whittaker, A. (eds) (2000), *Unlocking the Future: Developing New Lifestyles with People Who Have Complex Disabilities*, London: King's Fund.

McLaughlin, S.D., Melber, B.D., Billy, J.O.G., Zimmerle, D.M., Winges, L.D. and Johnson, T.R. (1988), *The Changing Lives of American Women*, Chapel Hill: University of North Carolina Press.

Melucci, A. (1988), 'Social movements and the democratisation of everyday life', in J. Keane (ed.), *Civil Society and the State*, London: Verso.

Merton, R. (1957), *Social Theory and Social Structure*, New York: Free Press.

Milardo, R. (1987), 'Changes in social networks following divorce: A review', *Journal of Family Issues*, **8**, pp. 78–96.

Mill, J.S. (1859), *On Liberty*, reprinted in J.S. Mill (1993), *On Liberty and Other Essays*, Oxford: Oxford University Press.

Miller, E. and Gwynne, G. (1972), *A Life Apart*, London: Tavistock.

Miller, P. and Ingham, J. (1976), 'Friends, confidants and symptoms', *Social Psychiatry*, **11**, pp. 51–7.

Mills, C.W (1970), *The Sociological Imagination*, Harmondsworth: Penguin.

Mistry, R., Rosansky, J., McQuire, J., McDermott, C. and Jarvik, L. (2001), 'Social isolation predicts re-hospitalization in a group of older American veterans enrolled in the UPBEAT program', *International Journal of Geriatric Psychiatry*, **16**, pp. 950–59.

Mitchell, J.C. (ed.) (1969), *Social Networks in Urban Situations*, Manchester University Press.

Mitchell, R. and Trickett, E. (1980), 'Social networks as mediators of social support: An analysis of the effects and determinants of social networks', *Community Mental Health Journal*, **16**, pp. 27–44.

Mitchell, W. and Green, E. (2002), '"I don't know what I'd do without our Mam": Motherhood, identity and support networks', *Sociological Review*, **50**, pp. 1–22.

Modell, J. (1989), *Into One's Own: From Youth to Adulthood in the United States 1920–1975*, Berkeley: University of California Press.

Monks, J. (1999), '"It works both ways": Belonging and social participation among women with disabilities', in N. Yuval-Davis and P. Werbner (eds), *Women, Citizenship and Difference*, London: Zed.

Moon, A., Lubben, J. and Villa, V. (1998), 'Awareness and utilization of community long term care services by elderly Korean and non-Hispanic white Americans', *The Gerontologist*, **38**, pp. 309–16.

Mor-Barak, M. and Miller, L.S. (1991), 'A longitudinal study of the causal relationship between social networks and health of the poor frail elderly', *The Journal of Applied Gerontology*, **10**, pp. 293–310.

Mor-Barak, M., Miller, L. and Syme., L. (1991), 'Social networks, life events, and health of the poor, frail elderly: A longitudinal study of the buffering versus the direct effect', *Family Community Health*, **14**, pp. 1–13.

Mor-Barak, M. (1997), 'Major determinants of social networks in frail elderly community residents', *Home Health Care Service Quarterly*, **16**, pp. 121–37.

Morris, L. (1988), 'Employment, the household and social networks', in D. Gallie (ed.), *Employment in Britain*, Oxford: Blackwell.

Morrow, V. (1994), 'Responsible children? Aspects of children's work and employment outside school in contemporary UK', in B. Mayall (ed.), *Children's Childhoods Observed and Experienced*, London: Falmer Press.

Morrow, V. (1998), *Understanding Families: Children's Perspectives*, London: National Children's Bureau.

Morrow, V. (1999), 'Conceptualising social capital in relation to the well-being of children and young people: A critical review', *Sociological Review*, **47**, pp. 744–65.

Morrow, V. (2000), '"Dirty looks" and "trampy places" in young people's accounts of community and neighbourhood: Implications for health inequalities', *Critical Public Health*, **10**, pp. 141–52.

Morrow, V. (2001a), *Networks and Neighbourhoods: Children's and Young People's Perspectives*, Report for the Health Development Agency Social Capital for Health series, London: Health Development Agency.

Morrow, V. (2001b), 'Using qualitative methods to elicit young people's perspectives on their environments: Some ideas for community health initiatives', *Health Education Research: Theory and Practice*, **16**, pp. 255–68.

Morrow, V. (2001c), Young people's explanations and experiences of social exclusion: Retrieving Bourdieu's concept of social capital', *International Journal of Sociology and Social Policy*, **21**, pp. 37–63.

Mulgan, G. (1997), *Connexity: How to Live in a Connected World*, London: Chatto & Windus.

Mulgan, G. and Briscoe, I. (1997), 'The society of networks', in G. Mulgan (ed.), *Life After Politics: New Thinking for the Twenty-first Century*, London: Fontana.

Mulgan, G. and Landry, C. (1995), *The Other Invisible Hand*, London: Demos.

Mullins, L., Sheppard, H. and Anderson, L. (1991), 'Loneliness and social isolation in Sweden: Differences in age, sex, labor force status, self-rated health, and income adequacy', *The Journal of Applied Gerontology*, **10**, pp. 455–68.

Murray, C. (1994), *Underclass: The Crisis Deepens*, London: Institute of Economic Affairs.

Nash, V. with Christie, I. (2003), *Making Sense of Community*, London: IPPR.

National Research Council (2001), *New Horizons in Health: An Integrative Approach*, Washington, DC: National Academy Press.

NCBS (1976), *Echstscheidingen in Nederland 1970–1974* [*Divorces in the Netherlands, 1970–1974*], Den Haag: SDU.

NCBS (1994), *Bevolking en Huishoudens Nu en in de Toekomst* [*Population and Households Now and in the Future*], Den Haag: SDU.

Nettleton, S., Burrows, R., England, J. and Seavers, J. (1999), *Losing the Family Home. Understanding the Social Consequences of Mortgage Repossession*, York: Joseph Rowntree Foundation.

Neugarten, B.L. (1969), 'Continuities and discontinuities of psychological issues into adult life', *Human Development*, **12**, pp. 121–30.

Newton, K. (1997), 'Social capital and democracy', *American Behavioural Scientist*, **40**, pp. 575–86.

North, F., Syme, S., Feney, A., Head, J., Shipley, M. J. and Marmot, M. (1993), 'Explaining socio-economic differences in sickness absence: the Whitehall II study', *British Medical Journal*, **306**, pp. 361–66.

Nunnally, J.C. (1978), *Psychometric Theory*, 2nd edn, New York: McGraw-Hill.

Oakley, A. (1992), *Social Support and Motherhood: The Natural History of a Research Project*, Oxford: Blackwell.

Offe, C. and Heinze, R. (1992), *Beyond Employment*, Cambridge: Polity Press.

Office for National Statistics (1997), *Health Inequalities: Decennial Supplement*, London: Stationery Office.

Office for National Statistics (2001), details to be found at www.statistics.gov.uk/socialcapital.

Ohlemacher, T. (1992), 'Social relays: micro-mobilisation via the meso-level', Discussion Paper FS III 92–104, Berlin: Wissenschaftzentrum.

Okwumabua, J., Baker, F., Wong, S. and Pilgrim, B. (1997), 'Characteristics of depressive symptoms in elderly urban and rural African Americans', *Journals of Gerontology: Biological Sciences and Medical Sciences*, **52A**, M241–6.

Oppenheim, C. (1998a), *An Inclusive Society: Strategies for Tackling Poverty*, London: Institute for Public Policy Research.

Oppenheim, C. (1998b), 'Changing the storyline', *Guardian*, Society, 1 April, p. 6.

Opportunity for All (2002), *Opportunity for All. Tackling Poverty and Social Exclusion*, London: Department for Work and Pensions, Stationery Office.

O'Reilly, P. (1988), 'Methodological issues in social support and social network research', *Social Science Medicine*, **26**, pp. 863–73.

Pahl, R. (1984), *Divisions of Labour*, Oxford: Basil Blackwell.

Pahl, R. (1991), 'The search for social cohesion: From Durkheim to the European Community', *Archives Euopéenne de Sociologie* **32**, pp. 345–60.

Pahl, R. (2000), *On Friendship*, Cambridge: Polity Press.

Pahl, R. and Spencer, L. (1997), 'Friends and neighbours', *New Statesman*, 26 September, pp. 36–7.

Parker, G. (1993), *With This Body: Caring and Disability in Marriage*, Buckingham: Open University Press.

Parsons, T. (1943), 'The kinship system of the contemporary United States', *American Anthropologist*, **45**, pp. 22–38.

Pearlin, L. (1985), 'Social structure and processes of social support', in S. Cohen and S. Syme (eds), *Social Support and Health*, New York: Academic Press.

Pearlin, L. (1989), 'The sociological study of stress', *Journal of Health and Social Behaviour*, **30**, pp. 241–56.

Performance and Innovation Unit (2002), *Social Capital: A Discussion Paper*, London: Cabinet Office.

Pescosolido, B. (2001), 'The role of social networks in the lives of disabled people', in G. Albrecht, K. Seelman and M. Bury (eds), *Handbook of Disability Studies*, London: Sage.

Peters, A. and Liefbroer, A. (1997), 'Beyond marital status: Partner history and well-being in old age', *Journal of Marriage and the Family*, **59**, pp. 687–99.

Peters, B. and van Nispen, F. (eds) (1998), *Public Policy Instruments: Evaluating the Tools of Public Administration*, Cheltenham: Edward Elgar.

Peters, G. and Kaiser, M. (1985), 'The role of friends and neighbors in providing social support', in W. Sauer and R. Coward (eds), *Social Support Networks and the Care of the Elderly: Theory, Research, Practice, and Policy*, New York: Springer Publishing.

Peterson, R. and Kern, R. (1996), 'Changing high brow taste: From snob to omnivore and univore', *Poetics*, **21**, pp. 243–58.

Phillipson, C. (1998), *Reconstructing Old Age*, London: Sage.

Phillipson, C., Bernard, M., Phillips, J. and Ogg, J. (2000), *Family and Community Life of Older People*, London: Routledge.

Pierson, J. and Smith, J. (eds) (2001), *Rebuilding Community: Policy and Practice in Urban Regeneration*, Basingstoke: Palgrave.

Portes, A. (1998), 'Social capital: Its origins and applications in modern sociology', *Annual Review of Sociology*, **24**, pp. 1–24.

Potts, M.K., Hurwicz, M.L. and Goldstein, M.S. (1992), 'Social support, health-promotive beliefs, and preventive health behaviors among the elderly', *Journal of Applied Gerontology*, **11**, pp. 425–40.

Pourat, N., Lubben, J., Wallace, S. and Moon, A. (1999), 'Predictors of use of traditional Korean healers among elderly Koreans in Los Angeles', *The Gerontologist*, **39**, pp. 711–19.

Pourat, N. Lubben, J., Yu, H. and Wallace, S. (2000), 'Perceptions of health and use of ambulatory care: Differences between Korean and White elderly', *Journal of Aging and Health*, **12**, pp. 112–34.

Power, A. (2000), *Poor Areas and Social Exclusion*, London: CASE paper 35, Centre for Analysis of Social Exclusion, London School of Economics.

Pressman, J, and Wildavsky, A. (1973), *Implementation: How Great Expectations in Washington are Dashed in Oakland or Why It's Amazing that Federal Programs Work at All, This Being the Saga of the Economic Development Administration as Told by Two Sympathetic Observers who Seek to Build Morals on a Foundation of Ruined Hopes*, 2nd edn, Berkeley, California: University of California Press.

Prime, D., Zimmeck, M. and Zurawan, A. (2002), *Active Communities: Initial Findings from the 2001 Home Office Citizenship Survey*, London: The Home Office.

Purdue, D., Razzaque, K., Hambleton, R., Stewart, M. with Huxham, C. and Vangen, S. (2000), *Community Leadership in Area Regeneration*, Bristol: The Policy Press.

Putnam, R. (1993), *Making Democracy Work*, Princeton: Princeton University Press.

Putnam, R. (1995a), 'Bowling alone: America's declining social capital', *Journal of Democracy*, **6**, pp. 65–78.

Putnam, R. (1995b), 'Tuning in, tuning out: The strange disappearance of social capital in America', *Political Science and Politics*, **28**, pp. 664–83.

Putnam, R. (2000), *Bowling Alone: The Collapse and Revival of American Community*, New York: Simon and Schuster.

Pynoos, J., Hade-Kaplan, B. and Fleisher, D. (1984), 'Intergenerational neighborhood networks: A basis for aiding the frail elderly', *The Gerontologist*, **24**, pp. 233–37.

Rands, M. (1988), 'Changes in social networks following separation and divorce', in R. Milardo (ed.), *Families and Social Networks*, London: Sage.

Ravanera, Z.R., Rajulton, F. and Burch, T.K. (1998), 'Early life transitions of Canadian women: A cohort analysis of timing, sequences and variations', *European Journal of Population*, **14**, pp. 179–204.

Rawls, J. (1971), *A Theory of Justice*, Cambridge, Mass.: Bellknap Press.

Rawls, J. (1996). *Political Liberalism*, New York: Columbia University Press.

Rayner, S. (1988), 'The rules that keep us equal: Complexity and the costs of egalitarian organisation', in J. Flanagan and S. Rayner (eds), *Rules, Decisions and Inequality in Egalitarian Societies*, Avebury: Aldershot.

Raynor, P, and Vanstone, M. (2002), *Understanding Community Penalties: Probation, Policy and Social Change*, Buckingham: Open University Press.

Regnier, V. (1980), *Community Analysis Techniques: Final Report*, Los Angeles: University of Southern California, Andus Gerontology Center.

Rex, J. and Moore, R. (1967), *Race, Community and Conflict: A Study of Sparkbrook*, London: Oxford University Press for the Institute of Race Relations.

Ritchie, J. and Spencer, L. (1994), 'Qualitative data analysis', in A. Bryman and R. Burgess (eds), *Analyzing Qualitative Data*, London: Routledge.

Ritchie, J., Spencer, L. and O'Connor, W. (2003), 'Carrying out qualitative analysis', in J. Ritchie and J. Lewis (eds), *Qualitative Research Practice*, London: Sage.

Rogers, R. (1996), 'The effects of family composition, health, and social support linkages on mortality', *Journal of Health and Social Behaviour*, **37**, pp. 326–38.

Rojek, C. (1995), *Decentring Leisure: Rethinking Leisure Theory*, London: Sage.

Rook, K. (1984), 'Loneliness, social support and social isolation', prepared for the Office of Prevention, National Institute of Mental Health.

Rook, K. (1994), 'Assessing the health-related dimensions of older adults' social relationships', in M. Lawton and J. Teresi (eds), *Annual Review of Gerontology and Geriatrics*, New York: Springer Publishing Company.

Room, G. (ed.) (1995), *Beyond the Threshold: The Measurement and Analysis of Social Exclusion*, Bristol: Policy Press.

Rosenthal, C. (1985), 'Kinkeeping in the familial division of labor', *Journal of Marriage and the Family*, **47**, pp. 965–74.

Rosser, C. and Harris, C. (1965), *The Family and Social Change*, London: Routledge & Kegan Paul.

Rowlands, A. (2001), 'Breaking my head in the prime of my life: Acquired disability in young adulthood', in M. Priestley (ed.), *Disability and the Life Course: Global Perspectives*, Cambridge: Cambridge University Press.

Rowles, G. (1978), *Prisoners of Space? Exploring the Geographical Experience of Older People*, Boulder, Col.: Westview.

Rowles, G. and Ravdal, H. (2002), 'Aging, place, and meaning in the face of changing circumstances', in R. Weiss and S. Bass (eds), *Challenges of the Third Age: Meaning and Purpose in Later Life*, Oxford: Oxford University Press.

Rubenstein, L.Z., Aronow, H.U., Schloe, M., Steiner, A. and Alessi, C.A. (1994), 'A home-based geriatric assessment, follow-up and health promotion program: Design, methods, and baseline findings from a 3-year randomized clinical trial', *Aging: Clinical and Experimental Research*, **6**, pp. 105–20.

Rubin, L. (1983), *Intimate Strangers*, New York: Harper and Row.

Rubinstein, R., Lubben, J. and Mintzer, J. (1994), 'Social isolation and social support: an applied perspective', *The Journal of Applied Gerontology*, **13**, pp. 58–72.

Russell Barter, W., McCafferty, P. and Woodhouse, L. (1999), 'Joining-up social exclusion: A report of research into current practice within local authorities', in DETR (ed.), *Joining It Up Locally: The Evidence Base*, Policy Action Team 17, London: DETR.

Salamon, L. with Lund, M. (1989), *Beyond Privatisation: The Tools of Government Action*, Washington, DC: Urban Institute Press.

Sauer, W. and Coward, R. (1985), *Social Support Networks and the Care of the Elderly: Theory, Research and Practice*, New York: Springer.

Saunders, P. (1990), *A Nation of Home Owners*, London: Unwin Hyman.

Scharf, T., Phillipson, C., Kingston, P. and Smith, A. (2001), 'Social exclusion and ageing', *Education and Ageing*, **16**, pp. 303–20.

Scharf, T., Phillipson, C., Smith, A. and Kingston, P. (2002a), 'Older people in deprived areas: Perceptions of the neighbourhood', *Quality in Ageing* **3**, pp. 11–21.

Scharf, T., Phillipson, C., Smith, A. and Kingston, P. (2002b), *Growing Older in Socially Deprived Areas: Social Exclusion in Later Life*, London: Help the Aged.

Schiepers, J.M. (1988), 'Huishoudensequivalentiefactoren volgens de budgetverdelings-methode' ['Family equivalence scales using the budget distribution methods'], *Supplement bij de Sociaal-Economische Maandstatistiek*, **2**, pp. 28–36.

Schmutzer, M.E.A. and Bandler, K. (1980), 'Hi and low – in and out: Approaches to social status', *Journal of Cybernetics*, **10**, pp. 283–99.

Schuller, T., Baron, S., and Field, J. (2000), 'Social capital: a review and critique', in S. Baron, J. Field and T. Schuller (eds), *Social Capital: Critical Perspectives*, Oxford: Oxford University Press.

Schwarz, M. and Thompson, M. (1990), *Divided We Stand: Redefining Politics, Technology and Social Choice*, Philadelphia: University of Pennsylvania.

Scott, J. (1991), *Social Network Analysis*, London: Sage Books.

Scott, J. (2000), *Social Network Analysis: A Handbook*, 2nd edn, London: Sage.

Scott, J. (2002), 'General introduction' in J. Scott (ed.), *Social Networks: Critical Concepts in Sociology*, Vol. 1, London: Routledge.

Secretary of State for Health, and Minister of State for Public Health (1998), *Our Healthier Nation: A Contract for Health*, Cm. 3852, London: Stationery Office.

Seeman, T. (2001), 'How do others get under our skin? Social relationships and health', in C. Ryff and B. Singer (eds), *Emotion, Social Relationships and Health*, New York: Oxford University Press.

Seeman, T., Singer, B., Ryff, C., Love, G. and Levy-Storms, L. (2002), 'Social relationships, gender, and allostatic load across two age cohorts', *Psychosomatic Medicine*, **64**, pp. 395–406.

Semenza, J., Rubin, C., Falter, K., Selanikio, J., Flanders, W., Howe, H. and Wilhelm, J. (1996), 'Heat-related deaths during the July 1995 heat wave in Chicago', *New England Journal of Medicine*, **335**, pp. 84–90.

Shanas, E. (1979), 'The family as a social support system in old age', *The Gerontologist*, **19**, 169–74.

Sibley, D. (1995), *Geographies of Exclusion: Society and Difference in the West*, London: Routledge.

Silburn, R., Lucas, D., Page, R. and Hanna, L. (1999), *Neighbourhood Images in Nottingham: Social Cohesion and Neighbourhood Change*, York: Joseph Rowntree Foundation/York Publishing Services.

Silver, H. (1994), 'Social exclusion and social solidarity: Three paradigms', *International Labour Review*, **133**, pp. 531–78.

Silverstein, M., Chen, X., and Heller, K. (1996), 'Too much of a good thing? Intergenerational social support and the psychological well-being of older parents', *Journal of Marriage and the Family*, **58**, pp. 970–82.

Sloggett, A. and Joshi, H. (1994), 'Higher mortality in deprived areas: Community or personal disadvantage?', *British Medical Journal*, **309**, pp. 1470–74.

Smart, C., Neale, B. and Wade, A. (2001), *The Changing Experience of Childhood. Families and Divorce*, Cambridge: Polity Press.

Smeenk, W. (1998), 'Een ruil tussen de seksen? Leeftijdsverschillen tussen mannen en vrouwen binnen samenwoonrelaties' ['An exchange between the sexes? Patterns and sources of age-differences in Dutch Couples'], *Mens en Maatschappij*, **73**, pp. 216–38.

Smith, A., Phillipson, C. and Scharf, T. (2002), *Social Capital: Concepts, Measures and the Implications for Urban Communities*, Keele: Working Paper 9, Centre for Social Gerontology, School of Social Relations, Keele University.

Social Exclusion Unit (1998), *Bringing Britain Together: A National Strategy for Neighbourhood Renewal*, Social Exclusion Unit, London: Stationery Office.

Social Exclusion Unit (1999), *Report of Policy Action Team 9: Community Self-Help*, London: Cabinet Office.

Social Exclusion Unit (2001), *A New Commitment to Neighbourhood Renewal: A Framework for Consultation*, London: Cabinet Office.

Solomon, D. (2000), Foreword to D. Osterweil, K. Brummel-Smith and J. Beck (eds), *Comprehensive Geriatric Assessment*, New York: McGraw-Hill.

Stansfeld, S.A. (1999), 'Social support and social cohesion', in M. Marmot and R. Wilkinson (eds), *Social Determinants of Health*, Oxford: Oxford University Press.

Steiner, A., Raube, K., Stuck, A., Aronow, H., Draper, D., Rubenstein, L. and Beck, J. (1996), 'Measuring psychosocial aspects of well-being in older community residents: Performance of four short scales', *The Gerontologist*, **36**, pp. 54–62.

Stevens, J. (1992), *Applied Multivariate Statistics For The Social Sciences*, 2nd edn, Hillsdale, NJ: Lawrence Erlbaum Associates.

Stevens, N. (1989), *Well-being in Widowhood: A Question of Balance*, unpublished dissertation, Katholieke Universiteit Nijmegen.

Stevens, N. (1995), 'Gender and adaptation to widowhood in later life', *Ageing and Society*, **15**, pp. 37–58.

Stewart J. (1995), *Innovations in Democratic Practice*, Birmingham: Institute for Local Government Studies, University of Birmingham.

Stewart, J., Kendall, E. and Coote, A. (1994), *Citizens' Juries*, London: Institute for Public Policy Research.

Stolle, D., and Rochon, T. (1998), 'Are all associations alike? Member diversity, associational type and the creation of social capital', *American Behavioural Scientist*, **42**, pp. 47–65.

Stone, R., Cafferata, G.L. and Sangl, J. (1987), 'Caregivers of the frail elderly: a national profile', *The Gerontologist*, **27**, pp. 616–26.

Strategy Unit (2002), 'Social capital: A discussion paper', www.cabinet-office.gov.uk/innovation.

Strauss, A., and Corbin, J. (1990), *Basics of Qualitative Research: Grounded Theory Procedures and Techniques*, Newbury Park: Sage.

Streiner, D. and Norman, G. (1995), *Health Measurement Scales: A Practical Guide to their Development and Use*, 2nd edn, New York: Oxford University Press.

Stuck, A., Walthert, J., Nikolaus, T., Bula, C., Hohmann, C. and Beck, J. (1999), 'Risk factors for the functional status decline in community-living elderly people: A systematic literature review', *Social Science and Medicine*, **48**, pp. 445–69.

Stueve, C. and Gerson, K. (1977), 'Personal relations across the life-cycle', in C. Fischer, R. Jackson, C. Stueve, K. Gerson, L. Jones and M. Baldassare (eds), *Networks and Places: Social Relations in the Urban Setting*, New York: Free Press.

Suttles, G. (1972), *The Social Construction of Community*, Chicago: University of Chicago Press.

Tadmor, N. (2001), *Family and Friends in Eighteenth Century England*, Cambridge: Cambridge University Press.

Tarrow, S. (1994), *Power in Movement*, Cambridge: Cambridge University Press.

Taylor, M. (1995), 'Community work and the state: The changing context of UK practice', in G. Craig and M. Mayo (eds), *Community Empowerment: A Reader in Participation and Development*, London: Zed Books.

Taylor, M. (2002), 'Community and social exclusion', in V. Nash (ed.), *Reclaiming Community*, London: Institute for Public Policy Research.

Taylor, M. (2003), *Public Policy in the Community*, London: Palgrave.

Teachman, J.D., Thomas, J. and Paasch, K. (1991), 'Legal status and the stability of coresidential unions', *Demography*, **28**, pp. 1–22.

Tebbutt, M. (1995), *Women's Talk: A Social History of 'Gossip' in Working-Class Neighbourhoods, 1880–1960*, Aldershot: Scolar.

Thoits, P.A. (1995), 'Stress, coping, and social support processes: Where are we? What next?', *Journal of Health and Social Behavior*, **Special Issue**, pp. 53–79.

Thompson, L. and Walker, A. (1989), 'Gender in families: Women and men in marriage, work and parenthood', *Journal of Marriage and the Family*, **51**, pp. 845–71.

Thompson, M. (1992), 'The dynamics of cultural theory', in S. Hargreaves Heap and A. Ross (eds), *Understanding the Enterprise Culture: Themes in the Work of Mary Douglas*, Edinburgh: Edinburgh University Press.

Thompson, M. (1996), *Inherent Relationality: An Anti-dualist Approach to Institutions*, Bergen: LOS Senteret.

Thompson, M., Ellis, R.J. and Wildavsky, A. (1990), *Cultural Theory*, Boulder: Westview.

Thompson, M., Grendstad, G. and Selle, P. (eds) (1999), *Cultural Theory as Political Science*, London: Routledge.

Torres, C., McIntosh, W. and Kubena, K. (1992), 'Social network and social background characteristics of elderly who live and eat alone', *Journal of Aging and Health*, **4**, pp. 564–78.

Townsend, P. (1957), *The Family Life of Old People*, London: Routledge & Kegan Paul.

Townsend, P. (1987), 'Deprivation', *Journal of Social Policy* **16**, pp. 125–46.

Townsend, P. and Davidson, N. (eds) (1982), *Inequalities in Health: The Black Report*, Harmondsworth: Penguin.

Tremethick, M. (2001), 'Alone in a crowd. A study of social networks in home health and assisted living', *Journal of Gerontological Nursing*, **27**, pp. 4–5.

Turner, R. and Marino, F. (1994), 'Social support and social structure: A descriptive epidemiology', *Journal of Health and Social Behavior*, **35**, pp. 193–212.

Turner, V.W. (1995), *The Ritual Process*, New York: Aldine de Gruyter.

Tyler, T., Boeckmann, R., Smith, H. and Huo, Y. (1997), *Social Justice in a Diverse Society*, Boulder: Westview Press.

Uhlenberg, P. (1993), 'Demographic change and kin relationships in later life', in G. Maddox and M. Powell Lawton (eds), *Annual Review of Gerontology and Geriatics*, Vol. 13, *Focus on Kinship, Aging, and Social Change*, New York: Springer.

Uhlenberg, P. and Chew, K. (1986), 'The changing place of remarriage in the life course', in Z. Blau and D. Kertzer (eds), *Current Perspectives on Aging and the Life Cyle*, Vol. 2.

UK Coalition Against Poverty (1998), *Eradicate Poverty!! A Resource Pack for Community Organisations*, London: UK Coalition Against Poverty.

van Hoorn, W., van Huis, M., Keij, I. and de Jong, A. (2001), 'Nog steeds liever samen' ['Still preferring to be together'], in J. Garssen, J. de Beer, P. Cuyvers and A. de Jong (eds), *Samenleven: Nieuwe Feiten over Relaties en Gezinnen*, Voorburg/Heerlen: CBS.

van Sonderen, E., Ormel., B., Brilman E. and van den Heuvall, C. (1990), 'Personal network delineation: A comparison of the exchange, affective and role-relation approaches', in K. Knipscheer and T. Antonucci (eds), *Social Network Research: Substantive Issues and Methodological Questions*, Amsterdam: Swets and Zeitlinger.

van Tilburg, T. (1995), 'Delineation of the social network and differences in network size', in C. Knipscheer, J. de Jong Gierveld, T. van Tilburg and P. Dykstra (eds), *Living Arrangements and Social Networks of Older Adults*, Amsterdam: VU University Press.

Vaupel, J. (1997), 'The remarkable improvements in survival at older ages', *Philosophical Transactions of the Royal Society London*, **352**, pp. 1799–804.

Vaux, A. (1988), *Social Support: Theory, Research and Intervention*. New York: Praeger Publisher.

Waite, L.J. (1995), 'Does marriage matter?', *Demography*, **32**, pp. 483–507.

Walker, A. (1997), 'Introduction: The Strategy of Inequality', in A. Walker and C. Walker (eds), *Britain Divided: The Growth of Social Exclusion in the 1980s and 1990s*, London: Child Poverty Action Group.

Walker, M.E., Wasserman, S. and Wellman B. (1994), 'Statistical models for social support networks, in S. Wasserman and J. Galaskiewicz (eds), *Advances in Social Network Analysis: Research in the Social and Behavioral Sciences*, Beverly Hills: Sage.

Warde, A. (1997), *Consumption, Food and Taste*, London: Sage.

Warde, A. and Tampubolon, G. (2002), 'Social capital, networks and leisure consumption', *Sociological Review*, **50**, pp. 155–80.

Wasserman, S. and Faust, K. (eds) (1994), *Social Network Analysis: Methods And Applications*, Cambridge: Cambridge University Press.

Weeks, J., Heaphy, B. and Donovan, C. (2001), *Same Sex Intimacies: Families of Choice and Other Life Experiments*, London: Routledge.

Weiss, R. (1973), *Loneliness: The Experience of Emotional and Social Isolation*, Cambridge, Mass.: MIT Press.

Wellman, B. (1990), 'The place of kinfolk in personal community settings', *Families in Community Settings: Interdisciplinary Settings*, New York: Haworth Press.

Wellman, B. (ed.) (1999), *Networks in the Global Village: Life in Contemporary Communities*, Boulder: Westview.

Wellman, B. and Berkowitz, S.D. (eds) (1988), *Social Structures: A Network Approach*, Cambridge: Cambridge University Press.

Wellman, B. and Wortley, S. (1989), 'Brothers' keepers: Situating kinship relations in broader networks of social support', *Sociological Perspectives*, **32**, pp. 273–306.

Wellman, B. and Wortley, S. (1990), 'Different strokes from different folks: Community ties and social support', *American Journal of Sociology*, **96**, 558–88.

Wellman, B., Carrington, P. and Hall, A. (1988), 'Networks as personal communities', in B. Wellman and S.D. Berkowitz (eds), *Social Structures: A Network Approach*, Cambridge: Cambridge University Press.

Wenger, C. (1984), *The Supportive Network*, London: George Allen & Unwin.

Wenger, C. (1992), *Help in Old Age*, Liverpool: Liverpool University Press.

Wenger, C. (1994), *Support Networks of Older People*, Bangor: University of Wales.

Wenger, C. (1995), 'A comparison of urban with rural networks in North Wales', *Ageing and Society*, **15**, pp. 59–82.

Wenger, C. (1995), 'Social network research in gerontology: How did we get here and where do we go next?', paper presented at the International Sociological Association Research on Ageing Intercongress Meeting, Melbourne, Australia.

Wenger, C. (1996a), 'Social isolation and loneliness in old age: Review and model refinement', *Ageing and Society*, **16**, pp. 333–58.

Wenger, C. (1996b), 'Social networks and gerontology', *Reviews in Clinical Gerontology*, **6**, pp. 285–93.

Wenger, C. (1997a), 'Nurturing networks', in I. Christie and H. Perry (eds), *The Wealth and Poverty of Networks: Tackling Social Exclusion*, London: Demos.

Wenger, C. (1997b), 'Social networks and the prediction of elderly people at risk', *Aging and Mental Health*, **1**, pp. 311–20.

Wenger, C. (1997c), 'Review of findings on support networks of older Europeans', *Journal of Cross-cultural Gerontology*, **12**, pp. 1–21.

Wenger, C. and Burholt, V. (2001), 'Differences over time in older people's relationships with children, grandchildren, nieces and nephews in rural North Wales', *Ageing and Society*, **21**, pp. 567–91.

Wenger, C. and Tucker, I. (2000), *Using Network Variation in Practice: Identification of Support Network Type*, Bangor: Centre for Social Policy Research and Development and Institute of Medical and Social Care Research, University of Wales.

Werbner, P. (1988), 'Taking and giving: Working women and female bonds in a Pakistani immigrant neighbourhood', in S. Westwood and P. Bhachu (eds), *Enterprising Women: Ethnicity, Economy and Gender Relations*, London: Routledge.

Wertheimer, A. (1995), *Circles of Support: Building Inclusive Communities*, Bristol: Circles Network.

Westergaard, J. (1975), 'Radical class consciousness: A comment', in M. Bulmer (ed.), *Working Class Images of Society*, London: Routledge.

Wheaton, B. (1980), 'The socio-genesis of psychological disorder: An attributional theory', *Journal of Health and Social Behaviour*, **21**, pp. 100–24.

Wildavsky, A. (1998), *Culture and Social Theory*, ed. S.-K. Chai and B. Swedlow, New Brunswick, NJ: Transaction.

Wilkinson, R. (1996), *Unhealthy Societies: The Afflictions of Inequality*, London: Routledge.

Williams, A., Ware J. and Donald, C. (1981), 'A model of mental health, life events, and social supports applicable to general populations', *Journal of Health and Social Behavior*, **22**, pp. 324–36.

Williams, C. and Windebank, J. (2000), 'Helping each other out? Community exchange in deprived neighbourhoods', *Community Development Journal*, **35**, pp. 146–56.

Willmott, P. (1986), *Social Networks, Informal Care and Public Policy*, London: Policy Studies Institute.

Willmott, P. (1987), *Friendship, Networks and Social Support*, London: Policy Studies Institute.

Wilson, W.J. (1987), *The Truly Disadvantaged*, Chicago: University of Chicago Press.

Winemiller, D., Mitchell, M., Sutliff, J. and Cline, D. (1993), 'Measurement strategies in social support: A descriptive review of the literature', *Journal of Clinical Psychology*, **49**, pp. 638–48.

Wister, A. and Dykstra, P. (2000), 'Formal assistance among Dutch older adults: An examination of the gendered nature of marital history', *Canadian Journal on Aging / Revue Canadienne du Viellissement*, **19**, pp. 508–35.

Wolf, S. and Bruhn, J.G. (1993), *The Power of Clan*, New Brunswick, NJ: Transaction.

Wolff, K. (ed.) (1964), *The Sociology of Georg Simmel*, New York: The Free Press.

Woliver, L. (1996), 'Mobilising and sustaining grass-roots dissent', *Journal of Social Issues*, **52**, pp. 139–52.

Yen, I. and Syme, S. (1999), 'The social environment and health: A discussion of the epidemiological literature', *Annual Review of Public Health*, **20**, pp. 287–308.

Young, M. and Willmott, P. (1957), *Family and Kinship in East London*, London: Routledge & Kegan Paul.

Zuckerman, D., Kasl, S. and Ostfeld, A. (1984), 'Psychosocial predictors of mortality among the elderly poor: The role of religion, well-being and social contacts', *American Journal of Epidemiology*, **119**, pp. 410–23.

6, P. (1997a), 'Social exclusion: Time to be optimistic', in I. Christie and H. Perry (eds), *The Wealth and Poverty of Networks: Tackling Social Exclusion*, London: Demos.

6, P. (1997b), 'Governing by cultures', in G.J. Mulgan (ed.), *Life After Politics: New Thinking for the Twenty-First Century*, London: Fontana.

6, P. (1998), 'Profiles, networks, risk and hoarding: Public policy and the dynamics of social mobility and social cohesion', unpublished paper presented at the PIU, Cabinet Office, London.

6, P. (2002), 'Governing friends and acquaintances: Public policy and social networks', in V. Nash (ed.), *Reclaiming Community*, London: Institute for Public Policy Research.

6, P. (forthcoming), *The Politics Of Social Cohesion: Public Policy and Personal Social Networks*, Cambridge: Cambridge University Press.

6, P., Seltzer, K., Leat, D. and Stoker, G. (2002), *Toward Holistic Governance: The New Agenda in Government Reform*, Basingstoke: Palgrave.

Index